EDWIN M. SCHUR, a sociologist well known for his work in criminology, is Professor and Chairman of the Department of Sociology, Tufts University. He has served as a member of the Governor's Special Commission on Crime and Violence (Massachusetts), and as Consultant to the National Institute of Mental Health. Among his previous books are *Crimes Without Victims: Deviant Behavior and Public Policy* (Prentice-Hall, 1965), and *Law and Society: A Sociological View.* Dr. Schur is also the author of numerous articles and reviews on crime and related social problems.

OUR CRIMINAL SOCIETY

The Social and Legal Sources of Crime in America

Edwin M. Schur

A SPECTRUM BOOK

PRENTICE-HALL, Inc.
Englewood Cliffs, N.J.

P 13-643882-2; C 13-643890-3.

*Library of Congress Catalog Card
Number: 72-79451.*

Printed in the United States of America

Current printing (last number):
10   9   8   7   6   5   4   3   2   1

Prentice-Hall International, Inc. (*London*)
Prentice-Hall of Australia, Pty. Ltd. (*Sydney*)
Prentice-Hall of Canada, Ltd. (*Toronto*)
Prentice-Hall of India Private Limited (*New Delhi*)
Prentice-Hall of Japan, Inc. (*Tokyo*)

To Amy, David, and Owen
—*that they may see a less criminal society*

CONTENTS

PREFACE

As a sociologist much concerned with issues of public policy, I have often tried—through my writings and other quasi-public activities—to reach beyond my own students and the readers of specialized professional journals to a wider general audience. In few areas have I felt this need more strongly than in that of criminology, where the great public concern and the widespread misconceptions about crime make dissemination of basic social science findings and perspectives of vital importance. Accordingly, this book was written, in the first instance, with the general reading public in mind. It should, however, also provide a useful overview of the field for students in basic courses on criminology, social problems, and American society. Hopefully, the combination of a strong policy orientation and a systematic review of key findings and theories about crime will prove valuable to both students and general readers.

I would like to thank my friend Lewis Coser—who knows that this project has not been without its perils—for suggesting to me in the first place that I undertake a book of this sort; and I am grateful also to Peter Grenquist and Michael Hunter (among others) at Prentice-Hall, for their active interest in and careful attention to the manuscript.

EDWIN M. SCHUR

INTRODUCTION:
THE NEED FOR A CALM
APPRAISAL

We Americans pride ourselves on being pragmatic and rational. In both our personal experiences and our public confrontations with national problems, we like to think of ourselves as acting in a calm, collected, and above all, sensible manner. How well we have managed to live up to this image of ourselves is debatable. But in at least a few major problem areas there is no doubt that we have failed to do so. With respect to these problems, we have allowed irrational outlooks and unworkable practices and policies to prevail. And we have been unable to assess these situations with the calm rationality that is needed. On the contrary our emotions have held sway, we have come to believe we were being overwhelmed by circumstances about which we could do little, we have in short—to adopt the common idiom—lost our cool. One such problem is war. Another is crime.

The war problem and the crime problem exhibit striking similarities. In each case, strong social sentiments develop to support a differentiation between the wrongdoers and the wronged. These categories are viewed as being clearly definable and separable—a conception that fits in well with the pervasive American tradition of the "good guys" and the "bad guys." In the case of war, as in the case of crime, it is widely believed that high values will be served by rendering the "enemy" his due. And, correspondingly, there is widespread distrust of any "soft" policies that seem to imply concessions to, or appeasement of the "other side." In each case, the very process of defining enemies seems to serve some important functions—psychological, social, or even economic—for the society confronting such wrongdoers. (With respect to war, this point was highlighted with satiric cogency in the recent book *Report from Iron Mountain*.) In each case, vicious-circle mechanisms are present. False beliefs and excessive fears may lead to reactions that actually increase the magnitude and intractabil-

1

ity of the very problems that caused them to arise in the first place. We know this is true of the arms race, and it is also true, I would submit, of the crime race. Both areas involve special susceptibility to, and considerable evidence of the "self-fulfilling prophecy."

War and crime have always existed. But in both cases the disturbing behavior seems now to be getting completely out of hand. We feel something must be done if we are to preserve our basic social institutions and values—indeed if we are to preserve ourselves. At the same time, we feel afraid and impotent in the face of war and crime situations. This breeds a dangerous combination of apathy and receptiveness to extreme and repressive appeals. While both war and crime are indeed fearful phenomena about which we should be intensely concerned, it will hardly do to panic. We must be alert to the real dangers, not the imagined ones, and our assessments must be informed by whatever authoritative evidence is available.

Muddled Thinking about Crime

Before I discuss a number of specific misconceptions about crime, and some of the irrational policies we have adopted in our attempts to control disruptive and disturbing behavior, let me merely cite some of the more common types of fuzziness we exhibit in thinking about crime problems. We are, to begin with, extremely hazy as to what the term crime really means—a point to which I shall return shortly. Furthermore, we often appear overly willing to accept unsophisticated assertions concerning the causes of crime. In particular, many people seem to find it easy to locate the trouble in some alleged shortcomings of the offending individual rather than in the general conditions of our society. (The interplay between these competing themes will occupy a good bit of space in the chapters that follow.) Americans also seem to be lamentably uncritical in their evaluation of public statements about crime rates and trends, perhaps because few of us have given much systematic thought to the very serious obstacles facing those who attempt to collect accurate data on such matters. And frequently, spurred on by the inflammatory statements of official or unofficial anticrime spokesmen, we too readily accept the view that a "get tough" response to crime problems is required. Actually, when we examine the facts a bit more closely, we often find that overreacting to crime may be even worse than not reacting at all.

There also tends to be a rather naïve optimism about potential solutions to the crime problem. Many people seem to believe that experts of one variety or another will somehow score a "breakthrough"—a characteristically American notion—that will enable us to eliminate most crime. The hope for this kind of comprehensive problem solving (particularly when it is seen as emanating from a sudden brilliant formulation by scientific experts) is a rather simple-minded one. It is futile to think about eliminating all crime. And it is a mistake to expect the experts to be able to "solve" our crime problems for us. As we shall see, systematic crime studies can help us to understand the nature and extent of these problems and can point the way to those policies that may constitute the most rational means of achieving our stated goals. But the basic attack on crime cannot be mounted by the specialists; we must take on this responsibility ourselves. It was not experts alone who created the social conditions out of which our crime problems have emerged, and it will not (or at least it should not) be the experts alone who make the necessary changes in those conditions. A wise citizenry will look to the specialists for learned guidance, but not for pat solutions. The responsibility for dealing with crime is a broad social one.

If we have tended to be overly optimistic about complete and "scientific" solutions, we have also probably been much more pessimistic than we need be about our own ability to effect less-than-complete but still very important changes in our crime situation. Control of crime is not an all or nothing matter. There are some specific measures we can take that will significantly reduce the magnitude and social danger of particular aspects of crime in America. There are also some very broad social policies we can adopt that are almost certain to appreciably reduce the overall level of crime in our society, even if we cannot hope for absolute elimination of criminal behavior. Crime is not a phenomenon that is completely out of our control, comforting as it may sometimes be to assert that this is the case. On the contrary, it is well within the power of American society to significantly shape and regulate its crime situation.

Just why we don't seem to be able to think more clearly about crime is an interesting and complex question. I shall return to it toward the end of this book. Clearly, very strong and perhaps even basic emotional reactions to crime and punishment hinder rationality in this area. Without doubt we are fascinated by these phenomena, which pose classic issues of human behavior and morality and which, psychoanalysts would maintain, strike very basic chords in the human psyche. On a more conscious level, our thinking about problems of crime and punishment is closely tied up with our ideas about right and wrong, and our legitimate concern that worthy values be maintained and socially desirable institutions preserved. The danger here lies in allowing a doctrine of horrible consequences to get the better of us. It is all too easy to say that our society is going to fall apart unless we "clamp down" on crime. It is more difficult, but nonetheless essential, for us to consider whether some aspects of crime in America constitute indicators of much needed social change. We must, in other words, be prepared to examine critically those values and institutions out of which the offending behavior arises. And we must also make sure that precipitous or unwise reactions to such behavior do not subvert the very values and institutions we consider most central to social well-being and progress in a democratic society.

At its core, our unwillingness to confront crime rationally is a political matter. Crime problems present the American people with major issues of public policy. Clear thinking about crime would force us to make a variety of legislative and other decisions that, at the present time, we may not really be prepared to make. We might have to admit, to ourselves and officially, that there are certain kinds of serious criminal acts no amount of lawmaking or preventive action can fully eliminate. We would also have to face up to the possibility that what we do *not* need (at least as a first priority item) is greater dedication to and funding of the "war against crime"—a phrase that has become all too standard in our political rhetoric. What is much more badly needed is a substantial shifting of anticrime energy and money away from specialized enforcement schemes and crash programs, and into basic long-term efforts at amelioration of the general socioeconomic ills of our society. As I shall show, these ills lie at the very heart of most serious crime in the United States today.

Americans would have to give sober consideration to finding ways of reducing the major discrepancies between many of our professed values and the values by which we actually live. To some extent general socioeconomic reform is directed to that end. The obvious case in point is the glaring discrepancy between our stated ideals of equal opportunity and equal rights and the persistence of major inequalities in our present social system. But American value discrepancies and inconsistencies go well beyond this—ranging across such diverse realms as economic competition, sexual morality, political freedom, and general fair dealing in business and other interpersonal relations.

While no society has ever been able to fully eliminate value discrepancies, there is good reason to believe that the gaps between the ideal and the real in modern American life have become so large as to represent a serious source of social confusion and personal alienation. Again, a central concern would have to be with the relation between such conditions and patterns of ongoing and incipient social change. In some instances a greater effort to live up to our stated ideals is called for. In other cases our professed values should probably undergo a certain amount of modification to permit greater flexibility in personal behavior. We will probably have to learn to live a bit more with some forms of behavior we now treat as criminal. As a major section of this book will indicate, our society has been unwisely eager to invoke criminal sanctions whenever confronted by individuals whose personal behavior diverged from or seemed to threaten a presumed societal norm or consensus.

A rational crime policy would require us to rethink just what we are trying to accomplish by employing criminal law as a means of social control. Are we in fact continuing to seek retribution in taking action against offending individuals—an aim generally disavowed by enlightened modern society? Or, if we are seeking to deter and to rehabilitate, how realistically are we gauging the prospects for and limitations on achieving those ends? With respect to deterrence, it may well be (as material to be presented below will suggest) that we employ the criminal law most vigorously in just those situations where the deterrent effect is least, and that we make relatively little use of criminal sanctions in those offense areas where they might more realistically be expected to deter violations of law. Unfortunately, it is not possible in this short book to consider in any detail the question of rehabilitation, or more specifically the role that might be played by our many and diverse types of correctional institutions and treatment programs. I will emphasize one related point, however—that concern with the "treatment" of offending individuals should not be allowed to overshadow the need for broader social reforms. As we shall see, a treatment focus has only limited usefulness in connection with broad segments of crime in America today.

If we are to rework our crime policies in line with these more realistic considerations, we must drastically revise our general outlook on crime and punishment. We must have an atmosphere within which policymakers (including political figures) can begin to advocate sensible measures without running the risk of political suicide. A few enlightened individuals have tried to speak out for such measures. But in general it remains extremely difficult for men of political power to make any statements concerning these issues without feeling compelled to speak in terms of "the crime menace," "the need for stronger law enforcement," and the like. Of course it is possible to use such terminology strategically—as window dressing under cover of which progressive policies may be advanced. But the overall impact of such rhetorical demands is to reinforce irrational fears and to support the call for repressive action. As I shall repeatedly emphasize throughout this book, the prime focus of crime policy must move away from law enforcement (and even treatment) toward general efforts at prevention and control. And the key to such efforts lies not in dealing with potential criminals, but rather in direct action against crime-encouraging social conditions.

To some extent, public resistance to changing outlooks may be attributable to relative ignorance of basic facts about crime. Sometimes it is suggested that no one in our society—not even the so-called expert—really knows very much about the nature and causes of criminal behavior. This is not true. Nor is it true—as some of their critics have sometimes claimed—that the academic specialists on crime have been so absorbed with abstract and esoteric theorizing that they have neglected problems of crime in "the real world." Actually, social scientists who have done research on crime have provided us with an enormous amount of information and much useful analysis of its meaning. And as I shall show, much of this work does provide important and fairly direct leads for those shaping public policy.

One of the major aims of this book is to bring some of these facts and theories into broader public view. To some extent, then, I shall be reviewing material included in standard college textbooks on criminology.[1] But the audience for such works is undoubtedly limited, and these books usually attempt a rather encyclopedic coverage of the relevant research—a coverage in which the most crucial findings and

[1] The "classic" sociological text on criminology is Edwin H. Sutherland and Donald R. Cressey, *Principles of Criminology,* 7th ed. (Philadelphia: J.B. Lippincott Co., 1966). Two other interesting basic texts are Don C. Gibbons, *Society, Crime, and Criminal Careers* (Englewood Cliffs, N.J.: Prentice-Hall, Inc., 1968), and Donald R. Taft and Ralph W. England, Jr., *Criminology,* 4th ed. (New York: The Macmillan Company, 1964). For an excellent brief overview, see Gresham M. Sykes, *Crime and Society,* 2nd ed. (New York: Random House, Inc., 1967).

ideas tend to get lost. Another potentially valuable source of information is the material recently brought together by the President's Commission on Law Enforcement and the Administration of Justice in *The Challenge of Crime in a Free Society* and in its "task force reports" dealing with various specific aspects of crime in America.[2] Here again, however, the audience for these works is not very large.

Perhaps relatively few Americans even realize that a great many sociologists and other social scientists have been devoting themselves to systematic empirical research in the area of criminology—a term that has unfortunately been adulterated in the public mind by its association with police science and detection work. Sociologists have carefully examined the spatial and social distribution of criminal offenses and known offenders. They have critically analyzed official crime statistics and methods of recording crime data. They have compared the social background characteristics of known offenders with those of samples of closely "matched" (i.e., otherwise more or less similar) samples of nonoffenders. They have asked samples of the general public about their involvement in activities for which they could be prosecuted under criminal law—with, as we shall see, some intriguing results. Researchers have recorded and analyzed the life histories of such diverse offenders as juvenile delinquents and adult professional thieves. They have done intensive observational studies of the structure and activities of delinquent gangs. They have analyzed the social organization and the success rates of various treatment programs and institutions. And, in numerous other ways, they have explored almost every facet of criminal behavior and our reactions to it.

As a result we know a good deal about the nature, extent, and distribution of offenses; the social correlates of involvement in crime; and the processes involved in the development of various kinds of criminal "careers." Unfortunately, sociologists of crime have themselves sometimes obscured the public relevance of their findings by displaying excessive caution and narrowness in defining their professional role. Since the primary aim of the social sciences is to develop a systematic understanding of society and its workings, sociologists frequently insist that concern with the uses to which such findings may

[2] President's Commission on Law Enforcement and Administration of Justice, *The Challenge of Crime in a Free Society.* See also the Commission task force reports on the police, the courts, corrections, juvenile delinquency and youth crime, organized crime, science and technology, assessment of crime, narcotics and drugs, and drunkenness (Washington D.C.: U.S. Government Printing Office, 1967).

be put is only secondary and that such decisions involve issues reaching beyond their special scientific competence. The scientist believes that he can provide a sound basis for decision-making, but that he cannot (as a scientist) establish the social ends to be pursued. Recognition of their supposedly "value neutral" role may lead some social scientists to shy away from publicly spelling out reasonable value implications of their research. In addition, sociologists sometimes are reluctant to state their findings in a clear-cut and decisive manner, because conclusions reached through scientific research are always viewed as being potentially revisable in the light of subsequent evidence. This outlook may not satisfy the policymaker, who seeks authoritative guidance and who needs to make definite decisions here and now. He cannot always wait until "all the evidence is in"—a condition that can never be fully met anyway. Of course, some sociologists have always been alert to policy needs, and researchers increasingly present their considered views for public examination. In this respect, the reports of the President's Commission are particularly noteworthy because they drew very heavily on a substantial body of already existing and specially commissioned social research.

The field of criminology itself has exhibited certain tendencies that may have helped to keep its public policy contributions to a minimum. Much of the traditional sociological research on crime has focused heavily on questions of individual causation. The researcher tried to determine (through statistical comparisons) patterns of association between the personal and social characteristics of individuals and rates of involvement in criminal behavior. Modern criminology has often prided itself on having brought about a concentration on "the criminal, not the crime." Certainly it was an advance to begin trying to understand crime instead of simply punishing it. Yet the emphasis on learning about crime through studying offenders, and the relative neglect of specific offenses, probably lent support to the popular view that crime is simply a function of individual maladaptation. Often all offenders were lumped together (as when the researcher compared a sample of "criminals"—usually incarcerated individuals—with one of "noncriminals"), regardless of the many different forms of offending behavior in which they had engaged. It was assumed that these offenders would display certain common characteristics that would significantly distinguish them from their law-abiding counterparts.

In the focus on comparing individuals, even the researchers sometimes lost sight of the broad social sources of crime. As we shall see, there has been a gradual shift in the emphasis of criminological studies from individual-centered approaches (viewing crime in terms of heredity, physical characteristics, and so on) to analyses of the ways in which an individual's position in society and patterns of social interaction (including his socioeconomic status, location in particular neighborhoods, family situation, and activities in and allegiance to primary groups) contribute to his involvement in crime. There has also been a growing and a salutary tendency to examine directly the structure of society itself and the nature of cultural value systems. It is increasingly recognized that approved social arrangements and values have a distinct bearing on the crime picture. In a sense, existing patterns of crime represent a price we pay for structuring society as we have structured it.

Compartmentalizing Crime

Some of these remarks should suggest what I consider to be our most basic misconception about crime—the tendency to see it as an alien, asocial phenomenon. We persist in thinking of crime as somehow existing outside of organized society. Crime is something done *to* society, criminals are enemies *of* society, society is at war *with* crime.

This leads us to compartmentalize crime problems, to ignore their close relation to the other conditions of our society, out of which criminals as well as conformists emerge. Certainly it is not necessary or desirable to welcome criminal offenders into the ranks of the approved citizenry. But disapproved behavior is a fact of social life. It represents part of our social system and cannot be relegated to some "external" location or attributed to forces viewed as being outside the regular workings of society.

That such an evasive conception is quite untenable becomes clear as soon as we stop for a moment and think just what we mean by crime. *Crime is behavior that violates the criminal law.*[3] As such, the categories of criminal behavior are not fixed and immutable. On the

---

[3] There is some debate among sociologists of crime as to whether *all* acts that technically violate the criminal law should be considered crimes, regardless of whether the individual committing the act and society at large really consider the behavior to be criminal. But sociologists are agreed that *only* acts in violation of the criminal law constitute crime. See the discussion in Sutherland and Cressey, *op. cit.*, pp. 19–20.

contrary, they may vary greatly over time and from place to place. To be sure, not all these categories are purely arbitrary. Virtually all modern societies have enacted criminal laws to cover certain very basic violations, such as homicide, incest, severe interpersonal assault, and major violations of property rights. Even in these areas, however, there is considerable variation as to the exact definition of offenses, circumstances accepted in extenuation, severity of official reaction, and so forth. To cite just one example, in capitalist societies today offenses against private property are considered to be extremely serious, whereas in socialist countries crimes against state property often have a more central place in the criminal code.

Naturally, the variations among countries are least with respect to these core offenses, and greatest as one gets into the more peripheral spheres of offending behavior. In such areas as sexual conduct, political behavior, and commercial regulation, one frequently finds crimes that "exist" in one country and not in another. What this means, of course, is simply that the social and official reactions to such behavior are different in the two situations. Just as the patterns of conforming and deviating behavior themselves reflect elements of cultural and social structure, so too do the patterns of reaction to such behavior. The definition of crimes is greatly confused in the United States by virtue of our federal system. We have not one, but 51 (state and federal) legal jurisdictions, each with its own set of criminal statutes.

We know too that what is a crime in a certain jurisdiction one year need not necessarily be criminal there the next. Prohibition is for Americans probably the best-known example of such changes over time, but in recent years we have seen frequent revision of the substantive definitions of crimes in the criminal laws of the various states as well as in the federal criminal code. There seems to be developing a slight tendency to "abolish" certain borderline crimes if the behavior is construed as essentially involving only private morality; on the other hand, the rapid expansion of industrial society has carried with it an enormous growth in "regulatory" crimes of all sorts.

Some of these points may seem rather obvious. However, it is essential that we place our thinking about crime in such a framework if we are to approach the topic with any clarity and reasonableness. For example, once we recognize that crime is defined by the criminal law and is therefore variable in content, we see quite clearly that no explanation of crime that limits itself to the motivation and behavior of individual offenders can ever be a complete one. Furthermore, in recognizing this essential legal aspect of crime, we come to realize that the statement "the major cause of crime is law" is not entirely a sophistical one. At least we are forced to see that by our control over the content of the criminal law we maintain a certain amount of influence in shaping the nature and extent of crime. Of course, to say that we are not going to treat a particular kind of offending act as criminal will not eliminate the behavior in question. On the other hand, the ramifications of charcterizing offending behavior as criminal may be extensive—and they are not always entirely socially desirable ones. In Chapter 6 of this book I shall discuss a number of areas in which what I have called the "criminalization of deviance" may actually do more harm than good.

Admittedly, the extent to which we can satisfactorily manipulate crime situations by changes in the criminal law is limited. Statutory manipulation will not solve the problem of a great deal of hard-core crime. To combat such crime we must, as I have already stressed, get at its basic social sources. Here again, the legal focus helps us keep our efforts in proper perspective, by underlining the fact that it simply will not do to act as though criminal offenders were somewhere "out there," beyond the bounds of society. Criminals are merely those citizens in our society who have engaged in acts that have been socially and officially defined as exceeding the limits of legally acceptable behavior. (We should keep in mind too, that in order for a specific individual to be labeled criminal he must, under our system of justice, have been tried and convicted of committing such an act. This requires that sufficient evidence link him with the act, that he be deemed "criminally responsible" for his behavior, without adequate extenuation, and so on.) Actually, we tend to be more or less oblivious to the subtle processes by which one day we view and describe John Doe merely as a person (perhaps a father, a factory worker, a churchgoer), while the next day (after he has been convicted of a crime, or perhaps even just charged with one) he has become a "criminal"—or possibly a "murderer" or "rapist."

I would suggest in fact that the common use of the term "criminal" has been extremely unhelpful. The usual unqualified reference to criminals serves only to reinforce popular assumptions about the offender's apartness and basic differentness which, as I shall stress repeatedly, are totally unwarranted in the light of our scientific knowledge of criminal behavior. It might be more useful to substitute more genuinely descriptive and less inflammatory terms—such as "convicted offender," "de-

fendant," and "suspect"—but the important thing is that we spend somewhat less time asking why individuals "go wrong," and a good deal
more asking just why it is that certain kinds of criminal behavior are
prevalent in our society.

A Criminal Society?

If we are not to speak of individuals as criminal, can we
then refer to a criminal society? As the title of this book indicates, I
think we can describe our society as criminal—indeed I think we must.
(In saying this I take the liberty of modifying somewhat my insistence
on semantic precision by adopting a largely figurative usage.) What I
mean by this is not, however, what would be meant by many pseudo-
alarmists and platitudinous soul-searchers who might also choose to
describe American society as criminal, or sick. On the contrary, it is
important that we reject a number of popular lines of reasoning about
America's criminality that are encouraged by such persons.

For example, it is sometimes asserted that we are a nation of
criminals, that American society is vitally menaced by an unprece-
dented tendency to "lawlessness," that we are experiencing a truly
alarming and ever-increasing "wave" of criminal behavior, behavior that
foreshadows the decline of civilized life in the United States and that
demands stern action to "stem the tide." This composite statement,
which I believe is not unrepresentative of a significant body of public
opinion about crime problems, is probably not without some slight
semblance of truth. But whatever truth is there is overwhelmed by
the fuzzy thinking and emotional appeals that inevitably characterize
this line of analysis.

Although studies have revealed that many citizens presumed to be
law-abiding have at one time or another engaged in some behavior for
which they might have been subject to criminal sanctions, there certainly is no evidence to suggest that we are becoming a nation of
hardened criminal offenders. Likewise, when public spokesmen refer to
a tendency toward lawlessness in modern American life, they often
obscure rather than clarify our view of the crime situation. "Lawlessness" has become a convenient category of disapproval for various
acts that should in many respects be distinguished from one another.
Ordinary street muggings; acts of civil disobedience protesting against

war and the draft; the major civil disorders that have shaken various American cities during the past few years; the assassination of public figures such as John F. Kennedy, Martin Luther King, Jr., and Robert Kennedy; on-campus student protests aimed at university reform; changing patterns of sexual morality; and even Supreme Court decisions safeguarding the procedural rights of defendants and suspects— all are lumped together, and the suggestion is made that in combination they indicate a pervasive decline in the authority of law in our society.

This is a very seductive conclusion. Some of these phenomena probably are indirectly related, and certainly each of them tells us something significant about the tenor of modern American life. However, it is extremely questionable to assert baldly—as did California Governor Ronald Reagan in the wake of Senator Robert Kennedy's assassination—that such an act is attributable to a growing permissiveness in the nation, to a growing attitude "that says a man can choose the laws he must obey, that he can take the law into his own hands for a cause, that crime does not necessarily mean punishment." [4] Our understanding of crime in America is hardly going to be enhanced by resorting to such glib and unsupported "explanations" of a variety of shocking and controversial events.

Similarly, as I shall indicate in more detail, the problems involved in determining crime rates and assessing trends are extremely complex. It seems that from time immemorial alarmists in all societies have deplored what seemed to them dangerous trends involving violations of custom and law. On balance, as we shall see, the available evidence does indeed suggest that crime in America is growing. Probably most criminologists believe that its present level exceeds by far what is "normal" or an irreducible minimum for a modern Western industrial society (although actually we have no idea how, scientifically, we might establish such a norm). Yet thinking in terms of a "wave" again blurs important distinctions among types of law violation, suggests an almost irreversible trend, and triggers emotions rather than constructive and clearly delimited policies. The self-righteous and get-tough reaction typified by Governor Reagan's statement, and the common assertion by political figures that crime will no longer be "permitted," only becloud the real issues. Crime in America is not a

---

[4] Quoted in the *New York Times*, June 6, 1968, p. 29.

consequence of governmental leniency. Ranting about people having the wrong attitude toward law (in the abstract) will only divert us from attention to the real sources of their behavior.

Another popular thesis concerning our society's criminality is that each of us must admit to his share of personal guilt for such major incidents of violence as the political assassinations just mentioned. In referring to our criminal society, I do not mean to cater to that pervasive social masochism which seems to afflict many Americans today —and which is especially concentrated among members of the informed white middle class. These people seem very receptive to public proclamations asserting that they are simply no damn good. If it takes the form of nebulous hand wringing and individual brooding about our sad state, "collective guilt" will not get us very far. As John Kenneth Galbraith nicely put it (in a commencement address at Tufts University), "Sometimes I think the greater danger in our day than violence is unfocused self-criticism. Nothing so serves as an excuse from reality." [5] What is needed in our country today is not an increase in personal soul-searching and feelings of guilt, but rather a widened sense of social consciousness that can be translated into concrete political action.

It is also sometimes suggested that what we must do to curb America's criminality is to perfect our ability to identify and control the increasingly large numbers of lawless individuals amongst us. Leaving aside for the moment the glib assumption that the proportion of the general population engaged in law violation is rapidly growing, can the criminality of our society be solved by dealing with so-called lawless individuals? I have already suggested that our penchant for emphasizing alleged differences between "criminals" and "normal people" is a misguided one—a theme that will indeed run throughout this book. When recent medical tests of defendants in certain highly publicized murder trials revealed the presence in each of a genetic deviation (an extra Y-chromosome) believed by some specialists to be related to extreme aggressive tendencies, the *New York Times* carried a front page article headed, "Genetic Abnormality Is Linked to Crime." [6] Note that the reference is to crime in general, and not simply to violent crime (or, as would have been more appropriate still, specific types of homicide). Even allowing for the vicissitudes of headline writing,

[5] John Kenneth Galbraith, "Escape and the Answer to Violence," commencement address delivered at Tufts University, Medford, Mass., June 9, 1968.

[6] *New York Times*, April 21, 1968, p. 1.

it would be a mistake not to recognize the appeal here (conscious or otherwise) to the public's wish for some scientifically certain key to crime problems. Certainly it is possible that systematic long-term research may reveal that some highly aggressive acts of crime are in part genetically determined. Yet, as we shall see, our knowledge of violent crime suggests that this is quite inadequate as a general explanation. Given the social and situational components of most violence in America, such "internal" factors are likely to have significance in only a very small proportion of violent offenses. And clearly the extension of such an explanation to crime in general is totally unwarranted.

The desire to isolate troublemakers runs deep. In American society its manifestations have included internment camps for wartime political enemies, institutions for the aged, proposed isolation centers for drug addicts, and the possibly excessive confinement of the psychologically disturbed (or disturbing)—as well as the strong reliance on imprisonment as a means of dealing with offenders against the criminal law. America's optimistic veneration of the "expert" reinforces the hope for specialized techniques by which to "head off" anticipated social problems. At the present time, psychiatric and psychological evaluation efforts are widely viewed as particularly relevant and "progressive" means toward that end.

Yet we must beware lest the psychiatric orientation be viewed as a satisfactory alternative to meaningful social reconstruction. The readiness of many Americans to accept efforts to identify and treat "predelinquent" children early in the school years—on the basis of asserted statistical probability that they will get into serious trouble later—is a rather ominous indication of where scientific "progressivism" may lead. As I shall make clear, psychiatric approaches undoubtedly have an important part to play in helping us understand and treat *some* criminal offenders. But, as the facts to be presented below also make evident, our overall crime picture massively reflects conditions that require collective social solutions. Social reform, not individual counseling, must have the highest priority in our program to reduce crime problems.

The Real Crimes of American Society

These popular ideas, then, only divert our attention from the real bases of America's criminality. If a sane, reasonable, and socially conscious man were asked to indicate the major grounds for legitimately describing American society as criminal, surely he would be compelled to come up with an answer emphasizing the following themes.

(1) *America is a criminal society because it is an unequal society.* At the time of this writing, many public figures are greatly exercised about domestic violence—and a special commission appointed by the President is studying this phenomenon. Yet, as I shall show, violence is considerably less central to American crime problems than is the tenacious persistence of widespread poverty and lack of economic opportunity. *The Other America* of the "invisible poor," so powerfully depicted by Michael Harrington in 1962, is still very much with us today.

The highly touted "war against poverty"—for which Harrington's book provided significant impetus—has made but fitful progress in eradicating the crying needs of the poor for decent jobs, adequate housing, and essential medical care. (The necessity in 1968 to organize a "Poor People's March on Washington," points up this depressing lack of progress.) Undoubtedly, present war expenditures have seriously hampered the government's efforts to curb poverty, yet one is left to query whether—even in the absence of the Vietnam conflict— the public and governmental commitment necessary for a systematic and uncompromising program aimed at decent living conditions for all Americans could in fact have been marshaled. It is noteworthy that even as the Poor People's March was pressing its demands in Washington, respondents to a Gallup Poll were expressing their disapproval of guaranteeing every American a decent income. When a national cross section of 1,570 Americans was asked in June, 1968, whether they would favor a guaranteed minimum income plan (". . . giving every family an income of at least $3,200 a year, which would be the amount for a family of four. If the family earns less than this, the Government would make up the difference."), 58 per cent indicated disapproval (although 78 per cent did approve of an alternative plan to guarantee enough work so that this income level might be reached). Disapproval of income guarantees was twice as strong among whites as among Negroes (60 versus 30 per cent), and perhaps not surprisingly disapproval varied directly with income level—the richer the person questioned, the less likely he was to approve the plan.[7]

---

[7] *New York Times*, June 16, 1968, p. 47.

Likewise, although recent racial disorders and the resulting Kerner Commission report (to be discussed below), as well as the assassination of Martin Luther King, Jr., led to a widespread public deploring of "white racism," national commitment and action to secure basic rights and equal opportunity for the black American have also lagged. As anybody who is willing to face up to social realities knows, Negro Americans have been trapped in all of the vicious circles that limit opportunity for the invisible poor—compounded by the special impact of prejudice and discrimination leveled against a highly visible minority. The situation of Negroes in our society has been one of multiple vulnerability, particularly with respect to involvement in criminal behavior. As we shall see, not only are they immersed in all those social conditions likely to promote criminal behavior, and subject to discriminatory treatment by the agencies of law enforcement, but in a certain sense Negroes also have been not too subtly defined by the white majority in America as Public Enemy Number One in the so-called "war against crime." To the extent that this is true, their dominant contribution to our crime problems has been ensured. The conscious or unconscious tendency among middle class whites to equate Negroes with crime has given the latter a final shove into total degradation and alienation, providing a powerful nothing-to-lose incentive to criminal acts.

It is, to be sure (and I shall discuss this point further in another chapter), a great oversimplification to attribute crime directly and solely to poverty. We know that many poor people do not resort to crime, and also that not all occasional or even persistent criminal offenders have come from poverty-stricken backgrounds. And the broad relation between societies' levels of affluence and crime rates is exceedingly complex. Furthermore, the social and psychological processes and situational influences involved in even the criminality of the poor are more intricate than a "poverty causes crime" theory would suggest.

Nonetheless—and notwithstanding the complicated and sometimes contradictory assertions of some of the sociological theories of crime causation to be reviewed below—many of the most serious aspects of our crime situation are integrally tied to the basic social and economic inequalities of our society. In part, this linkage occurs directly, through social and economic pressures, and the generation of feelings of deprivation and need. At the same time, indirect but equally potent attitudinal factors are involved. Poverty may breed generalized outlooks of profound frustration, hopelessness, and despair—which not surprisingly often activate aggressive impulses leading to hostile acts that the dominant middle-class majority then condemns as "criminal."

(2) *America is a criminal society by virtue of its involvement in mass violence abroad.* When President Lyndon Johnson addressed the nation following the assassination of Robert Kennedy, deploring violence and establishing a special commission to study it, many observers remarked on the glaring absence of any reference to the violent war in Vietnam. As *The Nation* commented editorially, "If it were sincere, what could such a commission tell him except truths about his own Administration so bitter that he has long since proved himself unable or unwilling to accept them? But this commission will not attempt to drive home any such hard facts: it is itself made up overwhelmingly of men who have supported his policy in Vietnam, men who believe that we can kill without scruple in Southeast Asia and by moral unction and police implacability suppress the consequences at home." [8]

For our purposes, however, the main issue is not the morality or legality of this particular war, but rather the potential impact it and other such military involvements may have on our domestic crime problem. Systematic evidence on the general relation between war and crime is somewhat inconclusive. And of course there has not yet been any systematic exploration of the impact of this particular conflict on crime in America. Actually, sociological researchers are hard put to test in any conclusive manner the subtle and long-term influence of such events. But it is certainly plausible that modern warfare does exert some significant if largely indirect influence on domestic crime problems. I shall return later to the issue of whether our society is "too violent." Suffice it to say here that the direct involvement of many Americans in acts of indiscriminate and mass violence, and the constant exposure of the entire citizenry to graphic depictions of these acts, can scarcely have any beneficial effects.

Various commentators have noted the increasingly depersonalized nature of much modern warfare. At least to some extent, push-button killing has allowed the perpetrator of violence to comfortably divorce himself from the consequences of his acts. Where this is not possible,

---

[8] *The Nation*, June 17, 1968, p. 780. With respect to legal issues raised by the war, see also Richard A. Falk, "International Law and the Conduct of the Vietnam War," in *In the Name of America* (New York: Clergy and Laymen Concerned About Vietnam, 1968), p. 27; Falk, *The Vietnam War and International Law* (Princeton: Princeton University Press, 1968); and Bertrand Russell, *War Crimes in Vietnam* (New York: Monthly Review Press, 1967).

efforts are made to depersonalize the enemy—as we see regularly in the language of modern war reporting, with its "mopping up operations," "body counts," and the like. Of course these phenomena are not entirely new, but more and more they are insidiously mediating what (despite our basic aggressive impulses) should be a natural human revulsion to extreme brutality.

Perhaps the more serious consequences of the current war are not those directly concerned with our feelings about violence. I have already alluded to the economic impact of military spending. This respresents a major obstacle to serious reconstruction of the basic social conditions of American life, and therefore has a very significant influence on the crime situation. Similarly, the attitudinal dimension is extremely important. Even among those who are not conscious political opponents of America's current military policies, the generalized discontent to which these policies give rise—particularly among Negroes (who poignantly reject the discrepancy between equal, even disproportionate, service and sacrifice abroad and unequal treatment at home)—contributes to an overall atmosphere that may be conducive to antisocial behavior. It is unlikely that we can expect to overcome the many methodological obstacles to a conclusive demonstration of the operation of subtle and indirect effects of this sort. But it would be a glib evasion to emphasize these technical problems. Everything we do know about structural and attitudinal causes of crime (discussed in Chapter 3 below) points to the potential relevance of the war's economic and psychological impact in shaping our present crime situation.

(3) *America is a criminal society because of certain emphases in our cultural values that help generate crime.* I have already referred to several areas of American life in which serious discrepancies or gaps exist between stated values and actual behavior. Certainly we need to examine our values in these areas. But we should also be concerned about some of the professed values we *do* live up to. Such highly esteemed values as dynamism, individualism, competition, and personal success (viewed largely in monetary terms) help to shape the nature of American life. As we shall see, our adherence to such dominant values may, in conjunction with structural aspects of our society, create pressures and frustrations that lead individuals into criminal behavior.

Criminologists commonly state that we cannot explain crime in terms of the general values of a society. In a narrowly scientific sense

—of trying to establish through statistical associations a basis for predicting individual criminality—this is quite true. A society's major values give rise to conformist achievement as well as to acts of law violation. The same drive for monetary success that leads one man into crime also produces the rags-to-riches story of the self-made millionaire. But in a more diffuse sense—of significantly coloring the typical social situations in which people in our society interact, and the overall outlooks they adopt—we ignore the role of basic American values at our peril. It is impossible to understand either the forms American crime takes, or the pressures underlying it, without some reference to them. It is, in this sense, quite proper to say of America, as it has been said more generally, that "a society has the criminals it deserves."

(4) *America is a criminal society because it has "created" much unnecessary crime.* As I have already pointed out, we establish the categories of crime by enacting criminal laws. In a subsequent chapter I shall indicate in some detail specific areas in which we have unwisely increased the dimensions of crime by succumbing to what seems almost a trait of our "national character"—a tendency to overlegislate. By such action we "produce" a great many "criminals" whose behavior may not warrant such designation. And often our criminalizing of a problem leads to a good deal of unnecessary secondary crime. In addition, our attempt to rely on criminal sanctions in situations where they are bound to fail may unwisely tax police and court resources, invite repressive enforcement practices and corruption, and do a good deal to undermine the integrity of the legal system.

(5) *America is a criminal society precisely because it has adopted an unseeing and unworkable orientation to crime problems.* This is an overriding theme I have already stressed—our misguided attempt to compartmentalize crime. Unfortunately, we seem addicted to the notion that crime problems always require special crime solutions. The more realistic stance, which sees general social reform as the *basic* path to reducing crime, has yet to gain wide public acceptance. Very gradually the American people are coming to realize the pressing need for antipoverty programs and improved race relations. But when confronted with crime issues, their vision tends to became blurred and the emotional reactions I have mentioned set in. The "get tough" outlook, stressing increased law enforcement, is activated. Among those sufficiently enlightened to recognize the shortcomings of this orientation, an increasingly popular tendency is to define individual offenders

as "sick." Even though this may result in less harsh treatment of some law violators, and hence may at least partially satisfy humanitarian impulses, it may also foist on doctors (and especially on psychiatrists) responsibility for managing social problems with which they are inadequately equipped to deal.

Crime, Law Reform, and Social Reconstruction

Implicit in the arguments I have presented so far is the conclusion that nothing less than a comprehensive restructuring of American society and of our system of criminal law can be expected to significantly alter our crime situation. Even though this seems an overwhelming and, at the same time, a somewhat nebulous goal, it is infinitely more realistic than continued reliance on inadequate short-term stratagems and semantic evasions. A good many years ago, an eminent criminologist, Hermann Mannheim, published a pioneering book entitled *Criminal Justice and Social Reconstruction,* in which he highlighted the necessary and intimate relation between crime and social and legal reform. While Mannheim was primarily concerned to examine critically various substantive and procedural aspects of the criminal law, his statement of the basic problems applies equally well to the broader task of simultaneous social and legal reform. He stated that,

We have to make up our minds as to what we regard as the *most important values* in a reconstructed world. . . . We have to decide whether these values should be protected *by the means at the disposal of the criminal law* [and implicit in his analysis was also the question of whether they *can* be so protected], or whether their protection should be left to agencies of a different character.[9]

Likewise, the recent presidential crime commission, in many respects a rather conservative and cautious body, asserted with a slightly different but complementary focus, the need for basic and comprehensive reform:

The underlying problems are ones that the criminal justice system can do little about. The unruliness of young people, widespread drug addiction, the existence of much poverty in a wealthy society, the pursuit of the dollar

[9] Hermann Mannheim, *Criminal Justice and Social Reconstruction* (New York: Oxford University Press, Inc., 1946), p. 2.

by any available means are phenomena the police, the courts, and the correctional apparatus, which must deal with crimes and criminals one by one, cannot confront directly. They are strands that can be disentangled from the fabric of American life only by the concerted action of all of society. They concern the Commission deeply, for unless society does take concerted action to change the general conditions and attitudes that are associated with crime, no improvement in law enforcement and administration of justice, the subjects this Commission was specifically asked to study, will be of much avail.[10]

Taking as our points of departure, then, the twin goals of a rational criminal code and an equitable and sane society, let us now examine more specifically some of the major findings of systematic research on crime in America. This will provide us with a more complete basis for stating the directions in which we must move if we are to have a sensible and effective policy to deal with the problems of crime that plague our society.

[10] President's Commission on Law Enforcement and Administration of Justice, *The Challenge of Crime in a Free Society* (Washington, D.C.: U.S. Government Printing Office, 1967), p. 1.

1

AMERICAN
CRIME PATTERNS

The general statistics of crime and criminals are probably the most unreliable and most difficult of all social statistics. It is impossible to determine with accuracy the amount of crime in any given jurisdiction at any particular time.

> Edwin H. Sutherland and Donald R. Cressey, *Principles of Criminology*

. . . if one goes from the "absolute" to the relative, to ask, as sociologists must, whether there is more crime now or less, whether it is here rather than there, whether the forms have changed and, if so, why, the answers to such questions have to come from facts and not from myths.

> Daniel Bell, "The Myth of Crime Waves"

Some Unrecognized Dimensions of Crime

In February, 1968, a Gallup Poll surveyed a representative sample of Americans in over 300 communities of all sizes, asking respondents "What is the most important problem facing this community today?" Crime and lawlessness was mentioned nearly twice as often as any other local problem. Queried about major national problems, respondents cited the Vietnam war most often, but crime (including riots, looting, juvenile delinquency) was the next most troubling condition, topping civil rights, high cost of living, poverty, and general unrest in the nation. According to the researchers, this was the first time that crime and lawlessness had been viewed by the pub-

lic as the top domestic problem facing the nation since the beginning
of systematic polling on such matters in the mid-thirties.[1]

These results seem to confirm both that Americans tend to compartmentalize crime and that their reactions to it are primarily emotional. Crime is viewed as being more of a core problem, requiring
urgent action, than poverty or civil rights—apparently with little
thought being given to the possibility that the latter conditions may
well breed the former. And apparently our reactions to crime and these
other national problems differ qualitatively as well as quantitatively.
We worry about and fear crime, whereas we rarely have such strong
feelings about poverty and racial difficulties. (The inclusion of riots
under "crime" in this survey does complicate our reading of the findings; however, the conclusion seems to hold that the public—somewhat abetted by questionnaire phrasing of this sort—is at least more
likely to subsume basic urban and racial problems under crime problems than the reverse.)

Is this uniquely intense concern justified? Without doubt there is
a great deal of crime in America today—it is a central theme of this
book that there is much more criminality than there "needs to be."
Yet our knowledge of just *how much* there actually is, exactly how
much of it is really *serious* crime, and our access to information and
reasoning on the basis of which we might gauge the extent to which
our present level of crime is excessive, are very slim indeed.

As Daniel Bell succinctly noted some years ago, "unfortunately,
crime statistics are as reliable as a woman giving her 'correct' age."[2]
This sensible warning, from time to time repeated by knowledgeable
commentators, has not been well heeded. On the contrary Americans
appear to be avidly receptive to the latest official crime figures, which
often are presented in a manner calculated to ignite intense alarm and
provoke impassioned reactions. For example, it is common for the
FBI in its annual *Uniform Crime Reports* to include "crime clocks"
graphically depicting the frequency of various major crimes: a murder
occurs somewhere in the United States every so many minutes, an

---

[1] *New York Times*, February 28, 1968, p. 29. For results of a later (mid-
July, 1968) poll, which apparently covered only opinion on national problems
and did not ask about "community" problems, see *New York Times*, August
4, 1968, p. 45. Again "crime and lawlessness" was rated as the second most
serious problem facing the nation.

[2] Daniel Bell, "The Myth of Crime Waves," in Bell, *The End of Ideology*
(New York: Collier Books, 1961). An earlier version of Bell's essay appeared in
Fortune, January, 1955.

auto theft every so many seconds, and so on. This technique would not be especially disturbing if it were in common use as a device to depict various aspects of American life. If accompanied on the one hand by a set of "clocks" showing the frequencies of births, marriages, college graduations, occupational achievements, crop harvests, and church attendance, and on the other by a set indicating infant mortality, highway accidents, war casualties, and unemployment, at least the crime clocks would be put in a reasonable perspective.

The inflammatory nature of the FBI's approach is brought home when it is compared with a much more reasonable device used by the President's Commission on Law Enforcement to show the nature and variety of American crime. Describing "Crime in a City Precinct"— the 365 diverse events reported as criminal behavior within a reasonably representative Chicago precinct during a typical week in 1966 —the Commission demonstrated the wide range and situational backgrounds of criminal acts. Such offenses as vandalism (often including "windows broken by rocks, bricks, snowballs, or eggs"), indecent exposure, gambling, narcotics violations, illegal fortunetelling, petty theft (including shoplifting), and lewd telephone calls combine with assaults, robberies, attempted rapes (two), and murder (one) to form the total crime picture. The Commission recognized that a great many crimes were never reported (see below), but it also noted that "Some 50 of the citizen reports proved to be unfounded, including 18 of 86 reported burglaries, 10 of 33 reported car thefts, 4 of 43 reported assaults, 2 of 9 reported robberies, and 1 of 31 reported thefts of over $50." After spelling out in some detail the complex social situations surrounding typical crime events, the Commission concluded:

What the crimes of that week strongly suggest is that, although there is always some danger in the city of being robbed and perhaps injured on the street and a considerable danger of being burglarized, what people have to fear most from crime is in themselves: their own carelessness or bravado; their attitudes toward their families and friends; toward the people they work for or who work for them; their appetites for drugs and liquor and sex; their own eccentricities; their own perversities; their own passions. Crime in Town Hall that week, like crime anywhere any week, consisted of the brutal, frightening, surreptitious, selfish, thoughtless, compulsive, sad, and funny ways people behave toward each other.[3]

[3] President's Commission on Law Enforcement and Administration of Justice, *Task Force Report: Crime and its Impact—An Assessment* (Washington, D.C.: U.S. Government Printing Office, 1967), p. 13. Commission findings cited in this chapter are taken from the same report, especially Chaps. 2, 5, and 6.

The Commission's report on assessment of crime is perhaps the most responsible and comprehensive statement available concerning the nature and extent of crime in America. It brings together and interprets wisely the relevant official statistics and also various data from special studies sponsored by the Commission. A major point emphasized in this report, and to which I shall return later, is that crimes of violence against the person comprise a very small proportion of the crime total. (In the 1965 FBI figures the Commission worked with, such offenses, *including* robbery [the taking of property from a person by use or threat of force with or without a weapon], made up only 13 per cent of major crimes; nonviolent property crimes accounted for the remaining 87 per cent.)[4] Furthermore, the common assumption and fear of attack by strangers lurking in the shadows is largely unwarranted. Studies cited by the Commission show that "about 70 per cent of all willful killings, nearly two-thirds of all aggravated assaults, and a high percentage of forcible rapes [64 per cent in a Washington, D.C. survey, and 57 per cent in a Philadelphia study] are committed by family members, friends, or other persons previously known to their victims." (Robbery, the Commission noted, does not usually involve this prior relationship between offender and victim.)

The Commission also initiated the first national study of crime victimization. In a survey of some 10,000 households, the National Opinion Research Center asked Americans in all walks of life whether they, or any member of their household, had been a victim of crime during the past year, whether the crime had been reported, and if not, the reasons for not reporting the offense. This research showed, as was anticipated, that the actual amount of crime is much greater than that reflected in the official police statistics—a matter which I shall discuss in some detail later in this chapter. An equally illuminating discovery was that there are significant variations among different income levels within the American population with respect to the risk of being a crime victim. As the Commission reported:

The risks of victimization from forcible rape, robbery, and burglary, are clearly concentrated in the lowest income group and decrease steadily at higher income levels. The picture is somewhat more erratic for the offenses of aggravated assault, larceny of $50 and over, and vehicle theft. Victimization for larcency increases sharply in the highest income group.

_____
[4] The same proportions prevailed during 1966, and again in 1967.

National figures on victimization also show sharp differences between whites and nonwhites. . . . Nonwhites are victimized disproportionately by all Index [major] crimes except larceny $50 and over.

. . . it is Negro males and females who are most likely to be victimized in crimes against the person. A Negro man in Chicago runs the risk of being a victim nearly six times as often as a white man, a Negro woman nearly eight times as often as a white woman.

Finally, in line with the findings of much past crime research, the Commission found a close correlation in race between victims and offenders. "Negroes are most likely to assault Negroes, whites most likely to assault whites. Thus, while Negro males account for two-thirds of all assaults, the offender who victimizes a white person is most likely also to be white."

Documenting the public's fear of crime mentioned earlier, the Commission noted that about one-third of the respondents in its national survey expressed fear about walking alone at night in their own neighborhoods, and that physical assaults are the most feared offenses. Basically, the Commission suggested, fear of crime appears to incorporate a "fear of the stranger" that in turn heightens distrust and social instability. Not only is it the case that "the public fears the most the crimes that occur the least—crimes of violence," but, strikingly, pervasive fears of violent crime persist despite the statistically much greater risks Americans face from other sources in their everyday lives—such as from traffic and home accidents, and improper emergency medical care.

Are We Experiencing a Crime Wave?

The most widely used official crime statistics are those brought together in the *Uniform Crime Reports* compiled by the Federal Bureau of Investigation. This annual source, which represents our main effort at developing a systematic and nation-wide tabulation of criminal offenses, involves the voluntary submission to the FBI by local police departments throughout the country of data on "crimes known" to them and on actual arrests—broken down in terms of various offense categories. Seven of these categories—considered to involve the most serious offenses—are brought together to form the Bureau's so-called Crime Index. During 1967 (the most recent year for which complete figures are available at the time this is written) the FBI reported the following numbers (and rates per 100,000 population) of Index crimes known to the police:[5]

Murder and nonnegligent manslaughter	12,093	6.1 *(per 100,000)*
Forcible rape	27,096	13.7
Robbery	202,053	102.1
Aggravated assault	253,321	128.0
Burglary	1,605,701	811.5
Larceny $50 and over	1,047,085	529.2
Auto theft	654,924	331.0

To put these figures in a broader perspective it should be noted that the non-Index (minor) offenses, on which the FBI reports only arrest rather than "crimes known" statistics, greatly outnumber the Index crimes. Thus, of a grand total in 1967 of 5,518,420 arrests (for all kinds of offenses), the total for the seven Index offenses was only 996,800. Drunkenness offenses were involved in 1,517,809 arrests and disorderly conduct violations contributed another 550,469, whereas the largest number for any of the seven major categories was 447,299 larceny arrests. The significant discrepancies between "crimes known" and arrest figures are apparent. Since the magnitude of such gaps varies among the particular offenses, it is next to impossible to systematically align available data for the Index and non-Index crimes. Nonetheless it is quite clear that dealing with so-called "peacekeeping" offenses, such as drunkenness, disorderly conduct, and vagrancy, represents a major police activity.

Of course the greatest deficiency of the official crime figures is that they cannot cover all criminal behavior. Crimes known to the police seem to come "closest" to the universe of actual crimes (and from this standpoint constitute a better gauge of the extent of crime than would arrest or prisoner statistics—both of which presumably understate badly the full amount of criminal behavior). But it is well known that a tremendous number of crimes is never even reported to the police. Thus the amounts of crime revealed in the victim survey conducted for the President's Commission were greatly in excess of the officially reported rates: "Forcible rapes were more than 3 1/2 times the reported rate, burglaries 3 times, aggravated assaults and larcenies of $50 and over more than double, and robbery 50 per cent greater

[5] U.S. Department of Justice, Federal Bureau of Investigation, *Crime in the United States*, Uniform Crime Reports—1967 (Washington, D.C.: U.S. Government Printing Office, 1968), pp. 62–63.

than the reported rate. Only vehicle theft was lower and then by a small amount. (The single homicide reported is too small a number to be statistically useful.)" Crucial to the relative reportability of an offense are the degree to which it is publicly visible and the presence or absence of a complaining victim. Private and consensual illicit behavior is most likely to be significantly underreported; gambling offenses, illegal drug sales, prostitution, and various other forms of illegal sex behavior are major examples.

Likewise, it has long been recognized that a great deal of shoplifting, minor embezzlement, and petty fraud never comes to the attention of the police. In the area of consumer fraud, 90 per cent of the cases disclosed in the national victimization survey had gone unreported to the police. It should be noted too that federal criminal offenses are not included in the *Uniform Crime Reports*. Although the number of such cases actually filed in court is relatively small (the President's Commission cites the following figures for the year 1966: antitrust, 7; food and drug, 350; income tax evasion, 863; liquor revenue violations, 2,729; narcotics, 2,293; immigration, 3,188), clearly federal data cover areas of behavior that are at least potentially of great significance for the effort to comprehend the total crime picture in the United States.

How useful are the official crime statistics if our aim is not simply to determine the present level of criminality but rather to assess short-term or long-term crime trends? Central to the problem of assessing trends is the fact that the official figures are (as we have already in part seen) far from being a "pure" reflection of actual criminal behavior. Rather they represent a mixture of the behavior of offenders and the behavior of the law enforcement officials who record the offenses. This mixture is subject to a number of kinds of variation that make efforts at comparison extremely difficult. Meaningful comparison would seem to require uniformity in the definitions of offenses and at least roughly comparable reporting and recording procedures in the units to be analyzed.

These conditions have never been fully met in the short run, let alone over long periods of time. Although the FBI provides local police departments with a special handbook of guidelines to be used in completing forms for the *Uniform Crime Reports*—including the definitions of offenses they are supposed to apply—we don't really know how scrupulously these instructions are followed. Local definitions and practices may produce substantial variations in the nature of the recording process. Similarly, changes in police practice over time confound the interpretation of statistics. This is most evident, of course, with respect to arrest figures; it is always difficult to know whether an apparent "trend" in arrests is the result of an actual crime increase or simply an indication of more vigorous enforcement activity. Even with "crimes known" statistics, however, the role of the police themselves in shaping apparent trends has been considerable. This point was sharply made by the President's Commission, which showed how changes in the reporting systems of New York City and Chicago had several times "produced large paper increase in crime."

Although Chicago, with about 3 million people, has remained a little less than half the size of New York city . . . it was reporting in 1935 about 3 times as many robberies. It continued to report several times as many robberies as New York City until 1949, when the FBI discontinued publication of New York reports because it no longer believed them. In 1950 New York discontinued its prior practice of allowing precincts to handle complaints directly and installed a central reporting system, through which citizens had to route all calls.

In the first year, robberies rose 400 per cent and burglaries 1,300 per cent, passing Chicago in volume for both offenses. In 1960 Chicago installed a central complaint bureau of its own, reporting thereafter several times more robberies than New York. In 1966 New York, which appeared to have had a sharp decline in robberies in the late fifties, again tightened its central controls and found a much higher number of offenses. Based on preliminary reports for 1966, it is now reporting about 40 per cent more robberies than Chicago.

This sort of crazy-quilt pattern of statistical distortions may not be at all untypical. Whenever one makes cross-jurisdictional, or longitudinal comparisons, or a combination of both, one faces this kind of problem. Naturally, when one attempts cross-national comparisons (where not even the incomplete effort at definitional and procedural uniformity is present), or the assessment of really long-term trends (in which one must compare time periods for which quite different— or in some cases no—systems of crime reporting and recording prevailed), the difficulties are greatly heightened.

It is not surprising, under these circumstances, that disinterested observers of crime much prefer to limit their trend assessment to relatively short periods, and to take data involving cross-cultural comparisons with a grain of salt. Americans in virtually every era, from colonial days to the present, have been much concerned about the level of crime in their society. And at numerous times they believed they were experiencing major upsurges of criminality, which they labeled "crime waves." Public concern about such alleged fluctuations often involves a misreading of actual events. Indeed it may even be the case, as sociologist Kai Erikson recently argued in his fascinating book *Wayward Puritans,*[6] that at least in a particular historical era the amount of deviant behavior (or crime) a community or society encounters is apt to remain fairly constant. Surveying deviance and social control in Puritan New England, and including an analysis of several apparent "crime waves" of that period, Erikson points out that to some extent the amount of deviation in a community necessarily reflects the size, and complexity, and activity of its social control system and that a community tends to establish "normal" bounds for deviation—only reacting strongly when these bounds are exceeded. If this analysis is correct, then many short-term "crime waves" may simply represent a sudden shifting of attention to one or another particular form of deviance or crime, or some abrupt change in the pattern of enforcement activity. Crime itself may not have changed as much as the reactions to it.

At any rate, it certainly seems futile to deliberate about crime trends in America from its founding to the present, or to conjecture whether modern societies display greater criminality than ancient or primitive ones. Although such inquiries might prove intellectually diverting, probably we would all agree that we have enough trouble on our hands right now without dissipating our analytic energies in such a manner. With respect to less ambitious assessments, there seems to be a general consensus among specialists that crime in America has indeed substantially increased between 1933 (the first year for which national figures are available) and the present time. Summaries of official data (to some extent adjusted to take account of deficiencies in national coverage of our reporting system prior to 1958) suggest roughly the following picture. With respect to violent crimes the overall trend is clearly upward (the President's Commission placed the adjusted rate for all violent offenses at about 150 per 100,000 population in 1933, whereas at the present time this rate well exceeds 200). Different trends are in evidence, however, for *particular* crimes of violence:

[6] Kai T. Erikson, *Wayward Puritans* (New York: John Wiley & Sons, Inc., 1966).

substantial increases have been shown for forcible rape and aggravated assault; robbery rates have fluctuated frequently but at present are lower than they were in the early thirties; the trend in willful
homicide has been slightly downward, with the current figure lower
than that for the thirties. Property crime increases have been much
more pronounced, with the burglary rate nearly doubling and the
rate for larceny of $50 and over reaching a level of more than 550 per
cent that of the early thirties. Since 1960 the official data have shown
upward trends for virtually all offenses, a point which the FBI is at
pains to emphasize in its press releases and through tables in its annual reports showing short-run trends. Notwithstanding the various
kinds of statistical inadequacy already mentioned (and some other
technical difficulties with the FBI figures), the President's Commission concluded that most forms of crime probably are in fact increasing more rapidly than the American population is growing, and it
pointed to a number of conditions that make this development understandable.

Shifts in the age composition of the population in part account for
growing crime—the high crime-risk group between 18 and 24 has
been increasing much faster than other groups in the population. Also,
it has long been recognized that urban crime rates exceed rural ones,
and a second major development in American society has been an increase in the proportion of the population located in urban areas. And,
ironically, the Commission noted that increased affluence may be directly related to upward crime trends—there is more around to steal
and it is less well protected than was previously the case. (Some sociologists have even suggested that if property crime trends were as-
sessed in terms of a level-of-property-available base rather than in
terms of a population base, the apparent long-term increases in these
offenses would be largely erased.) Finally, the Commission mentioned
two aspects of the crime reporting process that may especially contribute to the rising official crime rates: the growing expectation of
the poor and of minority-group members that they are entitled to their
rights and the correspondingly greater inclination to seek police protection and report wrongs done them, and the professionalization of
American police forces, which has made for more systematic care in
record keeping and an increased likelihood of processing complaints in
a formal, and hence recordable, manner. These factors do not, of course,
suggest that crime increases are not "real"; they (and other relevant

social conditions) merely help us to understand more fully the meaning of crime trends.

As regards crime trends and levels it is also worth noting that there exist significant regional and local differences *within* the United States. For many years the Southern region has displayed particularly high assault and homicide rates. The Pacific states, especially as they reflect the high California figures, had by the 1960's the highest overall rates for both serious crimes against the person and property offenses. New England showed the lowest rates for major crimes against the person, the East South Central states the lowest for major property crimes.

The highest crime rates are heavily concentrated in major urban areas—with the overall rural-urban differentials being accounted for largely by pronounced differences in the rates for major property crimes. Generally speaking, city size is closely related to the magnitude of average crime rates. Overall suburban rates have been increasing somewhat and are now similar to those of the smaller cities. Population concentration and degree of urbanization do not, however, explain all crime rate variations. Official statistics show, for example, considerable disparities in overall rates for major crimes among cities of the same size. Furthermore, specific cities seem to be high on certain crimes and not so high on others. Thus the President's Commission reported:

Los Angeles is 1st for rape and 4th for aggravated assault, but 20th for murder, with a murder rate less than half that of St. Louis. Chicago has the highest rate for robbery but a relatively low rate for burglary. New York is 5th in larcenies $50 and over, but 54th for larcenies under $50. The risk of auto theft is about 50 per cent greater in Boston than anywhere else in the country, but in Boston the likelihood of other kinds of theft is about the average for cities over 250,000.

The Commission was itself somewhat stymied by these strange variations, although it noted that undoubtedly some of them reflect, at least in part, differences in reporting.

In looking over these varied data on American crime rates, what in general can we conclude regarding the urgency of crime problems in this country? Unfortunately there are no meaningful criteria available through which we can authoritatively determine the extent to which American crime levels exceed those that "should" prevail in our kind of society. As I have already mentioned, comparisons with other countries are not much help—the variations in definitions of crime and reporting procedures, and the more general cross-cultural differences involved, greatly impair the comparability of such data. It is often said rather glibly that America is the most criminal of all societies (a view given world-wide credence through American gangster films and television programs, and questionably revived by the news of the several recent political assassinations in the United States), but whether this is true is not at all clear. The President's Commission noted that officially reported data indicate rapid rises in property crimes for most other countries, as well as for the United States. With respect to crimes of violence the apparent trends are less uniform: for example, between 1955 and 1964 reported violent crimes in England and Wales rose more than 150 per cent, but downward trends in crimes of violence were reported for Belgium, Denmark, Norway, and Switzerland. A comparison of homicide rates in various countries,[7] covering the years 1960–1962 (one of the three years for each country, depending on available data), showed the following:

Columbia	36.5	*(per 100,000)*
Mexico	31.9	
South Africa	21.8	
United States	4.8	*(1962 figures. As we have seen, the rate has gone up somewhat since then, but presumably it has also risen in the other countries listed here.)*
Japan	1.5	
France	1.5	
Canada	1.4	
Federal Republic of Germany	1.2	
England/Wales	.7	
Ireland	.4	

Limitations of our own national statistics also make it very difficult to assess the overall seriousness of our crime situation. Quite apart from the fact that the *Uniform Crime Reports* are neither really "uniform" nor complete, critics of these statistics have noted that the FBI's so-called Crime Index is—by virtue of the reporting procedures it

[7] United Nations, *Demographic Yearbook*, 1963, pp. 594–611, as reproduced in President's Commission on Law Enforcement and Administration of Justice, *op. cit.*, p. 39.

employs—on its face quite inadequate as a measure of the nature and seriousness of American crime.[8] The counting up of offenses to develop this "index" takes into account neither the number of victims of any offense, nor the nature and extent of their victimization. And where a given report to the police involves multiple offenses, only one (that which is considered more serious by the FBI) is recorded for Index purposes. All offenses are given equal weight in reaching the Index total, so that a $50 larceny and a murder contribute equally to the overall serious crime rate. Furthermore, it is questionable whether the Index crimes are always more serious than non-Index offenses. Critics have noted, for example, that neither arson nor kidnapping appears in the Index. The economic loss from certain non-Index offenses —such as embezzlement or fraud—may often be greater than that involved in larceny of $50 and over (which may include such acts as pocketpicking, shoplifting, and bicycle theft). This matter of economic loss suggests a final and very serious shortcoming—that this measure of the extent of major American crime does not at all reflect the substantial amount of serious economic crime (such as tax evasion and other white-collar offenses, to which we shall return later) that directly and indirectly may be inflicting great social harm in this country. Nor are such economically significant but notoriously underreported offenses as abortion in such a tabulation.

One of the implications of all of this may be that it would be wise for us to pay somewhat less attention to the *amount* of crime and to think a bit more about what *kinds* of crime are currently plentiful in the United States, and *why*. To continuously belabor the fact that Index crimes show a steadily upward trend—as the FBI is fond of doing—hardly enlightens us or produces steps toward effective reform. Certainly the high level of crime is an indication that something is seriously wrong in American life. But it tells us nothing about *what* is wrong. If we redirect our attention to the nature and sources of crime in America, then at least we will be confronting more directly the social and legal conditions *about which we can do something*. As I noted at the outset, our basic problem is not that burgeoning crime rates are producing social disorder and undermining the criminal law,

[8] For such criticisms and an alternative approach that tries to establish weightings that would allow meaningful indexing, see Thorsten Sellin and Marvin Wolfgang, *The Measurement of Delinquency* (New York: John Wiley & Sons, Inc., 1964); and *Constructing an Index of Delinquency* (Center of Criminological Research, University of Pennsylvania, 1963).

but rather that social disorder and unwise law breed crime. High crime rates are a warning and not an explanation.

Who Are the Offenders?

Similarly, to take the prevalence of crime as an indication simply that there are too many wrongdoers amongst us (and, as some would claim to do, to "explain" our crime problems by their presence) is also an evasion of basic causes. However, it is helpful—in seeking to understand the nature of crime problems in America—to explore, insofar as possible, the social distribution of individual offenders.

In attempting to do this we are, alas, once again severely limited by the nature of available statistics. "Crimes known" tabulations are not designed to provide information about offenders; there, the sole concern is to attempt a full recording of criminal acts. To get information about offender characteristics, we have to go to statistics on individuals who have been arrested, prosecuted, convicted, or imprisoned. Sociologists are pretty well agreed that not one of these categories provides us with a basis for obtaining accurate systematic information about actual offenders against the criminal law. As I noted earlier, many studies in criminology—at least in its formative stages—relied on comparing "samples" of imprisoned offenders with "matched" samples composed of otherwise similar (socioeconomically, etc.) non-prisoners. Yet sophisticated analysts now realize that neither kind of sample could be truly representative of the "universe" it was meant to represent. Not all actual criminal offenders are imprisoned, and some persons who are imprisoned did not in fact commit the acts for which they were convicted.

The characteristics of prisoners may tell us more about the kinds of people likely to be imprisoned than they do about the kinds of people who engage in criminal behavior. A key problem is referred to by some criminologists as "case mortality." Not all the crimes known to the police are "cleared" by arrest, not all arrests lead to actual prosecution, not all prosecutions result in convictions, not all those convicted are sentenced to prison. At each stage in our processes of administration of justice a certain proportion of cases drops out of the picture. For this reason, it is often asserted that prisoner statistics are probably the least useful as an indicator of the characteristics of actual offenders (reflecting as they do the stage "furthest away" from the criminal event itself). By the same reasoning, arrest data may be the most useful available source of information about offenders. Even the arrest figures, however, are generally recognized as being far from satisfactory.

Because of this realization, sociologists began in the late 1930's and early 1940's to devise means of obtaining more representative samplings of actual offenders. Researchers demonstrated, for example, that many young persons known to have engaged in delinquent acts never came before the juvenile court. Many were handled informally by school officials or police, or were quietly referred to private or public social agencies. And there were systematic variations in the socioeconomic characteristics of those individuals who were more likely or less likely to face formal judicial proceedings (for example, the extensive use of social agencies among Jews was reflected in low official delinquency rates for Jewish youth).[9]

Researchers also hit on the idea of asking people—in samples drawn from the population at large—whether they had ever committed any crimes. One study of college students found that almost all of them had previously engaged in some behavior for which they might have been judged delinquent, but virtually none of which resulted in any official action against them. In another inquiry, a sample of over 1,600 adults (in which the upper social classes were somewhat overrepresented despite efforts to obtain a balanced cross section) was given a questionnaire asking them to indicate which of 49 violations they had committed. Ninety-one per cent admitted having committed one or more offenses for which they might have been jailed or imprisoned. The findings showed an average of 18 adult offenses for the men and 11 for the women in the sample. At least one felony was admitted to by 46 per cent of the men and 27 per cent of the women.[10]

Studies of this sort indicated that there was a great deal more actual crime than was officially recorded. Sociologists thus came to recognize as an important feature of the crime picture the existence of "hidden" crime and delinquency. This finding has been borne out through the use of increasingly sophisticated techniques developed for such "self-reported behavior" research since those original studies. And as we have also seen, hidden criminality was indicated by the discrepancy

[9] A good example of this body of work is Sophia Robison, *Can Delinquency Be Measured?* (New York: Columbia University Press, 1936).

[10] Findings from this survey, conducted by J. S. Wallerstein and C. J. Wyle, were published under the pointed title, "Our Law-Abiding Law-Breakers," *Probation,* 25 (March–April, 1947), 107–12.

between the official crime rate figures and those discovered in the recent national study of victimization. Another apparent implication of the early "hidden crime" studies was that in the main it was lower-class crime that was officially dealt with, and middle- and upper-class offenses that remained hidden. The overwhelmingly disproportionate presence of lower-class individuals found in the official data largely vanished when you obtained a sample of offenders through self-reports from the general population. On the other hand, findings in at least one now classic study—of juvenile delinquency in the Cambridge-Somerville (Massachusetts) area—revealed that even among lower-class youth in high delinquency rate neighborhoods, a very large number of serious criminal acts went unrecorded. So, we know that there certainly is a good bit of hidden working-class crime too.

Sociological specialists continue to argue this issue of the social class distribution of crime. But the dominant view probably is that the most serious crimes *are* heavily concentrated in the lower-class sectors of our society. This is particularly true of the major varieties of urban male adolescent criminality in which some form of "delinquent subculture" (see Chapter 3) is involved. As one major study of such behavior notes, the development of a culture-within-a-culture geared to antisocial activity is not such a serious problem in middle-class areas. "In the lower class they seem to exhibit more distinctive and highly integrated forms of organization than in the middle class. For this reason . . . lower-class patterns of delinquency present the most costly and difficult problems in the area of delinquency control and prevention." [11]

Of course, any assessment of the relation between social class and crime is seriously complicated by the fact that official action is only rarely taken with respect to the "white-collar crime" (occupational offenses committed by persons of high socioeconomic status), which we know is highly prevalent in American society. It has been suggested by some criminologists that if such behavior were accurately recorded, both the lower class and the upper class would show very high crime rates, with only the middle classes evidencing low criminality.

Furthermore, research has indicated that in their dealings with suspects and known offenders (regardless of the forms of criminal behavior involved) the police and other officials often treat members of the different social classes differently. Thus, in a very revealing recent

[11] Richard A. Cloward and Lloyd E. Ohlin, *Deliquency and Opportunity* (New York: The Free Press, 1960), p. 28.

study of "Police Encounters with Juveniles," it was found that, next to prior record, the *demeanor* of youths brought into the police station was the most important factor affecting the police in their discretionary disposition of cases. Boys who were neatly dressed, who were contrite about their offenses and respectful and "cooperative" in manner, were most likely to receive reprimands and informal handling. However, those who dressed in a manner the police associated with "tough guys," and who were nonchalant or uncooperative in their dealings with the police, ran a much greater risk of formal arrest and court processing.[12] Basically, in other words, those who behaved like nice middle-class boys were let off.

We really do not know the extent to which such enforcement differentials, undoubtedly widespread, represent real bias against the lower classes (although, as we shall see, in this particular study police officers admitted certain biases). Some observers insist that at least to a degree tougher police action against lower-class youth reflects a realistic appraisal—based on long experience—that that they are more likely than their middle-class counterparts to make serious trouble for the community and to persist in crime if not curbed. (This kind of reasoning ignores the possibility that the harsh police reaction itself may increase rather than curb the likelihood of such persons following the path from isolated offense to criminal "career.")

However we feel about these matters, it would seem that the concept of "categoric risk" developed by sociologist Walter Reckless is extremely useful in describing class variations in crime. Persons in the lower socioeconomic strata probably run a greater risk (in a kind of actuarial sense) of engaging in common forms of serious crime. And we know they run a greater risk of being suspected; if suspected, arrested; if arrested, prosecuted; if prosecuted, convicted; and if convicted, imprisoned.

It probably does not come as a surprise to most readers that official reports show major conventional crime to be heavily concentrated in the 15- to 25-year-old age group. We tend to think of "criminals" as being strong and active—a stereotype that seems to be confirmed by such data. Actually youthful criminality has relatively little to do with such presumed sprightliness. On the contrary, age variations in crime are much more likely to reflect social position and the impact of social pressures—a point brought home by the fact that age ratios in crime

[12] Irving Piliavin and Scott Briar, "Police Encounters with Juveniles," *American Journal of Sociology*, 70 (September, 1964), 206–14.

vary for particular kinds of offenses, vary by sex, and probably also vary by area of residence.

In 1967, the FBI noted that 47.4 per cent of all arrests were of persons under 25, 36.5 per cent were under 21, 24.3 per cent were under 18, and 9.6 per cent under 15.[13] The figures for major offenses were even higher—75.3 per cent under 25, 64.4 per cent under 21, 49.0 per cent under 18, and 23.1 per cent under 15. Even within this category of major offenses, however, there were sharp variations with respect to specific offenses. Thus, whereas 88.7 per cent of auto thefts involved persons under 25, only 37.3 per cent of the murder and non-negligent manslaughter arrests fell into that age category—this differential becomes even more striking (61.8 per cent of the auto thefts versus 9.1 per cent of the homicides) when one considers the under-18 age group. Not surprisingly, such variations by offense become still more pronounced when one includes the crimes considered less serious. Thus 100 per cent of the arrests of runaways were of persons under 18, whereas for driving "under the influence" only 1.0 per cent of those arrested were under 18, and only 6.3 per cent under 21. Likewise, while 76.5 per cent of those arrested for vandalism were under 18 (and 85.1 per cent under 21), the corresponding figures for fraud were 4.2 and 13.8.

Such variations in the age concentrations for particular crimes strongly suggest the importance of situational factors (including occupational status), and in a broad sense reflect the relation between age and the opportunity to commit various crimes. As one text notes, with respect to some of the offenses that are concentrated in the older age groups:

It takes time to become an alcoholic or to become the kind of person who frequents the places where police are likely to arrest people for drunkenness. It takes time to become the kind of person police arrest for vagrancy. It takes time to become interested in the type of gambling activity which is located in places the police are likely to raid. It takes time to reach a position where the opportunity is presented for embezzling and fraud, where sufficient skill has been acquired to execute the deed, or where problems of middle age require solutions by manipulation of books, records, and checks.[14]

We also know that, generally speaking, the age of maximum crimi-

    [13] *Crime in the United States,* Uniform Crime Reports—1967, p. 123.
    [14] Walter C. Reckless, *The Crime Problems,* 4th ed. (New York: Appleton-Century-Crofts, 1967), p. 102.

nality is higher for females than for males; that children who become delinquent do so at an earlier age in areas having high delinquency rates than in areas having low rates; and that the younger a person is when he commits his first crime, the greater chance there is that he will go on to further offenses. However, it is significant that despite popular beliefs to the contrary, relatively few juvenile delinquents actually become adult offenders. As David Matza has pointed out, "Anywhere from 60 to 85 per cent of delinquents do not apparently become adult violators. Moreover, this reform seems to occur irrespective of intervention of correctional agencies and irrespective of the quality of correctional service." [15]

Sex ratios in crime are, as most of us would expect, pronounced. The evidence on this matter has been succinctly summarized by Sutherland and Cressey as follows: "The crime rate for men is greatly in excess of the rate for women—in all nations, all communities within a nation, all age groups, all periods of history for which organized statistics are available, and for all types of crime except those peculiar to women, such as infanticide and abortion." [16] Recently in the United States, male arrest rates have run around ten times the female rates. About fifteen times as many men as women are incarcerated in correctional institutions, if we include jails, and twenty times as many if we consider only prisons and major reformatories. About 85 per cent of juvenile court cases involve boys.

I often ask my sociology students, "Picture in your mind's eye a typical criminal." Invariably, an overwhelming majority has in mind a man. Yet women too are obviously quite capable of crime and in fact do engage in much criminal behavior. It is true that this particular stereotype or "picture in our minds" seems well borne out in a statistical sense (and the higher official male rates are in general also substantiated by data from the self-report studies mentioned earlier). Nonetheless, it is still revealing that most of us without much hesitation view crime as somehow a characteristically male activity, that we give very little if any thought to the crimes of women. (It is doubtful that the recent film *Bonnie and Clyde,* and the clothing fads that followed in the wake of its popularity, significantly affected this tendency.)

In 1950 sociologist Otto Pollak startled many of his professional col-

---

[15] David Matza, *Delinquency and Drift* (New York: John Wiley & Sons, Inc., 1964), p. 22.
[16] Sutherland and Cressey, *Principles of Criminology,* p. 138.

leagues when he published a controversial book entitled *The Criminality of Women.*[17] Asserting that available statistics regarding female crime are highly inadequate and misleading, Pollak noted that offenses particularly likely to be committed by women (including non-professional shoplifting, thefts by domestic servants, abortions, perjury, and disturbance of the peace) are among those that are most notoriously underreported. He emphasized also that certain prevalent offenses for which males are prosecuted go relatively unprosecuted when women are involved (citing as examples homosexual acts and exhibitionism). Developing further his central theme of "the masked character" of female crime, Pollak pointed to findings that women who kill use poison more than any other means, and he suggested that female homicide within the family circle may be much more frequent than we realize. Woman's social roles in preparing meals, nursing the sick, and caring for children, he argued, offer special opportunities to commit a variety of offenses that may go undetected.

Advancing the notion of woman's greater "deceitfulness" (though he recognized that such a condition could in large measure be imposed on women by their social situations), Pollak cited false accusation as another major female crime. He noted, "No matter whether the motive of the offense is revenge, concealment of actual misconduct, or a pathological flight from reality, the content of the false accusations committed by women is apparently, in the vast majority of cases, an alleged sexual attack on the accuser." The pattern that was common at least in the Southern states not long ago, of accusations of rape by white women against Negro men, represented a particularly virulent form of this phenomenon. That a young Negro boy was not so many years ago prosecuted in one Southern state for "assault by leering" at a white woman points up sharply the considerable opportunity that existed to employ legal accusation as a weapon in such situations. (We are now seeing considerable change in this regard as even Southern juries show increased willingness to convict white men of raping Negro women and to carefully scrutinize any allegation of sexual attack.) When the false accusation itself is not sexual in nature, Pollak contended, some sexual motive may nonetheless be involved.

In short, the greater attitude of protectiveness taken toward women in our society, and more generally the nature of their social roles and situations, permit them both to exploit their sex for criminal purposes

[17] Otto Pollak, *The Criminality of Women* (Philadelphia: University of Pennsylvania Press, 1950).

and to engage in various kinds of criminal behavior with relatively little fear of detection or prosecution. While perhaps few criminologists fully accept Pollak's suggestion that female crime may really be about as extensive as male crime, it is certainly worthwhile to recognize the significant relation between woman's social position and her crime patterns. Situational opportunities, relative visibility, and perhaps even male unwillingness to publicly admit to victimization by a woman, influence female crime. More broadly, woman's subordinate position in our society (socioeconomically, occupationally, sexually) affects the extent and nature of her criminality.

Woman's special situation pushes her into some kinds of crime and protects her from social pressures and opportunities that might lead her into others. Such offenses as prostitution and abortion, for example, have often been viewed as closely related to the economic and sexual subordination of women. At the same time, the limitations placed on women with respect to economic and occupational self-sufficiency, may shield them from financial pressures and from situational inducements to crime. The social and economic status a woman in our society typically attains by indirection from male providers—fathers and husbands—may leave women largely free from many of the needs, pressures, and frustrations that often drive men to criminal acts. On the other hand, anxieties concerning their sexual roles (constantly a focal point for women in modern American life) may work somewhat in the opposite direction—slightly promoting certain lines of criminal behavior.

Ironically, it may be that until modern woman is able to cast off more completely her role as the "other"—to adopt Simone de Beauvoir's perhaps exaggerated yet rather poignant phrase[18]—she will not be in a position to achieve her full share of criminality. Indeed cross-cultural data suggest a tendency for male and female crime rates to be most discrepant in countries in which women are kept in closely protected subordinate status, and least discrepant in countries in which a relatively high degree of social emancipation of women has taken place.

All of this seems to argue against a biological interpretation of low female crime rates. Even though some writers have attempted to relate female criminality to woman's physical, physiological, and psychological makeup, the sociological interpretation is infinitely more

[18] Simone de Beauvoir, *The Second Sex,* tr. H. Parshley (New York: Alfred A. Knopf, Inc., 1953).

persuasive. As Margaret Mead put it in *Sex and Temperament,* her classic demonstration of varying sex role expectations and behavior in three primitive societies, "We are forced to conclude that human nature is almost unbelievably malleable, responding accurately and contrastingly to contrasting cultural conditions." [19] There are few girl bank robbers in our society not because girls lack the necessary strength or daring, but rather because few girls experience the social and economic need to rob banks, and even more to the point, because it isn't considered a womanly thing to do. Women are infrequently arrested for drunken driving, because in so many drinking situations the man does the driving. More generally, most common serious crimes involve acts directly contradicting the behavior patterns and attitudes to which we try to condition girls from infancy onwards. A strikingly different situation pertains with respect to our expectations of boys—many of which are quite consistent with a variety of criminal behaviors.

While women in our society are freed from certain crime-producing pressures, men are not so lucky. For male adolescents and young adults, the complex of potentially criminogenic social pressures seems almost overwhelmingly powerful. Young men in our society are under strong pressure not only to establish their manly identity (and this alone may generate exaggerated efforts at toughness or even legally offending behavior), but also to achieve economic independence, to attain reasonable occupational success, and to find adequate meaning and satisfaction in some socially acceptable line of work. This situation is exacerbated by the fact that, in a society that prizes youth as much as ours does, many of the normal characteristics of adolescent and young adult life appear threatening and antagonizing to adults. Adults may envy youthful vigor and sexuality, as well as the adolescent's few remaining opportunities for freedom and self-expression. Sometimes the consequences are most unfortunate. As Edgar Friedenberg has nicely expressed it, "There is obviously something in adolescence itself that both troubles and titillates many adults. The 'teen-ager' seems to have replaced the Communist as the appropriate target for public controversy and foreboding, for discussions designed less to clarify what is going on than to let people vent their fearful or hostile feelings and declare themselves on the side of order and authority." [20]

[19] Margaret Mead, *Sex and Temperament in Three Primitive Societies* (New York: Mentor Books, 1935, 1950), p. 191.

[20] Edgar Z. Friedenberg, *The Vanishing Adolescent* (New York: Dell, 1959, 1962), pp. 176–77.

The present values of our society make the situation of youths extremely distressful and problematic, even for those who face no immediate and serious financial problems. It was not the nature of adolescence as such, nor the plight of lower-class youth alone, but rather the quality of our dominant life ways that prompted Paul Goodman's cogent and powerful characterization of young people "growing up absurd" in modern American society.[21] We shall have occasion below to look a bit more into the complex influences of American values on our crime problems. For the young men of the lower economic classes, the situation is of course infinitely more pressing. As various crime theories to be outlined below properly emphasize, such youths face not only all of the basic pressures confronting young people today, but in addition severe structural barriers to the kind of achievement that is expected of them as well as of their middle-class counterparts. And, needless to say, if the additional burden of being a black American is present, the problems are compounded even more.

Negroes and Crime

I suggested earlier that to some extent white Americans think of Negroes as soon as they start worrying about crime problems. It might be comforting, from the standpoint of white liberal rhetoric, if we could assert that Negro Americans do not really commit much crime, but in fact they do. To be sure, the accuracy of our information about racial differences in crime is greatly impaired by the fact that Negroes in our society traditionally and to the present day have been discriminated against at every level in our processes of administering criminal justice. Their "categoric risk" of being formally labeled criminal is extremely high. Various studies have shown that Negroes are more likely to be arrested, prosecuted, and convicted than are white persons who commit the same offenses. Furthermore, at least in some communities, it has been found that the racial membership of the victim has also influenced intensity of law enforcement: Negro-white offenses were considered most serious, and then in descending order, white-white, Negro-Negro, and white-Negro. (The precise impact this may have had on crime rates is somewhat obscure, since underreaction to intraracial offenses among Negroes could have balanced out the overreaction to Negro offenses against whites.) While discriminatory

[21] Paul Goodman, *Growing Up Absurd* (New York: Vintage Books, 1962).

law enforcement can hardly be considered a thing of the past, pressures being brought by the black community, combined with gradual recognition by whites of the legitimacy of the Negro complaints, cannot help but significantly reduce these differentials in the administration of justice.

Negro crime rates also reflect the fact that Negroes are concentrated in those sectors of the American population that show high crime rates for individuals of all races. Negroes in America are heavily represented in the urban and lower socioeconomic and educational categories, and also in the high-risk young adult age group. We cannot be absolutely sure what Negro crime rates would be like if this population distribution were different, but it is highly probable that they would be substantially altered. In this connection it is noteworthy that such studies as we do have show that there is a clear relationship between Negro education levels and crime rates. Thus not only are Negroes with more education less likely to commit crimes than their less well-educated brothers, but it has also been found that the crime rates for Negroes in the higher education categories are lower than those for poorly educated whites.

These facts go only so far in explaining the high crime rates of Negro Americans. The Negro arrest rate for major crimes is about four times as high as that of whites, though it is worth keeping in mind that these are *rates*—in absolute numbers, many more whites are arrested each year for serious crimes. The arrest rate differentials between Negroes and whites, however, vary considerably with the type of offense. By and large, the disparities are greater for violent crime than for crimes against property. For example, the Negro arrest rate for murder has been running almost ten times as high as that for whites, while the Negro burglary arrest rate has been only about three or four times the white rate. An interesting point uncovered by the President's Commission was that in recent years the Negro-white differences for certain crimes of violence have actually been *decreasing*. The Commission reported that between 1960 and 1965, "considering together the crimes of murder, rape, and aggravated assault, the rate for Negroes increased 5 per cent while the rate for whites increased 27 per cent. In the case of robbery, however, the white rate increased 3 per cent while the Negro rate increased 24 per cent. For the crimes of burglary, larceny, and auto theft the Negro rate increased 33 per cent while the white rate increased 24 per cent."

Though there have been many attempts to explain high Negro

crime rates in biological terms, the evidence against such an interpretation is now well recognized as incontrovertible. Certainly the day should be past when it can be seriously argued that Negroes are "basically" criminal—or inherently musical, athletic, or whatever. Quite apart from the fact that no people could be "basically" criminal, given the legal nature of crime, one has only to consider the substantial variations in crime rates *within* the Negro community to recognize how patently untenable such an idea is. As I have just noted, Negro crime rates vary by offense, they vary significantly along with socio-economic and educational level, they appear to vary to some extent by area of residence, and they vary also by sex (with Negro-white rate differentials for women exceeding those for men). Interestingly too, anthropological studies reveal that (even allowing for deficiencies in the data) homicide rates among Negroes in various African tribes are several times lower than those among Negro Americans, and indeed that they are even lower than American homicide rates for the general population.[22] As anthropologist Paul Bohannan comments, "If it needed stressing, here is overwhelming evidence that it is cultural and not biological factors which make for a high homicide rate among American Negroes."

Indeed it is incredible, in the light of the social situation of blacks in our society today, that anyone should find it necessary to look very far for an explanation of widespread Negro crime. On the contrary—and the racial disorders of the past few years should have served to warn whites on this point—it is probably remarkable that Negro crime rates in this country are not higher than they are.

During the past several years the American public has been bombarded with massive documentation of the conditions of urban Negro ghetto life in the United States—in the general news media; in a variety of best-selling books (such as Charles Silberman's excellent *Crisis in Black and White,* and Jonathan Kozol's prize-winning exposé of Roxbury Schools, *Death at an Early Age*); and through a number of widely publicized and authoritative government-initiated reports. The objective plight of black people in America—the widespread existence of unequal educational opportunity, high unemployment, inadequate income, and substandard housing—should by now (at least in general terms) be common knowledge among all reasonably well informed Americans.

[22] Paul Bohannan, ed., *African Homicide and Suicide* (New York: Atheneum, 1967), especially Chap. 9.

Likewise, the powerful force of slavery and its aftermath in shaping Negro life—especially Negro family structure—is widely recognized. Whether one agrees or not with the central theme of the controversial "Moynihan Report" on *The Negro Family*—that "at the center of the tangle of pathology is the weakness of the family structure"—surely there can be little doubt that the patterns of family instability and disruption and of male dependency bred in the slavery experience have at least been factors contributing to the vulnerable position of Negro American youth.[23] Certainly all available evidence supports the report's contention that "The combined impact of poverty, failure, and isolation among Negro youth has had the predictable outcome in a disastrous delinquency and crime rate."

More recently, the "Coleman Report" on equality of educational opportunity[24] has made clear that, almost fifteen years after the Supreme Court's historic school desegregation decisions, segregated schooling is the rule rather than the exception across the nation. Whatever precise influence this may have on educational achievement as such, there seems little doubt that on top of and in conjunction with the other burdens and indignities facing black Americans, the continuing segregation of school children is indeed, in Jonathan Kozol's poignant phrase, readily calculated to help "destroy the hearts and minds of Negro children."

Perhaps most important of all has been the Kerner (riot commission) Report on "civil disorders" issued in March, 1968.[25] I shall have occasion below, in discussing the relation between American poverty and crime, to review at some length the Commission's detailed documentation of the social and economic facts of Negro life in present-day America. However, a few of the Commission's eloquent and sober words of warning should be cited here. Stating as its basic conclusion that "Our nation is moving toward two societies, one black, one white —separate and unequal," the Commission insisted that "The alternative is not blind repression or capitulation to lawlessness. It is the

---

[23] U.S. Department of Labor, *The Negro Family, The Case for National Action* (Washington, D.C.: U.S. Government Printing Office, 1965). For a wide selection of commentary pro and con, see Lee Rainwater and William Yancy, eds., *The Moynihan Report and the Politics of Controversy* (Cambridge: M.I.T. Press, 1967).

[24] James S. Coleman, *et al.*, *Equality of Educational Opportunity* (Washington, D.C.: U.S. Government Printing Office, 1966).

[25] *Report of the National Advisory Commission on Civil Disorders* (New York: Bantam Books, 1968).

realization of common opportunities for all within a single society." Calling for a commitment to national action backed by massive resources (see Chapter 4 of this book for its specific recommendations), the Commission emphasized the responsibility of white Americans for the so-called Negro problem:

Violence and destruction must be ended—in the streets of the ghetto and in the lives of people.

Segregation and poverty have created in the racial ghetto a destructive environment totally unknown to most white Americans.

What white Americans have never fully understood—but what the Negro can never forget—is that white society is deeply implicated in the ghetto. White institutions created it, white institutions maintain it, and white society condones it.

In considering the question of crime among Negro Americans, some special attention must be given to the relations between black people and the predominantly white police. As late as 1961, the United States Commission on Civil Rights reported that its studies showed that "police brutality in the United States today is a serious and continuing problem in many parts of the country. Whether in the country as a whole it is increasing or decreasing is not clear. There seems to have been no marked overall abatement in recent years, although improvements have been reported in particular areas—such as Atlanta and Chicago." And the Commission went on to note:

The statistics suggest that Negroes feel the brunt of official brutality proportionately more than any other group in American society . . . among the complaints of police brutality received [by the Department of Justice] in the two and one half year period ending June 30, 1960, the alleged victims were Negroes (who constitute approximately 10 per cent of the total population) in 35 per cent of the cases. . . .[26]

It is probable, however, that cases of severe brutality have not had as much impact in shaping Negro views of the police and of "the law" they represent as have the patterns of routine harassment, humiliation, and discriminatory practice common in much everyday police behavior. Several studies have produced evidence of systematic differences in the way police deal with Negroes and whites. In the study of "police encounters with juveniles" mentioned earlier, it was found that Negro

---

[26] United States Commission on Civil Rights, *Justice*, Report No. 5, 1961, as quoted in Raymond J. Murphy and Howard Elinson, eds., *Problems and Prospects of the Negro Movement* (Belmont, Calif.: Wadsworth, 1966), pp. 228–29.

youths, as well as those white youths who looked and acted "tough" and failed to show the proper attitude, were particularly likely to receive the harsher dispositions. Eighteen of twenty-seven officers interviewed openly admitted a dislike for Negroes. However, the policemen attributed this outlook to recurrent experiences they claimed to have had with Negro youths. They stated that "Negro boys were much more likely than non-Negroes to 'give us a hard time,' be uncooperative, and show no remorse for their transgressions." As the researchers noted, this kind of police behavior comes to be "reflected in police statistics showing a disproportionately high percentage of Negroes among juvenile offenders, thereby providing 'objective' justification for concentrating police attention on Negro youths."

Equally significant perhaps has been the symbolic role white police have taken on for many black ghetto-dwellers—as a prototype of "the man," of all the white men who are responsible for their social subordination. An early statement by James Baldwin remains the most powerful depiction of this symbolism:

None of the Police Commissioner's men, even with the best will in the world, have any way of understanding the lives led by the people they swagger about in twos and threes controlling. Their very presence is an insult, and it would be, even if they spent their entire day feeding gumdrops to children. They represent the force of the white world, and that world's real intentions are, simply, for that world's criminal profit and ease, to keep the black man corraled up here [Harlem], in his place. The badge, the gun in the holster, and the swinging club make vivid what will happen should his rebellion become overt.[27]

Of course not all Negro Americans feel this way. Just as crime rates themselves vary greatly within the black community, so too do attitudes toward the police and toward law in general. Somewhat surprisingly, studies undertaken in several cities for the President's Commission on Law Enforcement disclosed generally favorable attitudes toward the police among all groups, including Negro males. For example, about half of the Negroes interviewed in Washington thought that Negroes get no worse treatment at the hands of the police than other people. Such views, however, were less likely to be voiced in the predominantly Negro districts than in other areas. And in any case questions of this sort may tap only surface attitudes—deep-seated

[27] James Baldwin, *Nobody Knows My Name* (New York: The Dial Press, Inc., 1961), pp. 65–66.

resentments reinforced by the symbolic presence of white police could well co-exist with such stated views.

Later, in considering the policy implications of various sociological theories of crime causation, we shall return to the matter of crime among Negro Americans. For the moment, let us simply have in mind that the black minority has been rigorously suppressed socially, economically, and psychologically; that Negroes in our society have been subjected to many conditions classically linked with crime involvement, and at the same time have received very few inducements to law-abidingness.

Although the objective conditions of the black's social situation have certainly been deplorable, even more pertinent for our purposes may be the psychological burden of low self-esteem against which the Negro in this country has had continuously to battle. As Abram Kardiner and Lionel Ovesey noted in their important study of Negro personality, *The Mark of Oppression*, "the Negro gets a poor reflection of himself in the behavior of whites, no matter what he does or what his merits are," a circumstance that leads to "endless vicious circles and blind alleys that are set in motion by the frantic efforts to remove the causes for self-hatred. . . ." [28] White Americans who deplore the high rates of Negro crime might well ponder the results of one study which found that such rates decreased noticeably in several communities at times when Negroes were actively involved in civil rights activity. The researchers concluded that "When he becomes aggressive *against segregation*, the Negro's sense of personal and group identity is altered; race pride partially replaces self-hatred, and aggression need not be directed so destructively at the self or the community." [29]

Criminal Acts and Crime Careers

Just as all sorts of people commit criminal acts, so too are there many kinds and degrees of crime involvement. As the President's Commission pointed out:

[28] Abram Kardiner and Lionel Ovesey, *The Mark of Oppression* (Cleveland: Meridian Books, 1951, 1962), p. 297. See also William H. Grier and Price M. Cobbs, *Black Rage* (New York: Basic Books, 1968).

[29] Fredric Solomon, *et al.*, "Civil Rights Activity and Reduction in Crime Among Negroes," *Archives of General Psychiatry*, Vol. 12 (March, 1965), as reprinted in Murphy and Elinson, *op. cit.*, p. 352.

An enormous variety of acts make up the "crime problem." Crime is not just a tough teenager snatching a lady's purse. It is a professional thief stealing cars "on order." It is a well-heeled loan shark taking over a previously legitimate business for organized crime. It is a polite young man who suddenly and inexplicably murders his family. It is a corporation executive conspiring with competitors to keep prices high. No single formula, no single theory, no single generalization can explain the vast range of behavior called crime.[30]

Clearly the individuals engaging in these diverse forms of behavior are not equally "criminal"—in terms either of how we view them or how they view themselves. Some offenders embark on lengthy criminal careers, others commit crime occasionally, and still others may commit only a single serious criminal act. Certain violations are committed by individuals acting alone, others are group offenses. In some cases an individual's criminal behavior is the culmination of a lengthy process of subtly assimilating a criminal "tradition," while, on the other hand, crime sometimes reflects a spur-of-the-moment act impelled by situational imperatives and engaged in by a person who has no substantial prior contact with "criminal" values or behavior patterns. Some people commit crimes to obtain money, some to obtain revenge, some "for the hell of it," and some without realizing it. For some persons crime is a job like any other; for some, it is a conscious act of rebellion against values they decry; for some, it is an unplanned consequence of other "normal" life patterns; in other instances a criminal act may be the result of deepseated phychological needs or drives.

The problems of classifying offenses and offenders have plagued criminologists for some time. Although numerous proposals have been advanced and classification schemes developed, there is no single generally accepted typology of either crimes or criminals. Given both the enormous diversity in the content of criminal offenses and the various levels of individual involvement in criminality, it seems most unlikely that any one classification system can realistically be expected to pull together the bits and pieces of our understanding of crime problems. It is not very surprising that each time a criminologist has developed some method of classifying offenses or offenders, his colleagues (in neighboring disciplines, and often those in his own field as well) have been less than eager to embrace it. At the heart of this difficulty has

[30] *The Challenge of Crime in a Free Society*, p. v.

been the fact that a scheme adopted for a particular purpose may prove unsuitable for other purposes.

Legal specialists on crime have generally been content to use the traditional categories of the criminal law—such as crimes against the person, crimes against property, crimes against public morals, crimes against the state—and where necessary to break these categories down further into their constituent and more specific offenses. Yet from a sociological standpoint such classification may not be very satisfactory. The sociologist seeks categories that will group offenses and offenders in terms of shared, sociologically significant characteristics. Very likely, crime (and offenders) against the person, against property, and so on are not sociologically homogenous categories; nor are the more specific legal groupings—such as murder (and murderers), assault, burglary. The people who legally fit into such a category may vary a good deal in their social characteristics, and also with respect to the nature and extent of their crime involvement.

Recognizing this, the sociologist may try to establish categories that seem to him more meaningful—such, for example, as professional and semiprofessional offenders, situational offenders, subcultural offenders, unintentional offenders, disturbed offenders. Likewise, the psychiatrist interested in crime may consider the surface behavior of criminality merely "symptomatic," and may therefore insist on a classification based on types of underlying disorders—organic or functional psychoses, neuroses, antisocial character disorders (and "psychopathic personality")—probably reserving a residual category for those offenders who do *not* appear to display serious psychic disturbance (in some psychoanalytic schemes they have been labeled "normal criminals"). Criminologists interested primarily in the informal social structure that develops within correctional institutions will tend to develop still other kinds of typologies. Thus, various studies in the sociology of prisons have elaborated a number of major "argot roles" present in correctional institutions—such as "rats," "right guys," "merchants," and "gorillas." Each of these approaches to the problem of classification (and there are still others) has some merit as a guide to understanding certain aspects of crime in America.

In this book, I am not going to be very much concerned with the technical issue of selecting the "proper" way of classifying criminal acts and offenders. To some extent, I shall at times be informally (and incompletely) adopting something rather like the legal approach to classification. This is because of my conviction that some forms of criminality arise from specific and identifiable complexes of social conditions and social values. Similarly, in those instances where I argue that we have unnecessarily "created" crimes through overlegislation, the offense itself clearly must be one major point of departure.

Another related perspective that colors my discussion of crime in America has to do with the nature and extent of crime involvement (or "commitment to deviant roles," as the sociologist sometimes puts it) exhibited by persons engaging in one or another sort of criminal behavior. This dimension may have a great bearing on the issue of what we can do about crime. Types of offenses that seem largely irrational or situational in nature, types that are heavily grounded in neighborhood tradition and group support, types of criminality that constitute "occupations," and types that are engaged in by citizens who are in the main perfectly "respectable," are likely to require distinct if somewhat related public policy efforts. And sometimes we find that our present policies themselves have had a considerable influence in determining the degree of commitment to criminal roles found in a particular offense category.

As I have already suggested, criminological specialists have been somewhat overconcerned with questions of individual crime causation —primarily with trying to predict why one individual becomes criminal and another does not. The hope that a single comprehensive theory will permit prediction of this sort with respect to *all* crime seems forlorn indeed. Even with respect to particular types of crime, it seems unlikely that such a focus on individual criminality will be very rewarding. Placing the major emphasis, as I do here, on crime rather than criminals, may help us to appreciate the broader social contexts within which criminal acts arise. At the same time, it should be useful to consider in brief some of the major efforts at causal theory. As we shall see, some of these formulations have been distracting or highly misleading, while others are of considerable value in our attempt to understand crime and to develop policies for dealing with it.

2

QUESTIONABLE
CRIME THEORIES

. . . crime will be explained differently, depending on which
frame of reference is the point of departure. Each approach
usually regards itself as self-sufficient; no view falls back on
any of the others for confirmation or verification; each considers
its explanations most nearly adequate, and none welcomes or
accepts the criticism of another point of view.

George B. Vold, *Theoretical Criminology*

"Innate" Criminality

Apparently people who more or less conform to societal
regulation—or who are at least fortunate enough to avoid entangle-
ments with society's agents of social control—find it highly comforting
to establish the "differentness" of known law-breakers. This probably
helps to explain the current white middle-class tendency to equate
Negroes with crime, and the active relish with which some adult
Americans villify the youth of our society for its alleged hoodlumism
and lawlessness. But differentness of this sort is not very extreme, and
is unlikely to fully satisfy the urge to establish criminals as a breed
apart. Hence the continuing appeal of theories of innate criminality.

Attempts to develop such "internal" explanations have a long and
not very happy history. As early demonic explanations of disturbing
human behavior gave way to more empirical analysis, the "scientific"
approach was taken to imply close scrutiny (physical, medical, and
psychological) of offending individuals. The emphasis shifted, as I
have mentioned, from crime to the criminal. A major contribution to
this line of thinking was made by Cesare Lombroso (1835–1909), an

55

Italian physician and psychiatrist who founded what is known as the "positivist school" of crime analysis and who, ironically, is often referred to as the "father of modern criminology." Unlike the so-called classical and neoclassical interpreters of crime (such men as Beccaria, Bentham, and Romilly)—who sought legal and administrative reform of criminal justice, and who by-passed close analysis of crime causes in favor of an emphasis on the self-determined free will aspects of human behavior—the positivists aimed at a more deterministic explanation of crime through scientific examination of individual offenders.[1]

While Lombroso and his followers performed a service in suggesting that criminal behavior was a natural phenomenon determined by scientifically discoverable causes (including, in Lombroso's later work and in other of the positivist interpretations, environmental ones), the emphasis in Lombroso's studies was on physical abnormality and the claim that crime was hereditary in nature. Lombroso studied a group of incarcerated Italian offenders (less than 400 in number), making use of extensive physical examination and measurement, and claimed that the presence in most of them of physical "anomalies" supported the idea of a "born criminal type." These physical "stigmata," he felt, indicated that criminals were "atavistic"—a kind of genetic throwback to an earlier form of animal life. Although his conception of research methodology was by modern standards inadequate, Lombroso did attempt a comparison of sorts (with a group of Italian soldiers), obtaining results that he believed supported his findings of biological anomaly in criminals. Whereas 43 per cent of his criminal subjects had five or more anomalies (such as "deviation" in head size and shape, eye "defects and peculiarities," receding chin, and "excessively" long arms), none of the soldiers displayed that many "stigmata" and only 11 per cent had as many as three of these allegedly revealing features.

Impressive as this research might have seemed at the time, it simply did not hold up in the face of careful testing. When an English research team, headed by Charles Goring, made careful measured comparisons of about 3,000 English prisoners and large groups of non-prisoners (including Oxford and Cambridge undergraduates), hardly

---

[1] My discussion of Lombroso, Hooton, and other theorists of "innate" criminality is indebted to the excellent discussion by George B. Vold, *Theoretical Criminology* (New York: Oxford University Press, Inc., 1958). Good reviews of some of the early crime theories are also presented in Hermann Mannheim, ed., *Pioneers in Criminology* (Chicago: Quadrangle Books, 1960).

any statistically significant patterns of physical difference were found. Although the criminals were found to be slightly shorter and, on the average, to weigh less, Goring and his associates concluded that "there is no such thing as a physical criminal type."

Notwithstanding this refutation, the Lombrosian influence continued to be strongly felt in numerous European and American research efforts. One of the best known and most recent American studies is that of Ernest Hooton, a Harvard anthropologist, who published his findings in a three-volume work *The American Criminal* (1939) and in a one-volume popularization entitled *Crime and the Man* (1931). On the basis of twelve years of anthropometric research, in which over 10,000 imprisoned offenders and a considerably smaller "control" group of nonoffenders were examined and measured, Hooton concluded that criminals are "organically inferior," "low grade human organisms," and that "the elimination of crime can be effected only by the extirpation of the physically, mentally, and morally unfit; or by their complete segregation in a socially aseptic environment."

Critics of Hooton's work (who were many and vocal) pounced on the many serious methodological shortcomings of his research. Hooton had assumed that prisoners comprise a representative sample of criminals, which as we have seen is most questionable. Furthermore, his "control" group (which included Nashville fireman, college students, hospital patients, patrons of a bathing beach, and others apparently chosen merely because of availability) was, as criminologist George Vold has noted, "a fantastic conglomeration of noncriminal civilians who for various reasons submitted to (or had to submit to) the required anthropometric measurements. What, or who, they may be representative of no one knows, since no criteria of selection were established (or apparently, even considered)." Hooton also emphasized only those findings which seemed to support his theory, ignoring others that would have brought it into question. Thus the Nashville firemen differed from a Boston control group more than either of these groups differed from the criminal sample. And needless to say, nowhere did he adequately explain the basis on which his Lombroso-like indicators of criminality (such as low sloping foreheads, tattooing, compressed faces, and narrow jaws) were to be judged as "inferior." There were other serious deficiencies in this work as well, but various commentators suspect that the basic difficulty was that Hooton was convinced from the outset that prisoners *must* be inferior—or else they wouldn't be in prison! As Sutherland and Cressey aptly comment, "by this logic males should be appraised as biologically inferior to females since a larger proportion of males are imprisoned."

Another variant of the theory of innate crime tendencies was developed under the rubric of "constitutional psychology." This was the school of thought in which "body types" were related to variations in temperament and behavior. Building on the earlier work of a German psychiatrist, Ernst Kretschmer, an American researcher, William Sheldon, conducted studies reported in a number of volumes published in the early 1940's—in which evidence purporting to show such linkages was presented. According to Sheldon three basic body types could be identified: the endomorphic (soft round type, with which a typically relaxed temperament was said to be associated); the mesomorphic type (muscular, and usually exhibiting dynamic, aggressive temperament); and the ectomorphic type (thin and fragile, and typically introverted and sensitive in temperament). Recognizing that a person would rarely qualify as a complete embodiment of one type, Sheldon worked out a system (called somatotyping) for numerically rating an individual on each of the three "components," and then using such a composite score or profile as the basis for associations with temperament and behavior.

In one of his books, Sheldon claimed to demonstrate that 200 young males dealt with by a Boston welfare agency, and whom he vaguely defined as delinquent, differed in dominant body types from nondelinquents he had studied. Critical analysts have concluded that Sheldon's own data did not justify such a conclusion, let alone his accompanying interpretations of inferiority and inherited tendency toward crime. While Sheldon's intellectual scheme and technical procedures were different, basically he agreed with Hooton that criminals were inferior organisms. Perhaps not surprisingly an eminent physical anthropologist referred to Sheldon's approach as a "new Phrenology in which the bumps of the buttocks take the place of the bumps on the skull." [2]

More recently, Sheldon and Eleanor Glueck, in their long-term studies of juvenile delinquents, have reported that somewhat more of their delinquent than their nondelinquent subjects displayed a predominantly mesomorphic body build. Even assuming that this finding

[2] S. L. Washburn, Review of W. H. Sheldon, *Varieties of Delinquent Youth*, in the *American Anthropologist*, Vol. 53 (December, 1951), as quoted in Sutherland and Cressey, *op. cit.*, p. 131.

was valid (and the Gluecks' work in many respects represented an advance methodologically over earlier work adopting this orientation), meaningful interpretation of it, in terms of the mix of relevant constitutional, environmental, and social psychological factors, is uncertain. As sociologist Don Gibbons has pointed out, "it could be argued that delinquent subcultures recruit new members selectively, placing a premium upon agile, muscular boys. . . . Excessively fat or overly thin and sickly youngsters make poor candidates for the rough and tumble world of delinquent behavior, so they are excluded. . . . If so, this is a social process, not a biologically determined pattern of behavior." [3]

Attempts have also been made to demonstrate the hereditary nature of criminal tendencies through investigation of so-called "degenerate family" trees, and through research involving comparisons between identical and fraternal twins. Neither of these approaches has produced satisfactory evidence. Case studies such as those of the "Jukes family" —in which of about 1,200 identified members 140 were found to be criminals (including 7 convicted of murder, 60 of theft, and 50 of prostitution)—were taken to suggest that "innate depravity" was a major cause of crime. (This family line was for some reason frequently compared with the descendants of Jonathan Edwards—large numbers of whom held high public office or attained success in learned professions. Actually more careful scrutiny of this comparison uncovered a good bit of criminality in the Edwards family line too.) But the real problems with such analysis were more basic. The family tree "studies" rested heavily on the questionable notion of inherited feeble-mindedness as a kind of carrier of degeneracy. And no real consideration was given to the very thorny question of sorting out hereditary and environmental influences. If the Jukes had in common some "bad genes" (even assuming that something as varied and changing as crime might somehow have a genetic source), they most assuredly had in common also unsavory family tradition and environment. Not all traits exhibited by families over several generations (sociological critic Edwin Sutherland cited the trait of using the fork in eating!) are inherited.

In the twin studies, the premise was that if heredity was a source of criminal tendencies, then identical (one-egg) twins should show more similarity with respect to criminal behavior than fraternal (two-

---

[3] Gibbons, *op. cit.*, p. 134.

egg) twins. One early study (involving thirty pairs of adult male twins in which one member of each pair was known to be criminal) found "concordance" (that is, both twins criminal) in 77 per cent of the thirteen identical pairs; only 12 per cent of the seventeen fraternal pairs exhibited this similarity. Subsequent twin studies by other researchers found less impressive differences with respect to similarity in criminal behavior of identical and fraternal twins. But even if it is true that identical twins tend to be more alike in criminality than fraternal ones, the inheritance of crime tendencies would not be established. Once again environmental factors—in this case the possibility of more similar environments for, and more similar reactions of other persons to identical twins—confounds the analysis.[4]

A final version of the innate crime approach was grounded in early efforts at intelligence testing. Here the assertion was that inherited mental defect was a major cause of crime. Most criminals, according to this explanation, were feeble-minded. Results from the application of intelligence tests to prison inmates convinced some observers in the early 1900's that there was a close association between lawbreaking and mental deficiency.[5] In the words of H. H. Goddard, one of the best known proponents of this view, "the greatest single cause of delinquency and crime is low-grade mentality, much of it within the limits of feeble-mindedness." A basic trouble with this research was that the investigators claimed the mental age level of prisoners fell substantially below a normal level, without really having any idea what the normal age level in intelligence actually was. No systematic comparisons provided a basis for this conclusion; there had, at that point, been no mass administrations of the tests among the general population. Intelligence testing of Army draftees in World War I provided devastating refutation of the claim that criminals were mentally deficient. It turned out that the mental age level of the draftees was much lower than anticipated (only slightly above the level Goddard initially considered to be the upper level of feeble-mindedness!), and systematic comparisons of prisoners and draftees soon made clear that intelligence differences between the two groups were negligible. As refinements in mental testing were developed, it became evident that such an explanation of crime was completely untenable.

Criminologists today are in general agreement that prisoners (and

---

[4] A good discussion of the attempts at hereditary theories of crime is provided by Sutherland and Cressey, *op. cit.*, pp. 123–28.

[5] See Vold, *op. cit.*, Chap. 5.

certainly actual offenders) exhibit a wide range of intelligence levels. There is no reason why this should not be so, and indeed we should realize that different levels of intelligence are required for various kinds of law violation. A person does not have to be very smart to commit an ordinary mugging, but great skill and versatility may be needed for confidence swindling. Ordinarily only persons of fairly high intelligence attain the position needed for the commission of certain offenses —such as major business crimes. And undoubtedly there are other offenses with respect to which the intelligence of the offender is a factor of only very slight relevance—an example might be the violent "crime of passion." Above all, it should be kept in mind that to commit any serious crime *and get away with it* usually requires considerable intelligence (or, in some cases, remarkable luck). Indeed, when a particular study does show slightly lower than average intelligence in a sample of prisoners, this may well reflect the fact that the brighter an offender the better chance he has of not being caught.

It is also widely recognized that most of the intelligence tests used in this country today are not "culture free." On the contrary, the content of the items in these tests is such that lower-class persons and Negroes are not as likely to achieve high scores as are middle-class whites. (The point has been vividly illustrated by the recent and only partly humorous development of an "alternative" intelligence test geared to the normal experience and knowledge of black ghetto-dwellers. The author of this "Chitling Test," which he designed "as a rebuke to standard intelligence tests," referred to his conviction that people were failing the regular tests, "not because they were stupid, but because the test was geared to middle-class white society.")[6] Those categories of persons especially likely to score low on the standard tests are also (for reasons quite apart from their intelligence level) the ones most subject to the forces likely to lead to imprisonment—to the crime-producing social conditions and the differentials in law-enforcement examined elsewhere in this book.

Are Criminals Sick?

Notwithstanding the lingering urge for a theory of innate criminality—on occasion reinforced by one or another public state-

[6] *New York Times*, July 2, 1968, p. 26.

ment or fictional contribution, such as the successful novel and movie
The Bad Seed—probably few even moderately informed Americans
nowadays really believe that crime is an hereditary condition or inclination. Gaining ascendancy in the wake of that view has been the
modern version of the "internal" crime explanations—the belief that
most if not all criminals are mentally ill. At a time when the phrase
"Freudian slip" has become common English usage, when such diverse
phenomena as race discrimination, the "hippies," divorce, and peace
demonstrations may be subject to psychoanalytic interpretation, and
when in certain circles having the right analyst can serve as a status
symbol, it is hardly surprising that the notion of the sick criminal has
wide appeal.

Let me comment at the outset that in criticizing this conception
sociologists are not attempting to deny either the considerable wisdom
of Freud or the social value of applying all the knowledge and insight
we can muster to the important task of treating mental disorders.
Criminologists generally agree that *some* persons who suffer from serious psychological disturbance commit crimes. The question remains,
what proportion of *all* the individuals involved in *major* crime falls
into such a category? Many sociologists believe there has been a tendency to greatly exaggerate the significance of psychopathology in the
analysis of crime problems.

Is there *any* category of our criminal law of which we can say that
all the offenders against it are, without question, mentally ill? One
sometimes hears the argument that all persons who commit murder
must be suffering from some psychological disturbance. And yet, as I
shall show in a later section, there is ample sociological evidence (in
terms of certain subcultural values and behavior patterns, and situational factors) to disprove this claim. Such a crime as incest, which
would probably strike many reasonable persons as definitely being a
"sick" form of behavior, may also be at least partly understandable in
terms of its sociological aspects.

. . . data on father-daughter incest contain indications that this activity
is carried on by males with relatively conventional sexual orientations. Involvement in sexual behavior with "inappropriate" partners seems related
to unavailability of more appropriate sexual partners, due to illness of the
spouse, social and physical isolation of the family unit, and related factors.
In some cases, seductive interaction between father and daughter may contribute to development of incestuous acts, as may covert collaboration of

the wife in the relationship, as she encourages the father to refrain from sexual acts with her and "winks at" sexual contact between him and his daughter.[7]

So-called "compulsive" crimes would also seem to carry a strong likelihood of psychopathology in the offender, but here again such an interpretation may rest more heavily on assumption than on reality. Thus the evidence shows, as Don Gibbons has noted, that "klepto-mania" by and large "turns out to be nothing more than a social label hung on 'nice people' who steal and withheld from 'bad people' who are simply 'crooks'!" Systematic studies have indicated that very little repetitive shoplifting by amateur thieves involves psychic disturbance. Supposedly compulsive shoplifters usually find themselves quite able to stop stealing once they have been caught, even though they had engaged in repeated thievery prior to being apprehended.

Perhaps the closest one can come to a crime category that does usually involve the acts of mentally disturbed individuals is that of the more esoteric nonviolent sex offenses. Even here systematic research is likely to reveal characteristic social patterns—the behavior in question clearly bears some relation to family background, learning experiences, and present social situation. Nonetheless, it seems reasonable to believe that the crimes of the exhibitionist or the "peeping tom," or of the man who derives his greatest sexual pleasure from rubbing up against strange women in the subway or from collecting women's satin shoes, do largely reflect individual psychopathology. It is significant that these nonviolent sex offenses, which of all crimes probably are the most "disturbed," represent but a small segment of the total crime picture. Furthermore, these offenders are generally recognized by criminologists not to constitute a serious social danger. (The supposed harms involved in nonviolent sex crimes—perhaps even the alleged traumatic effects of nonviolent child molestation—have often been exaggerated.) Studies have shown that most offenders in this category tend to be essentially passive individuals whose behavior is unlikely to "escalate" into violent crime.

Of course there are *some* violent offenders (including violent sex offenders) whose acts are likely to reflect a significant component of psychopathology. It seems clear that unless we wish to dismiss completely the very idea of mental illness (and that most certainly is not

---

[7] Gibbons, *op. cit.*, p. 375.

my intention here), we have to recognize that the "sniper" who climbs on top of a building and shoots as many people as he can before he himself is shot by the police, and the man who viciously attacks and mutilates unknown women, are seriously disturbed people. While it is true in these cases too that one cannot explain their disturbance without some attention to sociological and social-psychological factors in the broadest sense—early development in the family situation, current life failures, and so on—to say for that reason that these individuals cannot be described as sick does not make much sense. However, the important thing to keep in mind is that although such incidents receive a great deal of lurid publicity (on the day I write this the *New York Times* carries a five-column front page spread headlined "Gunman Terrorizes Central Park; 2 Dead, 3 Shot"),[8] they actually occur very infrequently. For every such occurrence there are thousands of petty thefts, well-planned and efficiently carried out burglaries, professional swindles, and middle-class occupational crimes.

When we try in this manner to place the crimes of obviously disturbed individuals within the broader framework of crime in America, the belief in mental illness as the major cause of criminality falls apart. The crimes of our society are incredibly varied, and they are committed by all sorts of people. As I have already noted, crimes of violence occur much less often than property offenses. And we know too that many acts of criminal violence are situational in character and nonrepetitive. Considering the enormity of the abominable social conditions breeding antisocial outlooks and behavior in certain segments of our society, the fact that for many individuals taking up a criminal "occupation" may be an almost rational decision given the nature of the available alternatives, and the prevalence of numerous acts that are at least technically criminal among otherwise "respectable" citizens, it becomes quite absurd to insist on the basic psychopathology of *most* American crime. Indeed, the only way in which such a claim could be substantiated would be as the corollary to a more general assertion that most if not all Americans are mentally ill.

According to some psychoanalytic discussions of crime, every one of us (not just Americans, but all human beings) is really a criminal at heart. Thus a major work on the psychology of crime and punishment proclaims that "within the innermost nucleus of the personality . . . it is impossible to differentiate normal from criminal impulses.

[8] *New York Times*, July 4, 1968, p. 1.

The human being enters the world as a criminal, i.e., socially not adjusted." [9] And Freud himself expressed a similar view:

> Civilized society is perpetually menaced with disintegration through this primary hostility of men towards one another. Their interests in their common work would not hold them together; the passions of instinct are stronger than reasoned interests. Culture has to call up every possible reinforcement in order to erect barriers against the aggressive instincts of man and hold their manifestations in check by reaction-formations in men's minds.[10]

Criminal tendencies, then, are seen as basic to the human condition. Even the sociologist, whose prime emphasis leads him away from notions of instinct and toward attention to processes of social learning and shaping of behavior (an emphasis so pronounced that one sociologist, for this and other reasons, has argued sociology may develop an "oversocialized conception of man"),[11] usually recognizes the significance of human aggressive impulses and accepts human conflict as a basic fact of social life.[12] But it is a big jump from this recognition to the idea that most crime is grounded in the human psyche. As some major post-Freudian psychoanalytic theorists have acknowledged (and some writings of Freud himself suggest this), it may be a major error to see only the impulses of hostility, aggression, and sexuality as basic to the nature of man. Erich Fromm, for example, has argued that such themes as creativity, love, and cooperation are equally basic to the psychological and social makeup of humanity.[13]

At any rate, sociologists are persuaded (on the basis of a great deal of impressive evidence from systematic research) that human behavior and outlooks are significantly shaped by continuous social interaction and subtle learning processes, by group situations and pressures, and at least indirectly by the broader structure of society itself. As Alex Inkeles points out, "man values others and seeks to re-

[9] Franz Alexander and Hugo Staub, *The Criminal, the Judge, and the Public,* rev. ed., tr. G. Zilboorg (New York: Collier Books, 1962), pp. 51–52.

[10] Sigmund Freud, *Civilization and its Discontents* (Garden City, N.Y.: Doubleday Anchor Books, 1930), pp. 61–62.

[11] Dennis H. Wrong, "The Oversocialized Conception of Man in Modern Sociology," *American Sociological Review,* 26 (April, 1961), 183–93.

[12] See Lewis A. Coser, *The Functions of Social Conflict* (New York: The Free Press, 1956).

[13] Erich Fromm, *The Sane Society* (New York: Holt, Rinehart & Winston, Inc., 1955).

late himself to them." He is "committed to mutual adaptation and adjustment to attain not only his individual and private ends but also the communal and public goals which he has *internalized* and made his own." [14] In the next chapter we shall examine the major concepts and theories through which this general orientation has been applied to efforts at understanding crime.

As these comments probably suggest, another aspect of the psychoanalytic approach that sociologists tend to question is the heavy concentration on the effects of very early childhood experiences. Sociologists agree that family situations are important, and that initial socialization (social learning) processes have great significance in the development of individual personality structure. They are not convinced, however, that either such personality structure or the behavior patterns a person adopts are clearly established for life in the earliest stages of childhood. On the contrary, they have unearthed considerable evidence of important changes that may be wrought in the individual by new situations and experiences throughout youth and adulthood. As we shall see, there is ample reason to believe that this observation is pertinent to our understanding of crime. Social pressures impelling criminality, group support for violations of law, specific opportunities to commit crimes, and the learning of major societal values that bear on law-abidingness and lawbreaking, are hardly concentrated in the first few years of life.

There have been many psychoanalytic and psychiatrically oriented discussions of crime and delinquency, presenting numerous and varied explanations of the development of crime tendencies.[15] As I have just indicated, most share an emphasis on basic human aggression and on the vital impact of early childhood experiences. Another common theme is that crime is merely a *symptom* of underlying psychic disturbance. It is the basic disturbance that must be understood and treated, not the offense itself. In many instances this contention implies that the particular form the offending behavior takes is not very significant. Some discussions suggest that if the offending individual's personality disorder had not led to crime, it undoubtedly would have

[14] Alex Inkeles, *What Is Sociology?* (Englewood Cliffs, N.J.: Prentice-Hall, Inc., 1964), p. 50.

[15] For sociological appraisals of these approaches, see Vold, *op. cit.*, Chap. 7; Gibbons, *op. cit.*, Chap. 7; Sutherland and Cressey, *op. cit.*, Chap. 8; also, Barbara Wooton, *Social Science and Social Pathology* (London: Macmillan & Co., Ltd., 1959), and Michael Hakeem, "A Critique of the Psychiatric Approach to the Prevention of Juvenile Delinquency," *Social Problems*, 5 (Winter, 1957), 194–206.

emerged in the form of some other "symptom." Others assert that frequently the (symptomatic) criminal behavior masks and distracts attention from the real problem—as in certain cases where the basic motivation of an arsonist or a burglar may relate to some sexual disorder.

One of the central difficulties with the symptom-of-underlying-disorder conception of crime is that it is almost impossible to prove or disprove, at least in a systematic way. Notwithstanding the tremendous insight psychoanalysis has brought to bear on aspects of human behavior (and no sensitive person who has read Freud's *Psychopathology of Everyday Life,* or other more complex psychoanalytic classics, can help but be impressed with their insight), diagnosis of mental disorders continues to rest very heavily on the interpretations made by the analyst himself. Although collective professional experience in studying and treating disturbed people has produced a repertoire of reasonably well-accepted clues to particular forms of psychopathology, existing diagnostic categories are far from being so clear-cut and uniform that their application will not vary according to the skills, experiences, insights, and inclinations of specific diagnosticians. Furthermore, most psychoanalysts and psychiatrists see their professional roles as centering around the treatment of the individual. They are quite properly committed to a depth understanding of each patient's problems, rather than to a statistical analysis of the variables associated with large numbers (let alone representative samples) of cases.

Because of the nature of his work the psychoanalyst or psychiatrist ordinarily assesses the problems of a law violator *after* he has committed a criminal act (or been held to have committed such a act), and after he has gone through various stages of official processing. In such a situation it is difficult to know exactly what to make of any personality characteristics, patterns, or problems psychiatric scrutiny may reveal. Did they *lead to* the criminal behavior, or did they develop *along with* or even as a *result of* involvement in such behavior? Might not *both* the criminal behavior *and* the "tell-tale" personality characteristics actually be attributable to some other unrecognized factor? Inability to provide conclusive answers to such questions has badly flawed various attempts to develop general statements about the relation between personality characteristics and disorders and crime. And the fact that the diagnostician *knows* that the person he is examining is believed to have committed a criminal offense cannot be ruled out as a potential obstacle to truly objective diagnosis. Even trained professionals may

find it difficult to avoid being influenced by the widespread moral re-
pugance toward certain behavior patterns.

Knowing that an individual is a murderer, a drug addict, a homosexual, or even a juvenile delinquent, some diagnosticians may more or
less *conclude at the outset* that "obviously" such a person is disturbed.
The nature of the diagnosis then shifts: the emphasis is no longer on
the question of *whether* psychopathology is present, but rather on *what
form it takes* or what underlying forces are *causing* it. (Of course,
when individuals voluntarily come to a therapist saying they are disturbed and want help, such an approach may be warranted. This is
rarely the case, however, with respect to the diagnosis of law violators.)
The danger of generalizing from studies based only on officially identified or incarcerated offenders (or patient populations) is suggested by
an intriguing research finding concerning homosexuality. Psychologist
Evelyn Hooker administered a battery of standard psychological tests
to homosexuals drawn from the general community—that is, individuals who were neither under psychiatric treatment nor experiencing
trouble with the law. When professionals examining the test results
were unaware that the subjects were homosexual, the test results revealed no greater indication of psychopathology than was found for
a sample of carefully selected nonhomosexual "control" subjects.[16]

In diagnosing the identified offender, then, a process of retrospective
interpretation often may occur. Review of the individual's case history
"reveals" early behavior patterns or personal characteristics that are
now construed as having led to the present crime involvement, and that
"should have tipped us off" earlier that the person was destined to get
into serious trouble. We suddenly realize that he was "all along" a
potential criminal. The kinds of early conditions that have been retro-
spectively applied in this way are myriad. Criticizing one psychiatrically oriented research project aimed at identifying and treating poten-
tal juvenile delinquents, a sociologist noted that the project had
developed a long list of personal characteristics and behavioral patterns
to serve as indicators that referral of children for professional diagnosis
and help might be called for. The list included both bashfulness and
boisterousness, both bullying and crying, both overactivity and under-
activity, both defiance and timidity—as well as such items as daydream-

---

[16] Evelyn Hooker, "The Adjustment of the Male Overt Homosexual," in Hendrik
M. Ruitenbeek, ed., *The Problem of Homosexuality in Modern Society* (New
York: E. P. Dutton & Co., Inc., 1963).

ing, hitching rides, nailbiting, quarreling, showing-off, silliness, teasing, and thumbsucking (to cite just a few). Asserting that such supposed clues "have not issued from valid research operations" but rather rest on "the untested preconceptions of the adherents of the psychiatric ideology," the sociological critic noted that scientifically established criteria by which to separate normality and deviation with respect to these characteristics were lacking. As a result they could be of little help in the prevention of delinquency and crime:

. . . suppose a child were discovered to evince a bothersome quantum of aggression, a characteristic which many clinicians insist is one of the cardinal signs of predelinquency. Should measures be taken to reduce the aggression? But aggression is not a trait that eventuates only in wanton rape and plunder. It can be quite handy in a corporation. Some generals have been aggressive. Some aggressive people have become noted explorers. Some have gone into medicine and law. Some have specialized in psychiatry. Some have entered teaching, as any student and any faculty member could attest. Aggression can find many happy uses.[17]

Furthermore, there is considerable lack of agreement among specialists themselves as to which characteristics are the most serious danger signs: "some harshly rebuke parents for being concerned about the very traits that others have painstakingly instructed and warned them to get exercised about." [18]

To some extent this particular critique may have involved tilting with strawmen. The project criticized appears to have been a rather unsophisticated one, and there have been some more systematic and carefully conducted researches aimed at providing a basis for the prediction of delinquency. The basic thrust of the criticism, however, has a lot of merit. Lack of specificity as to the linkages between crime and psychological disturbance, and the various methodological inadequacies that I have noted, make sociologists very leery about such terms as "predelinquency" and "latent delinquency" that crop up frequently in psychiatrically oriented discussions of crime.

Psychiatrists themselves tend to be in general agreement that only a very small proportion of (even incarcerated) criminal offenders dis-

---

[17] Hakeem, *op. cit.*

[18] *Ibid.*, on the problem of retrospective interpretation, see "The Medical Model and Mental Hospitalization," in Erving Goffman, *Asylums* (New York: Doubleday Anchor Books, 1961).

plays signs of those psychological disorders deemed sufficiently extreme to be labeled psychoses. The distribution of diagnosed offenders among the other categories of mental disturbance varies a good deal from study to study. Many of the relevant psychiatric findings and statements derive from studies of juvenile delinquents, with the only apparent agreement being that a large proportion of such youngsters is psychologically disturbed in one way or another (a famous study of 105 families, in which one child was delinquent and another was not, found that 91 per cent of the delinquents as compared with only 13 per cent of their nondelinquent siblings displayed signs of serious emotional disturbance). Some studies emphasize weak superego controls, others emphasize weak ego controls; one developed the idea of "superego lacunae" in which delinquent acts of the children were seen to be related to the parents' own problems and deviant impulses. One psychiatrist has identified two major types of delinquents, the adaptive and the maladaptive; it is only the latter in which serious emotional disturbance of the sort that primarily requires psychiatric attention is present. In the long-term studies of the Gluecks, a number of background and current characteristics (psychological, sociological, and even physical—the finding about body type that was cited earlier) distinguished the delinquents from control subjects. Reports of this research placed particular emphasis on factors relating to the family situation—such as parental affection, supervision, and discipline.[19]

A diagnosis that appears with special frequency in psychiatric crime studies is that of "psychopathic personality."[20] The term has probably been applied most often to certain highly aggressive but otherwise undiagnosable offenders, who are described as being able to commit acts of brutal violence without any sense of guilt, and as being largely incapable of establishing meaningful emotional relationships with other

[19] For discussion of a variety of psychiatric formulations regarding delinquency, see Sophia Robison, *Juvenile Delinquency* (New York: Holt, Rinehart & Winston, Inc., 1960), Chap. 6; and John M. Martin and Joseph P. Fitzpatrick, *Delinquent Behavior* (New York: Random House, Inc., 1964), Chap. 4, as well as materials cited in note 15 above.

[20] See Sutherland and Cressey, *op. cit.*, pp. 169–71. See also Hervey Cleckley, *The Mask of Sanity* (St. Louis: The C. V. Mosby Co., 1941); Robert M. Lindner, *Rebel Without a Cause* (New York: Grune & Stratton, Inc., 1944); William and Joan McCord, *Psychopathy and Delinquency* (New York: Grune & Stratton, Inc., 1956). A sociological interpretation of psychopathy—in terms of role-taking deficiency—is provided by Harrison C. Gough, "A Sociological Theory of Psychopathy," *American Journal of Sociology*, 53 (March, 1948), 359–66.

individuals. But the same diagnosis has been applied to drug addicts, various types of sex offenders, and—critics assert—to a wide variety of offenders the psychiatrist is convinced *must* be mentally ill but whom he can't fit into one of the better accepted diagnostic categories.

The vagueness involved in the application of this label is evident from striking variations in the frequency of its use. One study revealed that in roughly comparable prisons the proportion of prisoners diagnosed as psychopathic varied from 5 per cent to 98 per cent. Another study turned up over 200 terms that had been used more or less synonymously with "psychopath," over 50 traits and characteristics that had been linked with psychopathy, and 30 types of behavior that had been characterized as "forms of psychopathic behavior." Under the circumstances it is not surprising that even some psychiatrists consider it a "wastebasket" diagnosis; although there are others who insist strongly that there is a distinct category of violent offenders to whom the label psychopath—or, in some modern versions, "sociopath"—is meaningfully applied.

The extension of the term to cover highly diverse behaviors of individuals who do not display signs of the more standard mental disorders seems, however, clearly indefensible. It has also had some very unfortunate results, as in the case of the hastily passed "sexual psychopath" laws that still exist in certain states—under some of which almost any sex offender (violent or nonviolent, dangerous or harmless) may be committed for an indeterminate period to a correctional or "treatment" institution. As the Sutherland-Cressey criminology text succinctly notes, "Because no one has been able to identify a sexual psychopath any more than any other psychopath, the laws have been absurd in principle and futile in operation." Diagnosis of drug addicts as psychopaths has been similarly unhelpful. Of this and similar narrowly psychiatric views of addicts, sociologist Alfred Lindesmith wrote that apparently there was an unspoken assumption "that any trait which distinguishes addicts from nonaddicts is *ipso facto* a criterion of abnormality." He went on to note that,

Addicts are said to become addicted because they have feelings of frustration, lack of self-confidence and need the drug to bolster themselves up. Lack of self-confidence is taken as a criterion of psychopathy or of weakness. But another person becomes addicted, it is said, because of "curiosity" and a "willingness to try anything once" and this too is called abnormal. Thus, self-confidence and the lack of self-confidence are both signs of abnormality. The addict is evidently judged in advance. He is damned if he is self-confident and he is damned if he is not.[21]

These comments illustrate the problems of circularity and lack of specificity that may characterize a good deal of psychiatric diagnosis, and about which sociological crime specialists are, as I have indicated, quite uneasy.

Sociologists have often complained that psychiatric interpretations of delinquency and crime have failed to take adequate account of the variation in outlooks and behavior patterns that are given social approval in the different socioeconomic strata of our society. What is considered "normal" in one social class context may be adjudged "pathological" in another. The very definitions of mental health and mental illness, it has been asserted, are culture-bound. Whatever content is given to these terms is likely to have meaning only within a given culture, and then perhaps only within certain sectors of that culture.

This kind of perspective is increasingly recognized by the more sociologically sophisticated psychiatrists, who nowadays often take into account that the antisocial behavior and outlooks of even a hardened offender—in terms of the social milieu out of which they developed—are not always evidence of psychic abnormality. Accordingly, new types of psychiatric treatment programs have arisen, in which an effort is made to grapple with the group and cultural sources of the antisocial patterns and to create a "therapeutic milieu"—rather than simply attempting to utilize conventional forms of one-to-one psychotherapy.[22]

In summary, the limitations of an attempt to explain crime strictly in psychiatric or psychological terms are partly conceptual (failure to appreciate the significance of social factors in generating deviant behavior); but more centrally the problem is one of research method. Many of these formulations rest on inadequate evidence derived from clinical experiences with nonrepresentative groups of offenders. And

[21] Alfred R. Lindesmith, "The Drug Addict as Psychopath," *American Sociological Review*, 5 (1940), 920. See also Lindesmith, *Addiction and Opiates* (Chicago: Aldine, 1968).

[22] See, for example, Fritz Redl and David Wineman, *Children Who Hate* (New York: Collier Books, 1962); David Street, Robert Vinter, and Charles Perrow, *Organization for Treatment* (New York: The Free Press, 1966); also H. Ashley Weeks, "The Highfields Project," and Lamar T. Empey and Jerome Rabow, "The Provo Experiment in Delinquency Rehabilitation," both in Rose Giallombardo, ed., *Juvenile Delinquency* (New York: John Wiley & Sons, Inc., 1966).

the tendency to expand such selected findings into an overall theory alleged to explain all or most crime ignores the full range of criminal behavior in our society. Invariably the psychiatric "explanations" have been unable to explain adequately the patterned variations found in our crime rates.

A scientific basis for such a theory cannot be provided merely by inventing a fancy formula, as in the case of one psychiatric writer on crime who offers the following: $C = T + S/R$ ("A criminal act equals the product of a person's criminalistic tendencies elicited by the momentary situation, all of which results in his mental resistance being so decreased that he carries out the criminal act.")[23] It is highly questionable whether we can ever locate and measure (or in fact whether there really exists) such an entity as "a person's criminalistic tendencies." Such notions of predisposition to crime are quite out of line with our general knowledge of the constantly changing patterns of an individual's behavior, the complex variety of criminal offenses, and the fact that what is criminal is itself subject to variation through changes in the criminal law.[24]

The Mass Media and Crime

Turning to a rather different matter, what can be said of the fairly widespread view that a major contributing cause of crime in present-day American society is its treatment by the media of mass communication—comics, newspapers, movies, and television? As part of the national debate over the meaning of recent political assassinations and racial disorders, the question has been revived whether the media breed violence (and hence at least a certain proportion of major crime). Thus, the theatre section of the *New York Times* carried, on June 30, 1968, a selection of brief statements on the issue, "Are the Movies Teaching Us to Be Violent?" The views offered (by various people connected with the movie industry and a few outside writers) ran the usual gamut, including at least one outraged condemnation of vivid depictions of crime and violence, as well as several sober assertions that the basic sources of violence lie elsewhere.

[23] David Abrahamsen, *Who Are the Guilty?* (New York: Grove Press, 1958), p. 67.

[24] For a well reasoned general sociological assessment of psychiatric approaches, see Albert K. Cohen, "A Sociologist's View of Psychiatric Criminology," paper read at meeting of the American Psychiatric Association, May 10, 1966.

Systematic sociological research on media content and effects does not provide much direct support for the claim that the media are producing a nation of criminals.[25] Findings in these studies indicate that the dominant effect of media experience on the individual is the reinforcement of pre-existing outlooks. This conclusion is closely related to the discovery of three major processes involved in contact with the media: selective exposure, selective perception, and selective retention. People tend to expose themselves to media content that jibes with the attitudes they already hold, they tend to see what they want to see in this content (and to dismiss whatever they don't want to see or don't expect to see), and they tend to be impressed most by the items that are in line with their own views and earlier impressions. Although most of the selective exposure findings derive from studies of adults—and one night anticipate more indiscriminate exposure among children—it seems likely that selective perception and selective retention are general social psychological processes existing among children as well as among their elders. Similarly, while the basic finding of reinforcement effects was developed largely through studies of attempts at influencing and changing attitudes (particularly political and related attitudes), there is no reason to believe that this likely outcome would not hold for other situations too.

Another major conclusion from communications research which may have some bearing on the issue of the media and crime is that it is an oversimplification to think in terms of a direct transfer of ideas and attitudes from the medium to an undifferentiated mass audience. On the contrary, sociologists have found there is often a "two-step flow" of communication: first from the media to particularly influential individuals ("opinion leaders," informal group leaders), and then from these leaders to members of their "primary" groups and other individuals with whom they come into frequent contact. With respect to this process, we should keep in mind the possibility that the impact of any crime content in the media may well be "mediated" through the interaction processes of youthful peer groups, as well as by interaction within family situations.

Public concern about the treatment of crime and violence in the

[25] An excellent critical review of research findings in this area is provided by Joseph T. Klapper, *The Effects of Mass Communication* (New York: The Free Press, 1960). See also Charles R. Wright, *Mass Communication* (New York: Random House, Inc., 1959), and Otto N. Larsen, ed., *Violence and the Mass Media* (New York: Harper and Row, Publishers, 1968).

mass media probably reached a peak in the crime and horror comic book controversies of the early 1950's. One widely read statement condemning the media's performance in this area was presented by psychiatrist Fredric Wertham in his 1954 book *Seduction of the Innocent*.[26] Wertham saw in the comic books a frightening preponderance of violent, erotic, erotic-sadistic, and crime-condoning material—of which he provided many vivid examples (including reproduction of some of the more lurid pictorial content). He also related various cases, from his own clinical experience and elsewhere, in which young people showed serious disturbance which he felt was related to such content. Included were certain major crimes committed by youths who apparently had been influenced in one way or another (as revealed through the technique adopted, the costume worn, etc.) by comic books. The cardinal dangers, Wertham seemed to believe, were direct imitation of the criminal violence in the comics, and a more general distortion of values through exposure to a fairly explicit glorification of crime and violence (and sexual sadism).

Although Wertham was criticized for selecting particularly lurid content, there is little doubt that the comic books of that time contained a great deal of gratuitous and extremely unpleasant violence. For example, a systematic content analysis of some 350 comics, made during a 1954 study of this issue in the State of Washington, showed that a violent physical act appeared in one out of seven of the 44,653 frames examined. Even where pictures did not show the actual contact of weapons with victims, or the victim's mangled body, equally chilling effects were provided through the language used to describe killings. One of the examples cited was the following:

A man is shown lifting an axe preparatory to striking his wife on the floor. In the next frame he lowers the axe; the wife is not shown but the caption reads: "Bertha squealed as Norman brought the axe down. The swinging of steel and the thud of the razor-sharp metal against flesh cut the squeal short." In the next frame he holds the axe poised again, the body still is not exposed and the caption reads: "He brought the axe down again and again, hacking, severing, dismembering." [27]

[26] Fredric Wertham, *Seduction of the Innocent* (New York: Holt, Rinehart & Winston, Inc., 1954).

[27] Marilyn Graalfs, "Violence in Comic Books (Before Self-Regulation by the Comics Industry)," excerpted from *A Survey of Comic Books in the State of Washington* (1954), in Larsen, *op. cit.*, 91–96.

While it is doubtful whether the other media have achieved such heights of objectionable violence, there is little doubt that much violence is reflected in their output. Systematic studies conducted in the early 1950's for the National Association of Educational Broadcasters —in which all entertainment programs televised in New York during a one week period (in each of the study years) were carefully monitored and every act or threat of violence recorded—disclosed in 1953 a total of 3,350 incidents of violence for the week; in 1954, an even grander total of 6,868. This research also indicated that the frequency of violence was higher in the hours in which children's programs are concentrated than at other viewing times.

The comic book industry, under great pressure, adopted in 1954 a system of self-regulation which has probably served to eliminate a fair amount of the most objectionable content—though the resulting changes, deemed satisfactory by the industry and by spokesmen for some outside organizations, have not yet been sufficient to satisfy Dr. Wertham. And we know full well that production codes in the movie and television industries have hardly meant an absence of violence on their respective screens. But it is one thing to document the frequency with which violence or crime is depicted in the media, and quite another to demonstrate that this really has pernicious social effects. This is the issue on which Dr. Wertham and his more research-minded critics part company. From the outset, Wertham was criticized for relying on nonrepresentative clinical evidence only—selected cases he had encountered in which psychological disturbance seemed to have been produced through some impact of the media. Wertham countered with active criticism of questionnaires, interviews, and experimental studies, insisting that only an in-depth psychological study of the child can really tell us what is happening in and to his mind. As he recently expressed this view:

We must study the whole child and not just one facet. The only method that can give valid results is the clinical method. That is to say, the child has to be examined and all the psychobiological and psychosocial factors with a bearing on his life have to be considered. The influence of TV has to be taken up and analyzed unobtrusively and incidentally. Follow-up study of development is necessary and what young adults say later about their childhood is most relevant.[28]

[28] Fredric Wertham, "School for Violence," in Larsen, *op. cit.*, pp. 36–39.

Systematic researchers remain largely unconvinced. They want to be *shown* that Wertham has done more than turn up some sick viewers who most likely were disturbed *before* their experiences with the media. There is not yet any solid empirical evidence showing pronounced undesirable effects on individuals produced by the crime and violence content of the mass media. In a pioneering English study exploring the emotional effects of television on children (and involving a research sample of close to 2,000 children, half of them viewers and half nonviewing "controls"), the researchers came to the conclusion that, generally speaking, children are most unlikely to "translate television experience into action." Their findings suggested that even programs with particularly explosive content "do not initiate aggressive, maladjusted, or delinquent behavior," although they might "aid its expression." Similarly, American researchers who explored the effects of television viewing on some 6,000 children in eleven different communities, also concluded that little delinquency could be directly traced to television; at most, it might be a contributing factor in delinquency causation. The British study did find that a sizeable minority of child televiewers were frightened by some of the crime and violence fare (and it discovered also that the sheer amount of violence is probably not as significant in producing such fright as the nature of the setting in which violence occurs and the manner in which it is presented). While this investigation was geared largely to the children's own accounts of essentially short-term reactions, nothing in what they found led these researchers to think that long-range or serious psychological traumatization was likely to be a frequent occurrence.

Various studies have shown patterned variations among children in exposure to the media and in preference for particular kinds of media content. In one study of "exposure habits and cognitive effects" among over 600 fifth and sixth graders in the Boston area, a particular preference for "aggressive hero material" was found among boys who were in general highly exposed to the pictorial media, and who also exhibited certain distinguishing psychological characteristics (such as problems in their relations with parents and friends, high level of self-blame for difficulties, and "rebellious independence"). But the researcher asserted that these qualities did not appear to be media *effects*. She did find some indications that such children used the media in "escapist" ways, but that is a far cry from a showing of media-produced delinquency or crime. In general, students of media effects assert that most really disturbed reactions probably occur among previously disturbed children. As one well-known researcher puts it, "the kind and degree of vicarious experiencing depends upon the individual viewer's pre-existing interests and motives to some degree, and upon the match between these characteristics of the viewer and the events on the screen." [29]

Experimental laboratory studies of "aggression" conducted by social psychologists have produced somewhat mixed results. One early experiment purported to show a "cathartic" effect, that exposure to aggressive scenes may actually reduce aggressive drives by providing a vicarious release of latent hostilities. But there seems to be more evidence pointing in the other direction—suggesting that aggressive "stimuli" may trigger aggressive behavior immediately following such exposure. One has to be very cautious, of course, in transferring such findings (produced in largely artificial laboratory situations) into real life. Nonetheless, some researchers are convinced from studies of this sort that being exposed to aggression may heighten the likelihood in some individuals of committing aggressive acts afterwards. And punishment of the "villain" in the scene that is viewed does not provide a sure-fire guarantee that any aggressive impulses instigated by the exposure will be cancelled out. Punishment may have that effect, but it could also reinforce an attitude that hostile action against persons the viewer considers "bad" is justified. The role of pre-existing receptiveness to certain material remains, however, as a potentially important factor. One element in this may well be the viewer's level of discontent and frustration. When one group of schoolchildren in a study of film effects was given an easy task, and another a highly frustrating one, reactions to the subsequently shown film differed: the experimentally frustrated children retained much more of the film's aggressive content than those who had not been frustrated.

A few research projects have looked into the media habits of known delinquents and convicted criminal offenders. An early (1933) study involving interviews with convicted offenders found that crime movies were highly popular among these people. The researchers concluded that movies—by arousing the desire for easy money, by promoting toughness and adventurousness, by displaying criminal techniques, and so on—"may create attitudes and furnish techniques conducive,

[29] Eleanor E. Maccoby, "Effects of the Mass Media," in Larsen, *op. cit.*, p. 119.

quite unwittingly, to delinquent or criminal behavior." This suggestion, however, did not rest on any "hard" evidence of direct influence
from the films *to* criminal behavior. In a more recent investigation,
boys and girls who had been arrested for delinquent acts turned out
to be much more avid readers of crime, violent, and adventure comics
than a matched control group of nondelinquents. But the researcher
was careful not to conclude from this a causal relationship; in fact, he
pointed out that the influence could operate in either direction.

The overall evidence on direct and socially harmful effects of crime
and violence material in the media is, then, somewhat inconclusive.
We do not really know too much about the overall relative incidence
of harmful and harmless impact. But even if only a minority is ad-
versely affected, and even assuming that their pre-existing psychological make-up renders them susceptible to such effects, the possibility of
such socially undesirable influence provides some cause for public
concern (though not, it might be emphasized, any cause for panic).
As researcher Joseph Klapper comments, following his careful review
of all the evidence on this matter, "If depictions of crime and violence
have an unhealthy effect upon even 1 per cent of the nation's children,
it becomes socially important to inquire whether and how the situation
can be rectified." While few specialists favor outright censorship
(though the case for weeding out purely gratuitous and excessive
violence at least in the comics—a medium aimed almost entirely at
children—seems persuasive), a strong argument can be made for
continuous public pressure on the media to exercise greater care in
editing and programming, so as to reduce crime and violence content
not required by the basic needs of plot and atmosphere-creation, and
to minimize the exposure of children to such material. Such activity
may have *some* limited influence in preventing reinforcement of crime-
conducive outlooks; and it is unlikely to do any real harm to anyone.

As I have suggested, a basic shortcoming of most research on media
effects is that the findings relate to relatively short-term impact. It is
much more difficult to examine long-term and diffuse influence. Yet
it may be that subtle and diffuse effects actually are more significant
than specific and immediate ones. And if media content does not lead
directly to the commission of criminal acts, it may nonetheless be a
major factor shaping the public's view of crime problems. We have
already seen that the treatment of alleged "crime waves" is often
misleading. To the extent that they relay questionable statistics and
focus on alarmist statements, the media (particularly the newspapers)

are ill serving the public. On the other hand, the papers do sometimes point out the shortcomings of official statistics, and certainly that is to their credit.

By the use of unnecessary and prejudicial epithets in criminal cases the media may encourage the public to make snap judgments and unwise assumptions about suspects and defendants. To cite a recent example, the aforementioned article in the usually sober *New York Times*, entitled "Gunman Terrorizes Central Park," carried as a sub-head, "Thug on a Roof Duels Police for an Hour," even though none of the information about the suspect (provided on an inside page) in any way justified the use of the term "thug." The issue of free press-fair trial has, of course, been a controversial one for many years. However what concerns me here is not so much the potential impact of press coverage on the outcomes of particular cases, but rather that inflammatory coverage may reinforce and promote general patterns of stereotyped thinking about crime and "criminals." Similarly, many newspapers used to engage regularly in the practice of indicating when a suspect was a Negro, without referring to race at all when a suspect was white. This certainly inflated the public's impression of the relative contribution of Negroes to crime problems. The same kind of result is fostered by the use in crime stories of such descriptions as "a former convict" and "a former mental patient." As various sociologists have pointed out, if reporters provided comparable information whenever an offender was "a churchgoing Methodist" or "an active labor union member," "an officer of the local PTA" or "an active amateur gardener," a quite different crime picture would begin to come across.

To be sure, newsmen are becoming increasingly sophisticated and fair-minded in such matters, but in the more sensationalistic tabloids a great deal of biased material still appears. News reports of criminal acts may also promote highly questionable beliefs concerning crime causation. Thus, it has been suggested that a major tendency in modern crime reporting (particularly perhaps in the United States) has been for the reporter to seek at once a crime's motive.

The more shockingly trivial the alleged motive, the more newsworthy it becomes, particularly when heinous offenses are involved. "I wanted to see what it was like to kill someone." "I stabbed Pa because he was always criticizing me." "We set fire to the school because the gym teacher bawled us out." Such verbalizations of motive—even accurately reported—are really gross oversimplifications of human conduct, for they obscure the complex of attitudes, values, and group influences necessarily antecedent in some degree to all overt action.[30]

Even more deleterious in the long run may be the indirect impact on our crime problems of media content that does not at all involve a depiction of criminal behavior or relate in any apparent way to crime issues. The mass media at least reflect and reinforce—if they do not help to create—the value emphases of a society. As Vance Packard made clear in his best-selling *The Hidden Persuaders* the media certainly can exploit bases for receptiveness already present in the audience. When we consider statements by social researchers that play down the impact of the media, it may be well to keep in mind that advertisers have hardly despaired of the effectiveness of mass communication! Not just in the area of consumer behavior (where impact may indeed be quite forceful and direct), but in many other areas of outlook and behavior the media may very likely exert subtle long-term influences on Americans. For example, studies of soap-opera listening and viewing, and of other supposed "entertainments," have shown that often media content is not simply a diversion to be dismissed as unimportant. On the contrary, it may serve significant practical or symbolic functions for the individual. Likewise, factual material may exert some subtle influences of which we have little systematic knowledge. Thus, it is quite possible that wartime news reporting—which may now extend to virtually live battlefield coverage, brought into homes all over the country by television—may be having appreciable, if not really discernible effects in shaping American feelings and concepts about the value of human life. If, in any significant measure, such material is causing Americans to devalue human life (and of course we don't know that any effect runs in that direction), the impact on crime problems could, in the long run, be substantial.

For some years now, the media have been castigated for their contribution to a generalized debasing of American values (this was one of several shortcomings Newton Minow presumably had in mind when, as Federal Communications Commissioner, he described television as "a vast wasteland"). Without entering into the extensive debate about "high culture" versus "mass culture," it is difficult to avoid the conclusion that the media have helped to shape the texture of re-

[30] Donald R. Taft and Ralph W. England, Jr., *op. cit.*, pp. 211–12.

cent American life. Systematic studies have shown—and there is now growing public awareness—that the media have (by various kinds of selective emphasis and selective inattention) presented a distorted picture of the place and life of Negroes in American society. Very likely this distortion has in some degree affected the nature of interracial outlooks and behavior. There should be little doubt that the media have played a highly significant role in promoting what has been called the "cult of commodities" in American life, and in nurturing those patterns of "conspicuous consumption" and "pecuniary emulation" that economist Thorstein Veblen so unerringly diagnosed in his classic *The Theory of the Leisure Class.*

Since, as I shall indicate, the characteristically American emphasis on achieving monetary success, the structural obstacles to achieving such success, and the prevalence of feelings of relative deprivation, are central aspects of our current crime situation, the role of the mass media in this area should not be discounted. Not only do the media heighten lower-class frustration by making vivid to the poor person what he is missing, but they hammer home again and again—in subtle and not so subtle ways—that personal worth is to be measured in monetary and material terms. It is the guy with the snappy new car who gets the pretty girl; those who use their wits to make a "fast buck" achieve the big payoff. The media are strong in emphasizing the healthiness of competition and self-reliance; they are notably weak in pushing interpersonal cooperation, social consciousness and generosity, and basic human decency as major life values. They often convey the message that might makes right, and cynically disdain the presumably "lofty" embracing of meaningful human relationships and social altruism. While it is true that the prediction-oriented sociologist is leery of attempts to explain crime causation in terms of a society's general values (since such values do not by themselves help us differentiate between individuals who succumb to crime and those who do not), I hope to show in Chapter 5 that no attempt at meaningful understanding of crime in our society can afford to ignore the major value emphases of American life.

Church, School, and Family

"If we could only put God back in American life," the cry often goes, then we could do away with crime and delinquency.

Ideally it would seem that this notion should have a great deal of merit. Many if not most criminal acts in some sense contravene broad principles of religious morality. Training in and true acceptance of such principles, then, might not unreasonably be viewed as a major buffer against criminality.

Unfortunately, things are not so simple. While sociologists usually view religion as a broadly functional force in society—providing over-arching values that help to hold the society together and answering recurrent and compelling questions about the meaning of human ex-istence—they recognize too that in modern industrial society organized religion can be a source of division and conflict, and that the juxtaposi-tion of religious and social values may be extremely complex. In any area of human outlooks and behavior we might choose to consider, the role of religion turns out to be far from clear-cut and one-direc-tional.

We certainly find this to be the case when we approach the ques-tion of religion's relation to crime. The vast majority of Americans will, when questioned, state their belief in God (and even in an after-life), their view that religion is extremely important, their affiliation with a religious denomination, and their regular or at least occasional attendance at a church or synagogue. Yet notwithstanding this apparent Godliness, America continues to be plagued by a seemingly unstoppa-ble flow of crime problems. Our confusion may be compounded when we learn that various systematic studies have found high proportions (in one case, higher than in the general population!) of adjudicated delinquents and convicted adult offenders reporting both church mem-bership and church attendance.

Partial understanding of such evidence—which might on first glance seem inherently contradictory—lies in an appreciation of the relatively superficial nature of much religious behavior in modern American so-ciety. Undoubtedly there are a good many "truly religious" people in the United States today. Yet we know that a great deal of the post-World War II "revival" of religion represented an upsurge of religiosity more than of serious religious feeling and belief.[31] The same Americans who profess religious belief and affiliation also state that their religious beliefs have exerted little influence on their ideas concerning such important areas of everyday conduct as politics and business. And

---

[31] For an excellent discussion of this matter, see Will Herberg, *Protestant-Cath-olic-Jew*, rev. ed. (Garden City, N.Y.: Doubleday Anchor Books, 1960), espe-cially Chaps. IV and V.

religious doctrine as such seems to be only a secondary aspect of religion for many Americans. In his highly revealing analyis of contemporary American religion, Will Herberg pointedly quoted President Dwight Eisenhower, who had proclaimed, "Our government makes no sense unless it is founded in a deeply felt religious faith—and I don't care what it is." While Eisenhower undoubtedly intended to stress the value of harmony in a religiously pluralistic society, he unwittingly remarked on the nondoctrinal superficiality of much American religious practice. Religion as the right thing to do, the surface trappings of religion (such as attendance at major holidays, funerals, and marriages; utilization of relatively secularized Sunday schools; and development of church-related social programs)—these often seem at the center of religion in America, largely displacing deeply felt religious belief. Father Joseph Fichter, in a classic sociological study of a Roman Catholic parish in a Southern city, even analogized the modern urban church to a gas station—where parishioners come to be "serviced" impersonally on various routine occasions. If there is a body of widely relevant basic religious beliefs in present-day America, perhaps it is, as Herberg suggested, "the American way of life" itself. "By every realistic criterion," he stated, this is the "operative faith of the American people."

Religious affiliation and church attendance, then, are not of much use as indicators of commitment to religious ideals or to behavior patterns inspired by or consistent with religious beliefs. In American society the situation is complicated still further by the intersection of church membership with other significant social categories—in particular social class and race.[32] At the level of statistics, for example, substantial differences in the crime rates of various denominations turn out to be more likely attributable to the relative social class membership, racial composition, and level of urban concentration of the denominations than to any doctrinal factors. And with respect to the meaningfulness of religion for the individual, as well as its effectiveness as an institution of social control, these intersecting elements are again central. In one sense, religious belief often has provided some solace to the socioeconomically deprived. But, at the same time, as Father Joseph Fitzpatrick, a sociologist specializing in urban and crime problems, has noted:

[32] Gerhard Lenski, *The Religious Factor* (Garden City, N.Y.: Doubleday Anchor Books, 1963).

The morality which is enforced against the poorer people to preserve a system which benefits the wealthy is never equally applied against the wealthy to protect the interests of the poor. It is the situation which places the representatives of religion in a difficult position when they face the problem of using religious motivation to promote conformity to the expected norms of the society. If, as may be the case, the norms are operating in favor of the people of privilege and power, religion may appear to be another instrument for the protection of vested interests.[33]

We also know that throughout American life numerous behavior patterns and persistent values (actual if not professed) are quite at odds with major principles of Judeo-Christian morality, and this cannot help but undermine the potential influence of religion in socializing individuals to moral outlooks and ways of life.

It will not do, then, simply to argue that if we could arrange for all the individuals in our society to become tuned-in on the "message" of religion, we would drastically reduce crime. The overriding truth is that unless the socioeconomic context "encourages" patterns of cooperative and decent interpersonal behavior, many individuals will not accept religion's message. Or, alternatively, they will accept it and precisely for that reason believe in the justness of desperate criminal acts that violate the official dictates of a system they see as oppressive. Ironically, the conception of the nature of individual wrongdoing central to at least some religious thought—with its characteristic emphasis on man's freedom of moral choice and personal blameworthiness for the commission of "immoral" acts—may sometimes be used to buttress the views of those who refuse to recognize that some men are more free than others, and who are unwilling to admit the power of social forces in shaping patterns of crime.

We have to keep in mind also that, at least under the conditions of religious pluralism that pertain in the United States today, religious belief can positively motivate certain criminal acts. Mormon violations of bigamy laws, religiously motivated refusals to serve in the armed forces or accept even "conscientious objector" status, refusal of members of certain religions to accept various public health directives or medical procedures—these are just a few examples of ways in which religious tenets may generate crime. Indirectly, too, organized

[33] Joseph P. Fitzpatrick, S.J., "The Role of Religion in Programs for the Prevention and Correction of Crime and Delinquency," in President's Commission on Law Enforcement and Administration of Justice, *Task Force Report: Juvenile Delinquency and Youth Crime,* p. 321.

religion may be held partly accountable for the magnitude of American crime problems—through its frequent support for translating standards of private morality into criminal laws.

If a truly religious approach to crime problems requires a direct attack on immoral social arrangements and societal value emphases more than a reforming of individuals, it does not follow that religious groups as presently constituted are completely impotent with respect to reducing criminal behavior. Certainly, in particular cases, the teachings of religion may help to curb the inclination to crime. In the areas of prevention and treatment (largely outside the main focus of this book), there is little doubt that the efforts of religious groups may be very effective (the work of such organizations as the East Harlem Protestant Parish, the *Centro Catolico Puertorriqueno* in Jersey City, and the Jewish Board of Guardians, illustrates these possibilities). And even if certain religiously inspired efforts may be mocked and exploited by some offenders (as is often the case with respect to the chaplaincy in correctional institutions), the same efforts are usually of some real benefit to others.

While the influence of the church in modern American society has in recent years become somewhat attenuated, that of the public school has probably taken on increased importance. In a child-centered and education-oriented society such as ours, the schools—by virtue of their key role in determining the eventual placement of the individual in society, and also in terms of the sheer length and intensity of the child's exposure to educational institutions and processes—must be reckoned with as a major force shaping the lives of American youth. It has long been common to assert that crime and delinquency reflect a "failure of our schools." Usually what is meant by this is that the schools have neglected to inculcate respect for law and order and to teach the difference between right and wrong. But, as in the case of religion, to focus only on a vaguely and somewhat pretentiously defined function of consciously teaching morality and law-abidingness is to divorce the activity of the school from the social context in which it must operate, and to ignore both the intended and the unintended consequences of actual current educational practice.

Clearly the schools are not at present managing very effectively to prevent delinquency and crime. But the major conclusion to be drawn from what we know about the relation between the schooling process and these forms of behavior is even more depressing. Far from simply failing to inhibit the growth and spread of criminal outlooks and behavior patterns, the schools, as presently constituted, actively, if unwittingly, encourage their development. Sociologists Walter Schafer and Kenneth Polk, on the basis of a comprehensive review of relevant research findings, comment that "delinquent commitments result in part from adverse or negative school experiences," and that there are "fundamental defects within the educational system, especially as it touches lower-income youth," that actively contribute to delinquent outcomes. They insist further that "unless these underlying educational conditions that help produce delinquency are altered, efforts to deal with particular delinquent or delinquency-prone youth will have little effect in the long run." [34]

Since school success is a vital element in achieving favorable occupational and economic status, and since doing well at school is itself significantly dependent both on the conditions from which children come to school in the first place, and on the way they are treated once they get there, poor school performance becomes a major link in the vicious circle by which lower-class and Negro children are kept down. Most authorities now recognize that such children more likely than not come from so-called "culturally disadvantaged" homes—the social settings and informal learning processes they have experienced prior to school entrance have not prepared them for academic work or school procedures. At the same time, however, recent studies also show that educational aspiration is hardly limited to the middle and upper classes. Despite persisting social class differences in values relating to education, large proportions of lower-class parents appear eager that their children should do well in school. If few of them can see a good education as an abstract goal, the value of education as a path to relative economic security is readily understood. It is most unlikely that a great many lower-class children begin school with highly negative attitudes toward education. Indeed—as such teacher-writers as Jonathan Kozol, Herbert Kohl, and John Holt have made vividly clear —usually they are eager to learn, excited by the initial experience of school. It is the educational system itself, and not low motivation, or even low capacity on their part, that does them in.

They soon find that the system is unwilling to accept them on anything like their own terms, or even to credit them with being acceptable human beings. Most of the teachers come from middle-class back-grounds, have middle-class values, speak middle-class language, and demand middle-class styles of deportment and academic performance. Instructional material—as educators are just now beginning to realize —has itself had a heavy middle-class (and white) bias, and the child finds in its content practically nothing that seems to have any mean-ingful relation to his own experiences and urban ghetto environment. As one ex-delinquent commented concerning his early schooling:

It wasn't interesting to me. I liked the science books but I didn't dig that other stuff. Dick and Jane went up the hill to fetch a pail of water and all that crap. Mary had a little lamb. Spot jumped over the fence. See Spot jump over the fence. I mean I got this stuff in the seventh grade too. I got a little book no bigger than that. I opened it up. Dick and Jane was in the house. Mom and Dad went to the market. Spot was outside playing with the ball with Sally. I say, ain't this the cutest little story. And I took the book one day and shoved it straight back to the teacher and said I ain't going to read that stuff.[35]

Given the cultural deficiencies of their backgrounds (in white middle-class terms), and being badly prepared to score well on stand-ard IQ tests used to determine academic ability, many of the lower-class children are very early in the game relegated to the bottom of the class, the "slow learner" tracks, and so on. And many of their teachers consider it quite natural that they should be there. As various accounts make clear, particularly with respect to Negro pupils, there is a pervasive feeling that "you can't really expect these kids to do any decent work." Unwilling to consider a composition that graphically depicts the child's own poverty-stricken experiences as "acceptable," the teacher concludes that the child can't write. Failing to use imagi-native teaching methods that might meaningfully relate school tasks to the children's own lives, the teacher encounters apathy and blank-ness. Requiring rigidly middle-class standards of deportment, the teacher soon faces a hostile and unruly group of children.

Early academic failures build up cumulatively, and especially under the various "tracking" and "grouping" systems, students who are not performing well can hardly be expected to maintain satisfactory levels of "achievement motivation." As Schafer and Polk indicate, "students who fail tend to be progressively shunned and excluded by other achieving students, by individual teachers, and by the 'system as a

[35] Quoted by Schafer and Polk, *op. cit.,* p. 238.

whole.'" Not surprisingly, their view of themselves and of their future becomes progressively more dismal, and eventually "the school experience becomes highly unsatisfying, frustrating, and bitter." The potential in this situation for delinquent adaptations is evident. Often such a child can, quite realistically, anticipate greater feelings of competence and self-esteem, more group support, more varied and interesting experience, and in general increased social and financial pay-off from criminal acts than from continuing to knock his head against the wall of this alien and rejecting school experience.

For young Negroes there has been the additional factor that—even if they were able to perform adequately in the academic work—it was very difficult, at least until recently, to have any real hope that such performance would in the long run substantially open the doors to further opportunity and eventual success. Knowledge that even well-educated Negroes often were limited to menial and poor-paying jobs could hardly fail to convince many Negro youths that it was hardly worth the effort to try to do well in school. It is true that this situation is changing now, and that there is a growing interest in "compensatory" and remedial programs (both in school and at preschool age levels) to increase the chances that such children will achieve adequate performance levels. But it is quite clear that better job opportunities and special educational programs are not yet anywhere near to catching up with Negro and lower-class needs and aspirations. Such changes will have to be a great deal more extensive before they will begin to offset the resentments and frustrations bred through years of unconcern.

I have not even mentioned the deplorable conditions that we all know now exist in many ghetto schools. Overcrowding, dilapidated buildings, inadequate sanitary facilities, insufficient educational materials—these conditions are extremely prevalent, and the attitude taken toward their existence has often been one of passive acquiescence, of looking the other way. Jonathan Kozol describes well a frequently held reaction to ghetto school inadequacies:

"You children should thank God and feel blessed with good luck for all you've got. There are so many little children in the world who have been given so much less." The books are junk, the paint peels, the cellar stinks, the teachers call you nigger, and the windows fall in on your heads. "Thank God that you don't live in Russia or Africa! Thank God for all the blessings that you've got!" Once, finally, the day after the window blew in, I said to a friend of mine in the evening after school: "I guess that the building I teach in is not in very good condition." But to state a condition of dilapidation and ugliness and physical danger in words as mild and indirect as those is almost worse that not saying anything at all.[36]

Appalling as these physical conditions are, they are probably not as significant in promoting the drift into delinquent behavior as is the general social-psychological atmosphere surrounding the educational experience. As some of my earlier comments should make clear, the interpersonal reactions of teachers and other school authorities—the ways they respond to and handle the children's behavior and problems—may be especially crucial in establishing, and finally binding the child into, the vicious circle of academic failure and alienation from school and society. Unless these children are accorded some personal dignity, and unless efforts can be made to gear basic educational processes to content that will have meaning for them, the school will probably continue to bear a positive, rather than a negative, relation to crime causation. As Carl Werthman, a sociologist who has done extensive observational research on delinquency, points out:

. . . what is made of an act depends almost entirely on how it is defined and evaluated by the teacher, including the issue of whether or not the act is a violation of the basic authority rule. The boy is using the teacher to define himself as autonomous; and, like his behavior on the streets, he often creates or provokes the situation in which he then defends his honor. Yet if a teacher is willing to concede the fact that school is meaningless to some boys and therefore that other activities besides "teaching and learning" will necessarily go on in class, and if he is willing to limit the scope of his jurisdiction to the activity of "teaching and learning" itself, then his authority is likely to remain intact, regardless of how much it may be "tested." Whether or not he wishes to persuade the boys to join the learning process is another matter. . . .[37]

It follows from what I have said so far that an enormous amount of money and energy will have to be expended if educational conditions and programs that can both teach children and avoid these crime-generating tendencies are to be developed. This was recognized by the President's Commission on Law Enforcement, which recommended a major program of support for educational reforms, including sup-

[36] Jonathan Kozol, *Death at an Early Age* (New York: Bantam Books, 1968), p. 33.
[37] Carl Werthman, "The Function of Social Definitions in the Development of Delinquent Careers," in *Task Force Report: Juvenile Delinquency and Youth Crime*, p. 166.

port for personnel and facilities, reduction of racial and economic segregation, expanded "compensatory" programs, more relevant instructional material, and expanded guidance services. But the situation in the schools cannot be divorced from conditions in the ghetto generally (to which I shall return shortly). At best, improvement of the schools is one of several major efforts needed to free the ghetto-dweller from life conditions that breed crime.

For the present, then, the primary need in the schools is not so much a program that will teach children to be good as it is a system that will somehow nurture the desire to learn and be flexible enough so that most children can proceed at their own pace without discouragement. If accompanied by real reform in opportunities and living conditions outside the school, such a system could mean that the schools would begin to have a real anticrime impact, rather than a crime-producing one. Some efforts to "teach law and order" might also be useful. Any such program, however, would have to be well thought-out, realistic, honest, not overly "preachy," and geared to problems and situations that make sense to the audience. Particularly with "street-wise" youngsters, unsophisticated and fanciful (or downright dishonest) presentations are only likely to backfire. And in any case, teaching respect for law and order cannot hope to succeed in the context of a society for which the students can have no real respect. The likelihood of generating commitment in the classroom to values that have no real life meaning for the student is most slim indeed.

The "decline of the family" in American life is also frequently cited as a factor contributing to delinquency and crime. Actually the very notion of such a decline is rather questionable. Despite scattered groups of hippies and other independent-minded characters who make occasional attempts at communal living, and some young middle-class couples who live together outside of marriage (in most cases for short periods of time), there is no indication that the basic family system is on the way out in our society. It is true that the family is no longer a self-sustaining unit of economic interdependence (as the early American farm family sometimes was), and that many of the family's former socialization functions may have been taken over by other institutions. To some extent also the strength of family ties may not be what it once was. But some loss of reverence for family and marriage ties as ends in themselves may have been offset by the accompanying increases in freedom and independence of family members. If the child does not always unquestioningly obey the parent, at the same time he may be learning to think for himself in a way that formerly was less often nurtured. High divorce rates do at first seem to indicate a weakening of marriage ties, but this may be illusory— since low rates by themselves tell us nothing about the quality of marriages that do not break up. The casual assumption that absence of divorce implies marital harmony is unwarranted—the term "emotional divorce," adopted by one observer to describe conflict-ridden marriages that nonetheless persist, points up the danger of assuming that the absence of open disruption implies an underlying stability. It should be kept in mind, too, that while America has high divorce rates, it has high marriage rates as well. Americans do not appear to be disillusioned about marriage and family generally, even if they are increasingly unwilling to put up with unsatisfactory marital arrangements. And although average family size has, in long-run terms, declined, there is little indication that Americans today no longer want or care about children.

In thinking about the relation between family and crime it is a big mistake to assume that the family is always a force working *against* criminal involvement. "After a year of breaking into box-cars and stealing from stores, my stepmother realized that she could send me to the market to steal vegetables for her. My stealing had proved to be very profitable to her, so why not make it even more profitable." So reported a long-time delinquent whose story is retold in *The Jack-Roller*, a classic study of delinquency first published in 1930. "Stealing in the neighborhood was a common practice among the children and approved by the parents." [38] While this particular example is a bit misleading—since the stepmother in question was strongly hated and hence cannot represent the influence of loved and respected family members—the general point remains valid. Sometimes criminal behavior is learned at home. And even when parents actively try to inculcate anticriminal values, environmental conditions that support crime sometimes constitute strong forces competing for the child's allegiance and involvement.

In a neighborhood where crime and delinquency are dominant patterns, family factors may be significant in helping to determine which children do and which do not succumb to criminality. But it is equally important to keep in mind that in such situations the parents who try

[38] Clifford Shaw, *The Jack-Roller* (Chicago: University of Chicago Press, 1930; Phoenix Books, 1966), pp. 53, 54.

to keep their children out of trouble may well be fighting against almost overwhelming odds. To conclude that the "basic" causes of crime and delinquency invariably lie in the family is to ignore the extremely complex network of interrelationships between family influences and the simultaneous influences of community values, peer groups, neighborhood behavior patterns, socioeconomic pressures, and other relevant factors. The nature and extent of family influence is not a fixed entity; rather it will in all cases reflect this complicated mix of numerous "variables."

One of the most common explanations of delinquency has been that it is caused by "the broken home." It is true that various studies have indicated higher rates of broken homes for delinquents than for nondelinquents. However this difference has itself been subject to variation—depending on the types of offenses, and also the age level and the sex of the individuals sampled. The broken home seems to bear more of a significant relation to delinquency for younger boys and for girls than it does for older adolescent boys. Furthermore, most of the studies in which broken homes have been found to be highly significant relied on institutionalized youths for their samples of delinquents. When delinquent and nondelinquent samples are drawn instead from the general population, through the self-reported behavior technique, the significance of this factor appears greatly reduced. One major conclusion is that the existence of a broken home has special bearing on whether a child who gets into trouble is likely to be institutionalized, and it is this relation that was mainly responsible for the findings in the earlier studies rather than a direct relation between broken homes and delinquent behavior. It is also significant that a number of studies have concluded that family structure as such has considerably less impact in causing delinquency than does the *quality* of the child's family life. Marital happiness of the child's parents, consistent and fair discipline, and an atmosphere of parental affection and acceptance of the child, have all been found to be factors associated with low rates of delinquent behavior.

Because of its crucial role in "placing" a child in society—by establishing at the outset the neighborhood in which he lives, the values his environment fosters, and his socioeconomic status—the family is in some ways especially influential in leading to or fending off early crime involvement. In many respects it establishes the individual's "categoric risk" of contact with and immersion in criminal patterns. At the same time we know full well that not all children in high delinquency-rate neighborhoods get into trouble, and that some children from low-rate neighborhoods do. Hence we can say that while there is a close relationship between the influence of social class and of family factors, the two are not identical. The problem of sorting out these factors, and establishing some definitive explanation of their interrelationships, is one that continues to bother sociological researchers. All we know for sure is that the interaction of these elements is extremely complex.

Another focus we shall find increasingly stressed in theories of crime and delinquency is on the individual's developing self-image— how he sees himself, in other words. This in turn relates very closely both to how he has been viewed and treated by "significant others" and various authority figures in his personal life, and to his selection from the individuals and groups around him of those after whom he attempts to pattern his own outlooks and behavior. The family is, in this connection, of great potential significance—for it is largely here that the child first does or does not gain a sense of his personal worth, and does or does not have the opportunity to find an "acceptable role model" who can provide appropriate cues that may govern his own development.

This is one of the processes underlying the great concern in the "Moynihan Report" about the matriarchal (often fatherless) family structure among lower-class urban Negroes. As well as reinforcing the cycle of poverty and dependency, such a state of affairs may leave the male child without a significant and stable male figure on whom to model himself, and from whom to take on outlooks favorable to work, family stability, and law-abidingness. Again, however, we have to remember the difficulty in sorting out the relative impacts of what are undoubtedly interconnected forces. Thus one line of policy indicated by the Moynihan analysis would be to increase job opportunities as the first line of attack on the problems of the urban Negro. The glaring deficiencies in this regard will be outlined below. An improved family situation might well emerge in the wake of greater job and economic security; there is no reason to have greater confidence in the reverse cycle.

3

MAJOR SOCIOLOGICAL
PERSPECTIVES

The criminal is a social human being, he is adjusted, he is not necessarily any of the things that have been imputed to him. Instead of being unadjusted he may be quite adjusted to his group, and instead of being "unsocial" he may show all of the characteristics we identify as social in members of other groups.

Frank Tannenbaum, *Crime and the Community*

Extensive research in sociology has impressively documented the fact that, whatever area of human conduct is considered, "the way men behave is largely determined by their relations with each other and by their membership in groups." [1] As far as the applicability of this basic principle is concerned, it makes no difference what the moral standing of a particular form of behavior may be. Although we would not ordinarily tend to think of the rebel or the wrongdoer as a conformist, the outlooks and conduct of such people are—equally with those of conventional and law-abiding citizens—shaped by interpersonal influences, social traditions, and modes of social organization. Crime, like other human behavior, exhibits patterned variations. By studying these we begin to develop some understanding of crime's social nature and meaning.

In analyzing crime as a social phenomenon, the sociologist attempts to determine (by means of a variety of research techniques, some of which were mentioned earlier) both how individuals become criminals and why systematic differences exist between the crime situations (and rates) found in different sectors of the social order. As he con-

[1] Leonard Broom and Philip Selznick, *Sociology*, 4th ed. (New York: Harper & Row, Publishers, 1968), p. 17.

ducts such research, he does so with a special attitude of professional disinterestedness. No matter how concerned he is with the pressing nature of crime problems, the social researcher tries to set aside completely his own moral predilections, to maintain strict objectivity, to get beneath the surface of things as they commonly appear. As one sociologist has neatly expressed it, the sociological enterprise is often "subterranean" in character. Far from accepting official conceptions of social situations, "The sociologist often deals with very unofficial conceptions indeed. For the lawyer the essential thing to understand is how the law looks upon a certain type of criminal. For the sociologist it is equally important to see how the criminal looks at the law." [2] But, basically, the researcher is not at all interested in "taking sides." He realizes that we cannot expect to truly understand the phenomena of crime if our vision is blurred by prejudgments and engaged emotions.

We have already seen that systematic exploration has provided a great deal of factual knowledge concerning the details of crime in our society. At the same time, sociologists have been developing through their research findings theoretical formulations aimed at "explaining" crime. Such theories, it should be emphasized, are not armchair speculations that stand in contrast to the facts (as in the popular "that's all very well in theory" conception). On the contrary, these theories are closely related to the facts—which they seek to organize and explain. The number of existing sociological "theories" of crime is (if we give the term theory a loose, and not overly scientific meaning) quite large, and this body of theory contains a variety of sometimes contradictory strands. Yet there are some general perspectives and themes that pervade most of this work, and that can be seen as establishing a broadly sociological orientation to crime. Certain elements of this orientation also provide at least partial guidelines to formulating meaningful public policy measures in the crime area.

Learning Crime

One of the most central themes in the sociology of crime emphasizes the learned nature of criminal behavior. Here the sociolo-

[2] Peter L. Berger, *Invitation to Sociology* (Garden City, N.Y.: Doubleday Anchor Books, 1963), p. 29.

gist applies a very broad meaning to the term learning—so that it includes not only direct instruction, but also the long-term and often quite subtle influences of diverse socialization processes. All human behavior significantly reflects such influences, and there is no reason why we should expect criminal behavior to be an exception.

Indeed, as sociologists recognize, the very notion of an individual's "self" has little meaning apart from the subtle and continuous interplay a person experiences in relation to "significant others" in his environment from early childhood on. In all of his behavior, the individual looks to others for cues, for recognition, approval, and support, for overt or covert reactions in the light of which he can remake himself so as to conform with the image he would like to project. It is understandable then that individual behavior is strongly shaped both by directly experienced group interaction, and also by nonmembership "reference groups" from which a person almost imperceptibly seeks guidance in developing his own outlooks and patterns of activity.

These subtle influences, which are continuous and cumulative throughout a person's entire lifetime, bear a close relation to the emergence of both law-abiding and law-violating behavior. Even presumably sudden and inexplicable acts of interpersonal violence will usually have some kind of "social history" leading up to them—a stream of behavior and interaction (often between the actor and the specific victim) through which we can begin to understand the act's meaning. Sometimes the learning processes involved in crime are much more direct and immediate—as in the many criminal activities that are collective in nature. When the individual is acting as a member of a group (say, a delinquent gang), the reciprocal interpersonal influences may be readily apparent. And in other kinds of long-term, though not collective, criminal involvement, we uually find that the law-violating individual draws heavily on values and behavior patterns that are present (and probably common) somewhere in his environment. An individual offender very rarely "invents" crime. The necessary attitudes, opportunities, and skills are there to begin with; he simply takes them over.

The late Edwin H. Sutherland, usually considered the "dean" of American criminologists, made an enormous contribution to our understanding of crime as learned behavior. Sutherland was acutely aware of the varied nature of criminal behavior, and he was thoroughly disenchanted with attempts to explain *all* crime as the result of any particular concrete condition—such as poverty, low intelligence, or psychological disturbance. If we really want to formulate a valid theory of crime causation, he believed, we have to look for more *general processes* common to the development of diverse forms of criminality. This desire for a general explanation of crime informed all of Sutherland's research and writing, which ranged broadly across a large number of substantive crime areas and major criminological issues.

One of Sutherland's most notable works was his pioneering study of white-collar crime.[3] Uneasy about the contention that all crime stems from conditions we generally consider pathological (either psychologically or socially), Sutherland was convinced that many supposedly "respectable" upper class citizens in fact engage widely in criminal behavior. Because of the different social reactions to upper-class and lower-class crime, the former had remained largely hidden from view—but that didn't meant it wasn't there. Defining white-collar crime as, "a crime committed by a person of respectability and high social status in the course of his profession," Sutherland asserted that the financial cost of such behavior, "is probably several times as great as the financial cost of all the crimes which are customarily regarded as 'the crime problem.' " The financial loss from such violations, however, was—despite its enormity—not as serious a matter as the "damage to social relations." As Sutherland pointed out, "White-collar crimes violate trust and therefore create distrust; this lowers social morale and produces social disorganization. Many of the white-collar crimes attack the fundamental principles of the American institutions. Ordinary crimes, on the other hand, produce little effect on social institutions or social organization." [4]

Sutherland documented the existence of substantial white-collar crime through a careful tabulation and analysis of the decisions of courts and administrative agencies against seventy of the largest manufacturing, mining, and mercantile corporations in the United States. He uncovered 980 such decisions over the life careers of the corporations, or an average of fourteen decisions per corporation. Even when the administrative decisions were put aside, and just court decisions considered, 60 per cent of the corporations were found to have been convicted in criminal courts—with an average of approximately four convictions each. As Sutherland pithily noted, in some states in-

[3] Edwin H. Sutherland, *White-Collar Crime* (New York: Holt, Rinehart and Winston, Inc., 1949, 1961).
[4] *Ibid.*, p. 13.

dividuals with four convictions are labeled "habitual criminals." Major categories of crime revealed in the Sutherland study included: antitrust violations; illegal rebates; patent, trademark, and copyright violations; misrepresentation in advertising; unfair labor practices; financial manipulations (including embezzlement, "extortionate salaries and bonuses," other misapplications of corporate funds, and security misrepresentations and fraud); and violations of special wartime regulations. Clearly, these forms of criminal behavior (most of which are still prevalent today) can produce almost incalculable economic loss to the public or segments of the public—in addition to exerting the insidious effect on moral standards that Sutherland deplored. (In Chapter 5 I shall explore a bit further the place of white-collar crime in our present overall crime picture.)

Some criminologists question whether it is correct to treat white-collar offenses as constituting *real* crime. To these critics the relatively benign public attitude toward violations by businessmen, and the fact that such violators often do not view themselves as criminals, suggest that to group this behavior with "regular" crimes is unwarranted. Sutherland answered such criticism by pointing out that the acts in question violated laws that defined them as socially injurious and prescribed legal penalties for their occurrence—two major criteria for the definition of crime. The fact that the penalties actually imposed were rarely heavy ones, and the tendency to invoke administrative rather than criminal sanctions were not, Sutherland insisted, indications that the behavior was not really criminal. On the contrary, he felt, this simply showed that with respect to a large class of criminals the law was being differentially (and preferentially) enforced—because of their high social status.

From the standpoint of criminological theory, the issue of whether or when to include such behavior under the definition of crime may be a thorny one. As far as public policy is concerned, however, the problem is somewhat different. For the policymaker the relevant issue surely is *should* white-collar crime be treated as criminal, and *how severely* should it be punished? I shall come back to this question later on. At any rate, Sutherland's findings made it quite clear to him that not all crime could be attributed to either poverty, on the one hand, or mental illness, on the other. He recognized that the common understandings of businessmen, according to which law violation could often be justified or even approved, and the prevalence of the illegal behavior in certain social circles, had to be taken into account in formulating a theory of crime causation. Patterns of crime were fostered in such cases by collectively held values that were diffused among the violators. A theory focusing on the ways in which these values and the related behavior patterns led to individual criminality (to be described in a moment) seemed necessary for a general understanding of crime.

Sutherland also advanced greatly our knowledge of crime through his work on professional theft. *The Professional Thief*, by a Professional Thief, is a comprehensive description of the profession of theft which Sutherland obtained (in writing and through interviews) from a man who had been engaged in such activity for more than twenty years, and which he edited for publication (in 1937), together with his own sociological interpretation.[5] Here again, Sutherland broke new ground by showing that theft was a profession much like any other— "The professional thief has a complex of abilities and skills, just as do physicians, lawyers, or bricklayers." As "Chic Conwell," the author of this unusual document, pointed out, not just anyone can be a professional thief. A thief is not professional "until he is proficient." Although there are few restrictions on the kinds of people who could become professional thieves, acceptance and tutelage by professionals are absolute prerequisites for admission to the profession. Professional thieves, who steal systematically and carefully for a living, have little in common with amateurs; and they tend to look down on the use of violence. The principal rackets described by Conwell under the heading of professional theft—such as pocketpicking; systematic sneak-thieving, shoplifting, and hotel theft; confidence games; and shake-down (extortion) rackets—all involve "manipulation of suckers by nonviolent methods." The professional thief lives by his wits. His criminal activity is a well-planned effort (usually a group effort) in which interpersonal skills and general stealth are at a premium. He often comes to his present work from a legitimate occupation, and his family and other social life is not noticeably different from that of "respectables." He benefits from the willingness of many conventional persons to "make a fast buck" (a quality that is exploited in the many types of con games), and also from the possibilities of securing protection from law enforcement intervention through the political "fix."

In trying to frame a general theory of crime, Sutherland sought

---

[5] *The Professional Thief*—By a Professional Thief. Annotated and interpreted by Edwin H. Sutherland (Chicago: University of Chicago Press, 1937; Phoenix Books, 1956).

an explanation that would cover such phenomena as white-collar crime and professional theft, as well as those forms of criminality that could be more easily and directly tied to adverse social and psychological conditions. This search culminated in his statement of the principle of "differential association." An attempt to indicate how all persons who take up crime have in common that they have gone through a particular kind of learning process, the principle basically asserted that "A person becomes delinquent because of an excess of definitions favorable to violation of law over definitions unfavorable to violation of law." [6]

Criminal behavior, Sutherland insisted, is learned through interaction with other persons (especially intimate personal groups). The learning includes both techniques for committing the crime (which vary greatly in complexity) and a more subjective element—"the specific direction of motives, drives, rationalizations, and attitudes." This attitudinal dimension of learning about crime mainly depends on how those from whom one learns (or on whom one draws for cues) view the legal codes. It is the overall *balance* of the definitions favorable and unfavorable to crime to which a person is exposed that determines whether he turns to such behavior. Even though Sutherland did seem to stress the role of direct contact in small personal groups, his theory did not mean simply that a person who associates with criminals becomes one. The focus was less on *who* a person associates with than on content of the *definitions* or *patterns* to which he is exposed. Most individuals in a complex society are exposed to both anticrime and procrime definitions and patterns, and Sutherland recognized too that any of these associations may vary in "frequency, duration, priority, and intensity."

While Sutherland's approach did not ignore the importance of broad variations in crime rates (as I shall show in a moment), at its heart the differential association theory was an attempt to show how cumulative learning processes determine which individuals do and which do not engage in crime. Thus opportunity to commit an offense is always a necessary condition of crime, but different people presented with the same crime opportunities define them differently. The individual's past

---

[6] For this and other elements of the differential association theory, see Sutherland and Cressey, *op. cit.*, Chap. 4. Some interesting materials relating to this approach are brought together in Albert K. Cohen, Alfred R. Lindesmith, and Karl Schuessler, eds., *The Sutherland Papers* (Bloomington: Indiana University Press, 1956).

experiences (in particular the direct and subtle influences that have shaped his own "definitions" of law violating and law-abidingness) determine how he will define a potentially crime-engendering situation of this sort. Similarly, personality traits such as "aggressiveness" may seem to be involved in certain crimes, but Sutherland argued that differential association explained why some aggressive people engaged in crime while others did not.

There has been a great deal of debate among criminologists concerning the precise meaning, application, and status of the differential association thesis. Some critics have harped on the use of the word "association," claiming that in some kinds of crime there actually is little direct contact with criminal patterns. Yet as I have already mentioned, direct interpersonal contact with other offenders was not the key theme in this theory. The suggestion by one sociologist that the term "differential identification" be used in place of Sutherland's original formulation has the merit of broadening the apparent scope of the theory to cover the subtler ways in which procrime definitions and patterns may be diffused. It has been pointed out too that Sutherland didn't really explain what accounts for the particular patterns of associations that specific individuals do have. This is certainly a limitation of Sutherland's "theory." But it does not establish that his description of the general learning process in crime is invalid. And, as we shall see, in relating differential association to variations in crime rates, Sutherland did in fact have something to say about the determinants of a person's associations.

Perhaps the most potent criticism of the differential association principle has centered on the extreme difficulty of developing research instruments for testing it. "Definitions" favorable and unfavorable to crime are elusive qualities that are very hard to measure (in particular as they do vary in intensity, priority, etc.). A few attempts to devise questionnaire items aimed at tapping such definitions, which could then be related to an individual's involvement in crime, have been made—and generally the results of such studies do tend to support Sutherland's thesis. But whether or not the theory is completely testable, and even if it applies more fully to some kinds of offenses than to others, differential association remains a landmark principle in the development of sociological perspectives on crime. Sutherland demonstrated, to the satisfaction of most criminologists, that a general theory of crime must take into account basic learning processes—since crime, as he emphasized, is learned in much *the same way* as are other types of behavior. It is the content of the patterns learned, not the basic process involved, that varies.

Early Urban Studies

Another important body of work that called attention to the learning of crime was that of the so-called "ecological school" of urban sociology, developed at the University of Chicago in the late 1920's.[7] By then it was already recognized that urban crime rates greatly exceed rural rates. Consequently, it was natural to look directly at the organization of life in the city for clues to crime causation. Actually, the work of these Chicago sociologists that focused on crime was but one part of a broader research program in which the life patterns of individuals were related to the ecological (environmental) structures in which they were found. The Chicago researchers extensively documented the existence within the city of strikingly different "natural areas"—each with its distinctive structural features, population composition, styles of life, and social problems. And they showed, through a variety of techniques (including careful mapping to depict graphically the spatial distribution of social conditions and of different kinds of behaviors, as well as the collection of revealing life histories and other kinds of qualitative evidence), the close relation between the social structure of the city and the patterns of behavior found within it.

One of the major findings from this body of research was that various forms of socially problematic behavior were heavily concentrated in certain areas of the city. Ernest Burgess, building on the concept of "natural areas," pictured Chicago in terms of five concentric zones—running from the central business district at the core of the city out to the suburban commuters' zone. His colleague Clifford Shaw made a special study of rates of juvenile delinquency in Chicago, and found the highest concentration of offenders' residences in the transitional zone surrounding the central business district ("an interstitial area in the throes of change from residence to business and industry" which displayed a great deal of mobility owing to successive residential waves of the various ethnic immigrant groups). He also found a so-called "gradient tendency"—a progressive downward slope in delinquency rates from the zone in transition to the com-

[7] A good review of the work of this school is provided in Terence Morris, *The Criminal Area* (London: Routledge and Kegan Paul Ltd., 1958).

muters' area. Shaw later applied this same approach to the analysis of delinquency rates in other American cities—with roughly similar results—and therefore came to the general conclusion that the distribution of delinquency followed the pattern of the physical and social structure of the city. Furthermore, the studies showed that despite the invasion of these transitional slum districts by successive immigrant groups, delinquency rates for the various areas remained in more or less the same relationship to each other over time. The residence groups changed, but the high rate areas stayed the same.

Various subsequent "mapping" studies of American cities have challenged the "concentric circle theory" and the "gradient tendency" concept. Neither the physical nor the social structure of cities is sufficiently uniform that this single scheme of area analysis will fully "work" in all cases. At the same time, the more general finding that social problem behavior is concentrated geographically has held up strongly over the years. Studies of crime and delinquency consistently show offenders to be very heavily concentrated in particular areas of the major cities—not surprisingly, in areas that are usually among the most rundown and dilapidated, the most overcrowded, the most heavily populated by minority group members, and that have among the highest rates of other social problem behavior.

We shall return to a consideration of the relation between the modern urban slum and crime. Clearly the specific living conditions of the urban ghetto have become no less criminogenic since the days of the early Chicago studies; if anything, they have probably become more so. The lesson to be learned from this research, however, was not simply that slum living conditions breed crime (although these studies provided rich documentation that tended to support such a proposition). The Chicago researchers went beyond the mere demonstration of area variations in and geographical concentration of crime within the city to develop a theoretical framework for viewing this situation. Shaw and his co-workers saw crime and delinquency as but one aspect of a general pattern of social disorganization existing in the slum areas. The transitional zone surrounding the central business district exhibited the greatest amount of disorganization—owing largely to the breakdown of social control that accompanied the enormous mobility produced by successive migrations of immigrant groups to the area. In such a situation, competing and conflicting moral values arose, creating conditions under which delinquency and crime as a way of life competed strongly with conventional values and institutions. Children in the high-rate areas were exposed to a variety of contradictory standards and observed conflicting patterns of behavior. As a result, there existed in these areas a strong potential for the transmission of a "delinquent tradition." This tradition was passed over from one generation of boys to the next, much as language usage and other social traditions are transmitted.

This "cultural transmission" analysis of crime and delinquency, as it is sometimes called, came across most clearly in the detailed case histories the Chicago sociologists used to buttress their statistical analyses of crime rates. I have already quoted from Shaw's important work *The Jack-Roller* a passage indicating how families and neighborhood traditions positively supported criminal activities. In presenting and analyzing a delinquent's own story of his career, Shaw made clear how the various areas of Chicago in which "Stanley" lived had their distinctive traditions with respect to law-abidingness and law-violation, traditions which crucially shaped the lives of young residents. Through such studies in depth—all too often disdained by current sociology, with its emphasis on opinion surveys, statistical manipulations, and the like—Shaw was able to convey a sense of how it feels to live in and through situations that are quite remote from the lives of "respectable" middle-class citizens. (The same kind of thing has of course been done more recently in the autobiographical writings of James Baldwin, Claude Brown, and Piri Thomas—as well as in the ethnographic "novels" of Oscar Lewis. But the attempt to relate the subjective reactions indicated in these works to our systematic understanding of crime has, unfortunately, been rather slight.) "Stanley" provided a great many rationalizations of his criminal behavior, but his account does carry a sense of immediacy often lacking in more formal sociological studies. Having been presented with a close view of his early life, we begin to see why "life in the streets and alleys became fascinating and exciting," and to understand when he asserts:

The lures and the irresistible call drew me on like a magnet, and I was always helpless before them. I was like a canoe on a storm-swept sea, buffeted here and there, helpless and frail. I had about as much chance of controlling my desires to drift with the current of the underworld as the canoe had of braving the storm. But here I mingled with bums and derelicts like myself, and people did not stare at my rags and misery. Here I felt at home, for "misery loves company." So I drifted on with the rest of the human driftwood—carried on by the current of West Madison Street's exclusive "Four Hundred" or more.[8]

Out of the Chicago area studies too came the first major work on delinquent gangs. In his book *The Gang*, published in 1927,[9] Frederic Thrasher reported on research concerning over 1,300 gangs he had identified in Chicago—a fact which, in itself, is of more than a little significance. Again, the prime focus was on the neighborhood and its traditions; Thrasher viewed the gang as arising out of the spontaneous play group—although it does not become a gang "until it begins to excite disapproval and opposition and thus acquires a more definite group-consciousness." To the notion of learning in the neighborhood setting, then, Thrasher added the idea of group conflict. The behavior of gangs was seen to reflect closely adult social patterns that had prestige in the gang boy's limited environment, and also the demoralizing conditions in which he lived (with the gang satisfying those needs —for excitement, new experience, etc.—for which conventional society did not provide). And the crowded environment of "gangland" Thrasher found to be "full of opportunities for conflict with some antagonistic person or group within or without the gang's own social milieu."

The Chicago tradition in criminology, in short, combined an interest in the processes by which individual criminal careers developed with a systematic attempt to understand area variations in crime rates through an examination of the framework of social structure within which crime arose and prevailed. In focusing on neighborhood learning processes, and on the transmission of criminal traditions, these researchers laid the basis for later study of "delinquent subcultures." By using the life history as a major research device, and getting at the subjective reactions of law violators, they provided also a basis for recognizing the important role others (family members, teachers, police and other legal authorities) played in shaping the offender's self-conceptions and behavior. Similarly, they pioneered in realizing the intergroup conflict aspect of much crime and delinquency. And with respect to public policy, their studies should have made clear (although policymakers apparently did not very actively draw the necessary inferences at the time) the extent to which individual-oriented prevention and

[8] Clifford Shaw, *op. cit.*, pp. 50, 93.
[9] Frederic M. Thrasher, *The Gang* (Chicago: University of Chicago Press, 1927, 1960).

treatment programs could not really be expected to come to grips with the structural and cultural sources of crime.

Anomie, Subcultures, and Crime

As I have just mentioned, the ecological criminologists attributed variations in crime rates to the balance between elements of positive social organization and of social disorganization in the different neighborhoods. Sutherland too tried to apply his differential association approach not only to individual causation, but also to provide a (consistent) explanation of crime rate patterns. At first he also did this in terms of social disorganization, although sociologists gradually become somewhat uneasy about such a term—which seemed to suggest lack of any social patterning at all in slum areas, a misleading connotation. Eventually Sutherland framed his explanation of varying crime rates in terms of the alternative concept, "differential social organization." All segments of modern urban society are likely to contain both criminal and anticriminal patterns. Variations in the balance of differential associations to which individuals are exposed tend to reflect the balance of pro and anticrime influences in the social units to which the individuals belong (or with which they are less directly involved). If, in other words, we locate the individual in terms of his relevant units of social organization, and we know something about the crime-related "definitions" in them, then we can say something meaningful about the probabilities of his having a particular kind of differential association balance. Thus the broad variations in crime rates and the development of crime in the individual reflect but different sides of the same coin—the organization of attitudes favorable and unfavorable to law violating.

There has been a very long tradition in sociology of concern about patterned variations in the rates of different kinds of social behavior. A classic example of such analysis was provided by Emile Durkheim in his famous study of suicide.[10] Durkheim was interested in developing a general explanation of suicide which would account for the many diverse patternings of variation in suicide rates (between different groups, societies, over time, etc.). He found that one could make

---

[10] Emile Durkheim, *Suicide,* tr. J. Spaulding and G. Simpson (New York: The Free Press, 1951).

sense of virtually all these rate differentials by looking at them in terms of the extent and stability of social cohesion in the various groups and under various conditions. A by-product of this analysis was the concept of *anomie* (roughly definable as "normlessness")— referring to a state which might be brought about by abrupt or disturbing changes in social conditions (particularly as these affect the satisfaction of human wants), and which Durkheim saw as producing at least a certain amount of suicide. This concept lay the groundwork for some of the most important recent sociological thinking about crime.

In a widely discussed and highly influential professional journal article entitled "Social Structure and Anomie," [11] sociologist Robert Merton followed up this lead to develop a penetrating analysis of the relation between American social structure and the generating of deviant behavior—including crime and delinquency. Concerned to explain "how some social structures exert a definite pressure upon certain persons in the society to engage in nonconforming conduct," Merton focused on two important aspects of social control—first, the "culturally defined goals, purposes and interests, held out as legitimate objectives for all or for diversely located members of the society," and second, the ways in which the social structure "defines, regulates, and controls the acceptable means of reaching out for these goals." It is through the interrelation of these two elements, the cultural goals and the institutionalized means, that the patterns of conformity and deviation within different sectors of our society are shaped. If the goals and means are not well integrated, Merton claimed, we may expect a condition similar to Durkheim's *anomie* to arise.

Merton graphically illustrated his thesis with a typology in which the various possible combinations of individual acceptance or rejection of both goals and means were pictured as giving rise to one or another general type of conformity or deviation (Merton's major categories being conformity, innovation, ritualism, retreatism, and rebellion). For our purposes, "innovation," in which the individual accepts the cultural goals but rejects the approved means (or at least accepts also resort to disapproved means), is the most relevant "outcome"; presumably this is what is involved in a great deal of crime and delinquency. Merton saw this kind of outcome as crucially tied

[11] Robert K. Merton, "Social Structure and Anomie," *American Sociological Review*, 3 (October, 1938), 672–82; revised and extended in Merton, *Social Theory and Social Structure*, rev. ed. (New York: The Free Press, 1957).

in with the inordinate American emphasis on monetary success, which had not been adequately accompanied by concern about the means for achieving such success. He wrote that "It is only when a system of cultural values extols, virtually above all else, certain common success goals *for the population at large* while the social structure rigorously restricts or completely closes access to approved modes of reaching these goals *for a considerable part of the same population,* that deviant behavior ensues on a large scale."

Having been determined at the outset to explain why the frequency of deviant behavior varies within different social structures, Merton was alert to the importance of the social class system in shaping the distribution of problematic behavior. Clearly we could expect lower-class persons in our society—who are largely expected to meet common success goals, but are without the resources needed to do this by legitimate means—to turn to illicit means. Merton also considered the role of the family in generating the strain toward anomie. Particularly where lower-class parents—who were in a very bad position to offer access to legitimate means of success—projected their own frustrated ambitions onto their children, the strain would be greatly exacerbated.

In developing this formulation, Merton laid at least part of the groundwork for subsequent analysis of the "delinquent subculture." Sociological attention to the notion of subculture (which means quite simply a culture within a culture) came to the fore with the publication in 1955 of Albert Cohen's important study *Delinquent Boys: The Culture of the Gang.*[12] As we have seen, the Chicago sociologists already had shown that delinquent and criminal traditions existed in certain sectors of the city, and that these traditions were transmitted much as are other cultural elements. To this recognition, Merton had added a focus on the rigidity of the stratification order in its relation to commonly held cultural goals, especially standards of monetary success. In this way he spelled out to some extent how common modes of individual adaptation generated by pressures inherent in our social system led to high rates of deviance and crime in the lower socioeconomic classes.

Building on all this, Cohen turned to yet another aspect of delinquency—the *content* of the delinquent subculture. Agreeing with

---

[12] Albert K. Cohen, *Delinquent Boys: The Culture of the Gang* (New York: The Free Press, 1955).

Merton that serious delinquency and crime are heavily concentrated in the urban lower class, Cohen nonetheless questioned the "illicit means" theory by which Merton explained resort to crime. If crime simply involved finding alternative means to the kind of economic success held out to all Americans as a major life goal, then one would expect such criminality to be motivated by the prospect of financial reward. Yet Cohen found that much youthful crime was not of this sort. On the contrary, he contended, the behavior exhibited by subcultural delinquents is largely "non-utilitarian, malicious, and negativistic." Urban lower-class male youth engages in a great deal of crime just "for the hell of it," and furthermore displays the qualities of extreme "versatility" and "short-run hedonism" which seem rather at odds with the Merton thesis.

To explain these phenomena, Cohen—who was concerned with the mechanisms of individual motivation, as well as with the impact of broad factors of social structure—centered his theory around the idea of collective problem-solving. Accepting, along with Merton, that persons at all levels in our society are held to the common goal of financial success, Cohen spelled out in somewhat more detail a still wider complex of middle-class values (such as ambition, individual responsibility, development of specialized skills, rationality, deferred gratification, and control of aggression) to which lower-class, as well as middle-class children are often subjected. Against this almost universal "measuring rod" in our society, the working-class boy is almost bound to end up at "the bottom of the heap." Although the child's family background and early experience clearly have not prepared him to meet such standards, the pervasive agencies of middle-class society (in particular the school, with its middle-class orientations and middle-class teachers) seek to impose them nonetheless. The result, according to Cohen, is a severe "status anxiety," that in turn—through the psychological process of "reaction formation"—leads to a complete repudiation of those standards and creation of a system of norms and values in terms of which the working-class youngster can achieve satisfactory standing. The delinquent subculture, in other words, represents a turning-upside-down of the oppressive system of middle-class values; its hallmark is "the explicit and wholesale repudiation of middle-class standards and the adoption of their very antithesis."

This theory has been subjected to a great deal of analysis and criticism since it was first presented, and Cohen himself now states that it is not a completely adequate formulation. Even at the time, he realized that it did not explain the motivation underlying middle-class delinquency (for which he provided a special discussion, emphasizing the masculine-identification problems of middle-class boys). However, Cohen's work had the great merit that it paid attention to the quality of delinquent behavior, as well as its distribution and transmission, and (as we shall see) it led to considerable exploration of and debate about the nature of the values held by delinquents. The concept of delinquent subculture, although sometimes qualified, continues to be an important one in the sociology of crime.

A major amplification of this concept was offered by Richard Cloward and Lloyd Ohlin in their 1960 study *Delinquency and Opportunity*.[13] Working in the Durkheim-Merton-Cohen tradition, Cloward and Ohlin focused on the failure of previous theories to consider very much the different kinds of delinquent adaptations individuals might make. They defined three major types of delinquent subculture: the criminal ("rackets"-oriented) subculture, the conflict (fighting gang) subculture, and the retreatist (drug-oriented) subculture. Each of these, according to Cloward and Ohlin, arises out of a fairly distinctive set of social conditions. Though most lower-class youths are under substantial pressure of the sort Merton indicated (if not because of actual desire for middle-class membership, at least because of the wish for monetary success), the blockage of legitimate opportunities is not all that is involved in determining specific delinquent solutions. Cloward and Ohlin point out that the distribution of *illegal opportunities* is also very significant. Each of the major types of subculture "requires a specialized environment if it is to flourish." Youngsters will turn to the criminal rackets only in fairly stable and cohesive slum neighborhoods where there exist well-organized criminal patterns that are also to some extent integrated with the conventional values and structures of the community. Only in situations exhibiting a reasonably long-term stability of this sort will criminal values and skills circulate, and will youths find criminal role-models after whom to model their behavior. Conflict patterns, on the other hand, are likely to thrive in less well-integrated neighborhoods:

The many forces making for instability in the social organization of some slum areas include high rates of vertical and geographical mobility; massive housing projects in which "site tenants" are not accorded priority in occupancy, so that traditional residents are dispersed and "strangers" re-

[13] Cloward and Ohlin, *op. cit.*

assembled; and changing land use, as in the case of residential areas that are encroached upon by the expansion of adjacent commercial or industrial areas. Forces of this kind keep a community off balance, for tentative efforts to develop social organization are quickly checked. Transiency and instability become the overriding features of social life.[14]

Not only are legitimate avenues to achieving success-goals blocked in such situations, but "access to stable criminal opportunity systems is also restricted." Such conditions may well give rise to subcultures through which violence becomes the most readily available means of achieving social status. When violence becomes the major avenue to obtaining "rep," the qualities needed for success shift radically—neither the factor of socioeconomic resources for legitimate achievement nor access to established criminal traditions is any longer necessary. Cloward and Ohlin suggest that the third type of subculture—the "retreatist" drug-use variety—largely accommodates certain lower-class youth who, for one reason or another, have not managed to find legitimate means to success, *and* who have also failed to find adequate illicit opportunities in either the criminal or conflict subcultures.

Without wishing to see a strengthening of the criminal rackets in the urban slums, Cloward and Ohlin at the same time deplore the conditions that are progressively breaking down social cohesion in slum neighborhoods—such as badly thought-out and massive urban "renewal" and relocation programs. The reorganization of slum communities, they argue, should be the major thrust of efforts at reducing delinquency. If legitimate substitutes for the forces that traditionally maintained cohesion in the slum (such as the rackets, the urban political machine, and so on) could be developed, it might be possible to stave off all three of the major types of delinquent subculture.

Cloward and Ohlin's work, in emphasizing the relation between neighborhood social structure and delinquency, has had a significant impact on public policy. While the notion of "treating" communities rather than individuals has been very slow in gaining public support (despite early and impressive efforts, such as those in the multifaceted crime prevention-oriented Chicago Area Project begun many years ago), this study gave new impetus to such an enterprise. Their book provided much of the framework for the varied efforts (to increase individual opportunities and community involvement) of the Mobilization for Youth program in New York City—which became the proto-

[14] *Ibid.*, p. 172.

type for many of the federally sponsored "war on poverty" programs now existing in major cities throughout the United States.

As I have noted, the concept of subculture has not been without its sociological critics. Some have claimed the notion was too vague and untestable. Others have challenged the "reaction formation" explanation of delinquent value systems. Thus, one alternative analysis claims that no such severe reaction need be posited for us to understand the values and behavior of urban male working-class youth. On the contrary, lower-class culture itself exhibits certain "focal concerns" (including "trouble," "toughness," "smartness," "excitement," "fate," and "autonomy") which help to account for the high rates of lower-class crime. According to this thesis, lower-class male youth do not engage in any complicated repudiation of middle-class standards; instead they are drawn into behavior that violates the law simply by their efforts to achieve status in terms of the values most highly prized within their own cultural milieu.[15] And in another discussion of delinquency it is asserted that far from being thoroughly committed to a system of values and norms that repudiate and stand in opposition to the dominant standards of "respectable" society, the delinquent in fact often continues to share these standards (as seen in his frequent guilt or shame on detection, his resentment if illegal behavior is imputed to others he cares about, the admiration he often exhibits for law-abiding persons, and his unwillingness to victimize certain persons—all of which seems to indicate his realization of the wrongfulness of his behavior). Because the delinquent often does act in violation of standards he basically accepts, he develops, according to this theory, "techniques of neutralization" that neutralize guilt and justify his deviance. Thus he claims he can't help himself, denies that he's really causing much harm, says the injured party deserved what he got, and so forth.[16]

Similarly, critics have questioned just how well organized, how completely structured urban working-class delinquency really is. According to one sociologist who has worked with and observed delinquent gangs, the gang tends to be a much more amorphous and changeable gathering than the "delinquent subculture" concept might

[15] Walter B. Miller, "Lower Class Culture as a Generating Milieu of Gang Delinquency," *Journal of Social Issues*, 14 (Summer, 1958), 5–19.

[16] Gresham M. Sykes and David Matza, "Techniques of Neutralization: A Theory of Delinquency," *American Sociological Review*, 22 (December, 1957), 664–70.

suggest. He prefers the term "near-group" for this phenomenon—which he sees lying somewhere in between the truly organized group on the one hand and the collective behavior of the crowd or mob on the other.[17] Likewise, in a more recent study of delinquency, the author suggests that the notion of the delinquent subculture incorporates assumptions of greater constraint on individual behavior than are warranted. Although delinquency does develop in a cultural milieu in which knowledge of such behavior is widespread, and in which techniques of neutralization are used to justify it, to view the delinquent as acting through simple conditioning to the dictates of a subculture directly opposing dominant values is an oversimplification. Instead it is likely that the urban lower-class setting provides opportunities for a "drift" into delinquency, and that whether or not such a drift occurs will depend on a great many factors, including the experiences the individual has of contact with the agents of formal control, such as the police and the courts.[18]

Sociologists do not entirely agree, then, as to extent, complexity, and degree of constraint imposed by the delinquent subculture. However one does find in the literature leading up to the subculture idea, and in that dealing directly with subcultures, a number of points that are more or less held in common. These include the following:

1. Delinquent and criminal "traditions" develop, persist, and are transmitted within certain sociocultural milieus. Although these traditions may not hold absolute sway over the destinies of those individuals subjected to them, they constitute a potent force shaping involvement in criminality.

2. In such situations, values conducive to crime may have high currency, and individuals already engaged in criminal behavior may become major "role-models" for and "teachers" of the young.

3. When this happens, the conventional agencies for training young people—such as the family and the school—are, as we saw in the last chapter, up against powerful competing forces.

4. Social pressure emanating from the extreme emphasis on financial success plays an important role in generating delinquent and criminal behavior in modern American society.

5. Likewise, restrictions on socioeconomic advancement represent a significant factor contributing to law violation.

[17] Lewis Yablonsky, "The Delinquent Gang as a Near-Group," *Social Problems*, 7 (Fall, 1959), 108–17.
[18] David Matza, *op. cit.*

6. And the social structure of the city itself—including patterns of residential succession and degrees of neighborhood integration, as well as the more concrete living conditions existing in various areas—is closely related to the distribution of crime and delinquency, and probably also to the types of criminality that develop and thrive within the city.

7. Opportunities to commit crimes, as well as opportunities to pursue success-goals by legitimate means, are unevenly distributed within our society and in given community settings. Such opportunities also help to shape crime patterns.

Labeling Criminals

Another important sociological perspective, in which there has been a marked renewal of interest recently, emphasizes the role played by society's reactions to offending behavior in shaping social problem situations. Sociologist Howard S. Becker has stated this view succinctly:

. . . social groups create deviance by making the rules whose infraction constitutes deviance, and by applying those rules to particular people and labeling them as outsiders. From this point of view, deviance is *not* a quality of the act the person commits, but rather a consequence of the application by others of rules and sanctions to an "offender." The deviant is one to whom that label has successfully been applied; deviant behavior is behavior that people so label.[19]

This does not, of course, mean that the *acts* we commonly term homicide, theft, and drug use would never occur if they were not considered deviant or criminal. Rather the point is that their nature, distribution, social meaning, and implications and ramifications are significantly influenced by patterns of social reaction. Society, in other words, determines what we make of these acts socially.

"Criminal" in this view is in some measure what sociologists call an "ascribed status." An individual's designation as an offender depends crucially on what *other people* do with respect to him and his behavior; it does not result simply and directly from his own acts. This means that research on crime problems must pay a good deal of attention to the substantive nature of these reactions (how and why we react to

[19] Howard S. Becker, *Outsiders* (New York: The Free Press, 1963), p. 9.

particular "offenses" as we do); the direct reactors and "labelers" (agencies of formal control, such as the police and the courts); and the typical processes of interaction between these control agents and the individuals they treat as criminals (with special reference to how this interaction may affect the development of criminal self-images and "careers" among the people so "labeled"). This point about inter-action is important, because a great value of this orientation is the stress it places on *processes* involved in the development of criminal outlooks and behavior. Crime is not simply a matter of static condi-tions—under which some individuals clearly "are" criminals (for all time and in all places) whereas others clearly "are not." On the con-trary, both the individual's behavior and his self-conceptions are constantly undergoing change, and they are highly responsive to the reactions of others.

To a large extent, this view is little more than a recasting or ampli-fication of a classic sociological dictum of W. I. Thomas to the effect that "when men define situations as real, they are real in their con-sequences"—a theme developed further by Robert Merton as the "self-fulfilling prophecy." If we treat a person like a criminal, he is likely to become one. This point was nicely described by Frank Tannenbaum in an early work on crime and delinquency:

> No more self-defeating device could be discovered than the one society has developed in dealing with the criminal. It proclaims his career in such loud and dramatic forms that both he and the community accept the judg-ment as a fixed description. He becomes conscious of himself as a criminal, and the community expects him to live up to his reputation, and will not credit him if he does not live up to it.[20]

We have already seen how the identification of young people as "troublemakers" by teachers and school officials may backfire—rather than acting as a preventive technique, such labeling may drive the child into new trouble and progressively greater alienation. Clearly the police and the courts also have substantial power to activate and reinforce criminal careers and self-concepts. I have mentioned the ease with which we often "change" a person into a "criminal" (that is, our view of him changes) during the course of his trial on criminal charges. Indeed, the criminal trial is a prototype of what one sociologist has called the "status-degradation ceremony"—a ritualized process by

---

[20] Frank Tannenbaum, *Crime and the Community* (New York: Ginn and Com-pany, 1938), p. 477.

which a condemned individual is stripped of his old identity and given a new (degraded) one. It is very difficult for an individual to sustain a favorable image of himself under the pressure of such public definitions. And if the defining process is clearly unfair (recall the criteria for official disposition in the "police encounters with juveniles" study), then however unwilling the "offender" may be to define himself as such, and even if harsh sanctions are not invoked in his particular case, he is likely to develop a hostility toward the official "system" that may increase the likelihood of antisocial behavior on his part in the future.

Under the impact of negative social reactions the individual may, then, be propelled from isolated acts of criminality into more complete involvement in criminal ways of life (heightened "commitment" to criminal roles), and he may come increasingly to view himself as an enemy of society (since society seems so determined to consider him one). Sociologist Edwin Lemert has suggested the distinction between "primary" and "secondary" deviation, the latter occurring when an individual comes to employ his deviance "as a means of defense, attack, or adjustment to the overt and covert problems created by the consequent societal reaction to him. . . ." [21]

Concern with the impact of social reactions on individual self-conceptions and behavior (that is, focusing not on the pressures that initially drive the person into deviating behavior, but rather on the *consequences* for him of engaging in such behavior and being publicly identified as doing so) is but one aspect of this orientation to crime. Another involves examining the general impact, *on the society*, of defining a particular form of behavior as criminal. I have already referred to a prime example of this sort of impact—seen in the consequences of treating as criminal various borderline "offenses." As we shall note in more detail, the "criminalizing" of certain types of behavior may exacerbate the social problems in question in ways that take us quite beyond the level of individual social psychology. Thus, we may find significant economic consequences flowing from "criminalization" (as when a society's reaction to some form of deviating behavior provides the groundwork for a thriving black market) and also significant effects on the behavior and outlooks of law enforcement officials— as well as the predictable proliferation of much "secondary" crime among the "offenders" themselves.

[21] Edwin M. Lemert, *Social Pathology* (New York: McGraw-Hill Book Company, 1951), p. 75.

Finally, the emphasis on social reactions suggests still another broad area of research which should increase our understanding of crime problems. This has to do with the social meaning of the "creation" of crimes (by lawmaking), both generally and with respect to particular offenses. Thus we are led to ask what general functions are served by ensuring that there are *some* crimes and "criminals" in a society (do we, in other words, really need crime?). And we are also drawn to comparative and historical analysis of rule-making in particular behavior areas (for example, what led up to our present drug laws, why do they differ from those in other Western countries, etc.). Unfortunately it will not be possible in this book to deal with such questions at any length—important as they may be for a comprehensive analysis of crime problems.

Summary

In presenting a few of the major sociological orientations on crime, I have attempted to sift out what seem to me the most important of the numerous and diverse formulations developed by sociologists working in this field. It should be understood that this summary is a highly compressed and selective one; a glance at the discussion of sociological theories in standard criminology texts will immediately reveal how much more extensive is any attempt at comprehensive coverage. I have tried to spare the reader from a debilitating immersion in the many intricate strands of detailed research and competing theory, as well as from much of the rather ponderous professional jargon.

Even so, we have been forced to recognize that sociologists do not entirely agree as to where the prime emphasis should be placed in analyzing and explaining crime. Nonetheless, there is in this body of work a core of key themes that stand out for their general acceptance, their central sociological importance, and (notwithstanding the "so what" reaction that frequently is elicited by sociological formulations) their relevance to public policy. These include the facts that crime is learned (and neither inherited nor invented by the individual); that crime cannot be understood unless we examine its relation to approved social values and arrangements; that the role of the social class system is especially crucial in shaping crime problems, particularly through the structuring of opportunities for achieving success by approved means; and that crime situations are shaped by the social and official reactions to them, both in the broad sense of the "creation" of crimes by lawmaking, and in terms of the direct social-psychological impact on individuals produced by the responses of others to their behavior.

Such perspectives reflect a still broader sociological orientation toward social problems in general—not just crime problems—that has been developing over the years.[22] Sociologists are now pretty well agreed that the problems of any society reflect its forms of social organization. Disorganization and organization are theoretically inseparable; the types of problems we find in a given social order represent the price that is paid for maintaining that particular structure. Because of these linkages the problems themselves are in some indirect ways "functional"; any attempts to ameliorate them must take account of the effects change would be likely to produce in related aspects of the social system. As we shall see in considering some more specific aspects of crime in America, it is indeed the case that much crime is closely related to other aspects of the American social order. It is not enough to think simply in terms of eliminating criminal activities; as the sociologist would put it, "functional alternatives," approved ways of satisfying the same needs (individual or social), must often be developed.

The social class system is, as we have seen, particularly significant because individuals located variously within it are differentially subject both to pressures and opportunities leading to crime. But it is also true that individuals at different socioeconomic levels tend to view crime situations and policies quite differently. Proposed solutions to specific crime problems are likely to be in line with the interests of some sectors of society, but counter to the interests of other sectors. Thus it is not surprising that there is far from a complete consensus within American society as to what kinds of offenses in general should be reacted to most stringently, as to the merits of particular proposals for legal change, as to how criminal laws should be enforced, and so on. And since social and political power is far from being evenly distributed among the various social strata, we have to recognize that crime situations almost invariably embody an important element of

[22] See Robert K. Merton, "Social Problems and Sociological Theory," in Merton and R. Nisbet, eds., *Contemporary Social Problems* (New York: Harcourt, Brace & World, Inc., 1961); also Edwin M. Schur, "Recent Social Problems Texts: An Essay-Review," *Social Problems*, 10 (Winter, 1963), 287–92.

group conflict. Those holding the power in society have a great deal to do with the making of laws; those with less power must be content to try to obey them—and sometimes to suffer because they are differentially enforced to their disadvantage. In modern American society, the criminal law in some respects represents the efforts of the middle and upper classes to control the working and lower classes; of whites to control Negroes; of men to control women (the laws against abortion being a case in point); of adults to control youth (through the juvenile court and related institutions). Out of the conflicts of interests and values between such strata emerge both the substance and administration of our criminal law and the nature and distribution of our crime problems. From this standpoint, as well as from that of the "labeling" orientation, the focus on differing reactions to crime is an essential one.

A final sociological proposition of great importance to our consideration of crime problems (one that is implicit in the points I have just been making) is that social problems are inevitable. Precisely because there can never be a full consensus on values and behavior norms in any society, we will always find a great diversity in outlooks and activities—which will also range across a wide continuum of degrees of social approval and disapproval. Although a minimum degree of consensus is probably necessary if a society is to continue as "a going concern," a complex modern society invariably exhibits a pluralistic value structure rather than a single uniform one. There will always be fairly distinct groups and sets of values that are to some extent in conflict with one another. It is difficult to see, therefore, how one could ever have a problemless society. For what some people view as socially desirable, others invariably see as a problem (a consideration of the vast range of behaviors that some persons in our society are prepared to view as problematic—including long hair, premarital sex, and pacifism, as well as more generally condemned "offenses"—should make this point clear). There always have been and always will be crimes. The realistic aim is to shape crime situations in accordance with meaningful social goals, rather than to hope that we can eliminate crime entirely.

4

POVERTY, VIOLENCE, AND CRIME IN AMERICA

. . . the city jail is one of the basic institutions of the other America. Almost everyone whom I encountered in the "tank" was poor: skid-row whites, Negroes, Puerto Ricans.

> Michael Harrington, *The Other America*

I guess it was harder on the girls than it was on anybody. Dixie started tricking when she was thirteen. She was big for her age, and "nice" ladies used to point at her and say, "Oh, ain't that a shame." But it wasn't. The shame of it was that she had to do it or starve. When she got hip and went out there on the street and started turning tricks, she started eating and she stopped starving.

> Claude Brown, *Manchild in the Promised Land*

The background of disorder in the riot cities was typically characterized by severely disadvantaged conditions for Negroes . . . a local government often unresponsive to these conditions; federal programs which had not yet reached a significantly large proportion of those in need; and the resulting reservoir of pervasive and deep grievance and frustration in the ghetto.

> *The Kerner ("riot commission") Report*

As we have seen, our understanding of the relation between poverty and crime is complicated by the patent inadequacies of official statistics. Furthermore, the inability or failure to vigorously prosecute white collar offenses greatly distorts our picture of the social class distribution of crime. In the next chapter I shall return to the matter of white-collar crime. For the moment, let us set it aside and consider only the common varieties of serious crime about which Americans more typically express strong concern.

If one has in mind the known facts about the social and spatial distribution of such offenses (discussed in Chapter 1), and the central themes of the sociological orientation which I have just outlined —including the conditions under which crime subcultures and traditions are likely to arise—it seems difficult not to conclude that a great deal of American crime is attributable, at least indirectly, to poverty.

Somewhat surprisingly, criminology textbook writers appear rather reluctant to assert that poverty causes crime. This hesitancy is understandable, however, in terms of the attempt to offer a systematic framework for the scientific understanding of criminal behavior. As Sutherland insisted, poverty cannot provide the basis for a universal theory explaining all crime—for clearly much crime does not stem from that condition. Also, even where conditions of poverty are relevant to the involvement of particular individuals in crime, the relation is not a simple and direct one. Thus, Sutherland would say that the person's location in the social order and his living conditions might well affect his associations, and the crime-related definitions to which he is exposed, and that it is the pattern of these associations and definitions that in the end "determines" whether or not criminal involvement occurs.

Then too, data from studies of the relation between fluctuations in the business cycle and overall crime rates are somewhat inconclusive. While there has been a slight but inconsistent tendency for the most serious crimes to increase in times of depression and to decline in periods of prosperity, the overall crime rate does not seem to increase significantly during depressions. There has been a tendency for property crimes involving violence to increase somewhat during depressions, but no pronounced tendency in this direction has been found for nonviolent property crimes. And there appears to be no consistent pattern of association between crimes against the person and business cycle fluctuations.[1] Similarly, comparative studies of crime rates suggest that the general level of prosperity in a society does not by itself determine the extent of criminality. As one consultant to the President's Commission on Law Enforcement noted in analyzing the relationship

[1] A summary of the various findings is presented by Sutherland and Cressey, *op. cit.*, pp. 234–42.

between affluence and adolescent crime, "the relationship between subjective dissatisfaction and objective deprivation is more complicated than was at first thought. Poverty cannot cause crime but resentment of poverty is more likely to develop among the relatively deprived of a rich society than among the objectively deprived in a poor society." [2]

Of course, our own society is precisely the sort in which this high level of "relative deprivation" might be anticipated, and indeed does exist. Even if poverty is not a direct cause of crime, it is still fully appropriate to conclude that a great deal of the crime we are now experiencing bears a very close relation to the conditions of poverty that persist in the United States.

At the same time, it is true (as my previous remarks have suggested) that no amount of socioeconomic reform will eliminate all crime, and also that there is no alternative economic system that provides a panacea for crime problems. Orthodox Marxist writers have long tried to attribute crime to capitalism, and there has been at least one effort to develop a broad criminological theory based on Marxist principles. Thus the Dutch writer William Bonger suggested in an early work that the "egoistic tendencies" fostered by the capitalist system breed crime, whereas one could expect much less criminality under more cooperative modes of living.[3] Unfortunately, available evidence from those societies that have been founded on and supposedly governed by Marxist principles has not borne out the claim that socialism would eradicate crime. Soviet spokesmen just after the revolution were optimistic about the eventual demise of criminality—just as they were about the "withering away" of the state and of law. More realistic adaptation to the conditions of postrevolutionary life and to the apparent requirements of maintaining a viable social and political system impelled a revision of these rather grandiose projections. We know very well (notwithstanding our somewhat limited sources of information) that the Soviet Union has not abolished crime. Indeed, American sociologists who have visited Russia recently report that their Soviet colleagues are now willing to admit openly the existence of serious problems of crime and delinquency in their society—something they were unwilling to do not so many years ago. On the other hand, it is undoubtedly the case

[2] Jackson Toby, "Affluence and Adolescent Crime," in *Task Force Report: Juvenile Delinquency and Youth Crime*, p. 143.

[3] W. A. Bonger, *Criminality and Economic Conditions* (Boston: Little, Brown And Company, 1916); also J. M. van Bemmelen, "Willem Adriaan Bonger," in Mannheim, ed., *Pioneers in Criminology*, pp. 349–63.

that Soviet values and programs have served to appreciably reduce certain kinds of crime—even though this may simply have brought to the fore other types of offenses. It is revealing (and perhaps supportive of the general principle that any society is by definition plagued by those crimes it concentrates on most) that the Soviets have been almost continuously confronted with a rash of "crimes against state property." To this extent, the dissemination of socialist values has been far from effective in eliminating property offenses—with respect to which perhaps the strongest case for linking crime with capitalism might have been built.

This does not mean that in trying to understand crime in our own society we have nothing whatsoever to learn from Marx. I have already alluded to the group and class conflict aspects of crime problems; in using such concepts we are, of course, indirectly indebted to the Marxist heritage. It is probably also true (as I shall suggest in the next chapter) that some rather extreme forms of "egoistic" behavior present under our form of capitalist enterprise do encourage certain types of criminality. The existence of vested economic interests in the persistence of some kinds of crime further suggests the partial relevance of at least a vaguely Marxist type of analysis.

Nor should we conclude that since socialism cannot eliminate crime, it is futile to try to curb criminality through social and economic planning. On the contrary, such planning can be expected to have an enormous impact on crime problems. There is reason to believe, for example, that democratic socialist systems (such as those in the Scandinavian countries) have achieved considerable success through their extensive welfare programs in reducing crimes related to economic deprivation, even if they have not eliminated all other types of crime-producing situations and motivations. I believe we should be leery of the argument that if we manage to control one type of crime, the urge to violate law will pop up in some other form. Although we are in no position to eliminate crime across the board, we do maintain the power to drastically alter the face of our crime picture. Since there is no basis for believing that most of our current offenders are "basically criminal," we would be quite mistaken to assume that they would commit crimes under any and all conditions. If the social and economic conditions now driving many of them into criminality can in fact be ameliorated—and there is every reason to believe that they can—we should proceed on that basis, and worry later if and when new crime problems arise.

The Social Structure of Violence

At the present time, America is going through a highly vocal crisis of conscience concerning the recently discovered violent nature of life in our society. Actually, of course, violence is nothing new to the down-trodden in America; they have been subjected to it systematically and persistently over many years. From the historic campaign of violence that eradicated a large proportion of the American Indians to the substantial violence that characterized the early days of the American labor movement, from the six-shooter justice of the frontier to the lynch-law brutality visited on generations of black Americans, violence has long been part of the American scene. In such conflicts, it has invariably been the poor and relatively powerless who have most strongly felt the impact of this tradition. And even more recently, as we have seen, violent crimes against the person have been largely internal to the lower classes and the black community in the United States. Indeed, as Michael Harrington recently observed, it is only because violence today seems to be overstepping these bounds that widespread concern is being expressed: "As long as it stays in the ghetto, it is ignored; when it threatens the white middle class, it becomes a national problem." [4]

We have seen that orthodox psychoanalytic theory views the potential for interpersonal violence as basic to the human condition. A similar conception has received considerable publicity lately through best-selling books on animal behavior—particularly Konrad Lorenz's *On Aggression*—in which intraspecies aggression is seen as having both an instinctual basis and a definite survival value for the species (by preventing too dense a population, ensuring survival of the most adaptable organisms, and so on). [5] While these works—with their colorful and interesting illustrations of animal aggression—are certainly intriguing, it is not at all clear that the claim of an *innate* aggressive instinct has been adequately demonstrated. To do so, the operation of supposedly internal drives would have to be systematically separated from that of environmental and situational factors. This has not been done satisfac-

[4] Michael Harrington, "Is America By Nature a Violent Society?" *New York Times Magazine*, April 29, 1968, p. 111.

[5] Konrad Lorenz, *On Aggression* (New York: Bantam Books, 1967).

torily for animals, let alone humans. As other observers have concluded, "The study of animals has not yet uncovered evidence that aggression is a product of an instinctive, innate urge in the organism."[6]

With respect to humans, there is a great deal of evidence showing that the tendency toward violence in the individual is learned in specific social contexts, varies according to position in the social order, and is in large measure a response to pressures generated by particular kinds of social conditions (especially those giving rise to intense feelings of frustration).[7] Single acts of violence often appear to reflect situational factors, a point which does not accord well with any "internal" explanation. We have already seen that offender and victim in crimes of violence frequently are known to each other (sometimes intimately) prior to the offense. In the most complete and sytematic analysis of homicide data undertaken thus far—involving study of all known cases of criminal homicide in Philadelphia for the years 1948–1952—the three most frequent types of motivation for homicide were found to be "general altercations" (35 per cent), family or domestic quarrels (14 per cent), and jealousy (12 per cent). Furthermore, 26 per cent of the homicides in this study were deemed to have been "victim-precipitated"; that is, they arose out of situations in which it appeared that the eventual victim had in fact been the initial aggressor or had provided substantial provocation of one sort or another.[8]

Undoubtedly there is a close connection between the likelihood of situations being defined by participants as ones in which a violent solution may be appropriate, and the broad (statistical) patterns exhibited by rates of violent crime. Situations conducive to violence, in other words, are not specific to the individuals involved but are likely to arise because of broader social configurations. An example of this is seen in the finding from the Philadelphia homicide study of especially high rates for this offense on weekends, with a peak rate for Saturday nights. Noting that it is largely Negro males who produce a high incidence on Saturdays, the researchers also pointed out that "drinking is a common accompaniment of crimes of personal violence, and Friday and Saturday nights are traditional periods for social drinking and drinking

[6] Marvin E. Wolfgang and Franco Ferracuti, *The Subculture of Violence* (London: Social Science Paperbacks, 1967), p. 193.

[7] See works cited in Wolfgang and Ferracuti. Some useful essays are also brought together in Elton B. McNeil, ed., *The Nature of Human Conflict* (Englewood Cliffs, N.J.: Prentice-Hall, Inc., 1965).

[8] Marvin Wolfgang, *Patterns in Criminal Homicide* (Philadelphia: University of Pennsylvania, 1958), Chaps. 10 and 14.

sprees. Homicide is generally committed against persons who are relatively close friends or relatives, and the opportunities for such personal
contacts are probably much greater during the leisure hours of eve-
nings and week-ends." [9] The relationship between this situational finding and the more general conditions relevant to violence in our society
is suggested when one considers along with it some of Claude Brown's
autobiographical comments about Saturday night in Harlem. Any policeman who has been in Harlem, Brown states, "for a month of Saturday nights has had all the experience he'll ever need, as far as handling
violence is concerned." On Saturday night "there is something happening for everybody in Harlem, regardless of what his groove might be."
Saturday night is "a time to try new things. Maybe that's why so many
people in the older generation had to lose their lives on Saturday night.
It must be something about a Saturday night with Negroes. . . .
Maybe they wanted to die on Saturday night. They'd always associated
Sunday with going to heaven. . . ." [10]

Systematic social studies of homicide have led to the conclusion that
there exists among certain groups of low socioeconomic standing (particularly Negro males in this category) a "subculture of violence"—a
sociocultural milieu in which the social controls that help inhibit violence among middle-class citizens are weakened and the likelihood of
resorting to physical aggression is greatly heightened. To some extent
this thesis is implicit in the claim I cited earlier that lower-class culture
embodies certain "focal concerns"—including "toughness"—which may
have among their consequences the generation of certain crime patterns.
Also significant are the findings that while homicide correlates highly
with low socioeconomic status, high suicide rates tend to be associated
with high socioeconomic standing. Given the enormous amount of
objective deprivation among the lower classes, this finding is at least
consistent with the idea that there is a lower-class value system under
which frustration-induced aggression is likely to be directed outwards,
whereas dominant values among the middle and upper classes tend to
direct such aggression inwards. [11]

As we have noted earlier, it is unlikely that many crimes of interpersonal violence are committed by psychotic or otherwise seriously

[9] *Ibid.*, p. 109.
[10] Claude Brown, *Manchild in the Promised Land* (New York: Signet Books,
1965), pp. 313, 315.
[11] On this matter see Andrew F. Henry and James F. Short, Jr., *Suicide and
Homicide* (New York: The Free Press, 1954).

disturbed individuals. Furthermore, it has been estimated that probably "fewer than five per cent of all known homicides are premeditated, planned intentional killings, and the individuals who commit them are most likely to be episodic offenders who have never had prior contact with the criminal law." [12] Most homicides, and probably most other serious crimes of violence, result from situations "not unlike that of confrontations in wartime combat, in which two individuals committed to the value of violence came together, and in which chance, prowess, or possession of a particular weapon dictates the identity of the slayer and the slain [or in nonfatal incidents the victim and the victimizer]." [13] Perhaps the use of the word "committed" in this statement is a bit strong. But it is certainly reasonable to assert that the willingness to resort to interpersonal violence, and the tendency to do so under specified conditions, varies considerably and systematically among the different socioeconomic sectors of our society. On the basis of his Philadelphia homicide study, sociologist Marvin Wolfgang states:

> . . . the significance of a jostle, a slightly derogatory remark, or the appearance of a weapon in the hands of an adversary are stimuli differentially perceived and interpreted by Negroes and whites, males and females. . . . A male is usually expected to defend the name and honor of his mother, the virtue of womanhood . . . and to accept no derogation about his race (even from a member of his own race), his age, or his masculinity. Quick resort to physical combat as a measure of daring, courage, or defense of status appears to be a cultural expectation, especially for lower socioeconomic class males of both races.

When various individuals with these same basic response patterns interact, the prospect of some violent act resulting may be substantial. Situations that middle-class values might define as trivial are taken very seriously in such contexts, and middle-class legal norms are to some extent rendered ineffective by this alternative set of cultural standards.[14]

Sociologists have related the "subculture of violence" to social class differences in child rearing and to the resulting general differences in the value systems of the various strata. Patterns of discipline experienced in childhood may well affect the adult's tendency to act violently

[12] Wolfgang and Ferracuti, *op. cit.*, p. 141.
[13] *Ibid.*, p. 156.
[14] Wolfgang, *op. cit.*, pp. 188–89.

toward other persons. Thus studies show that working-class parents are more likely than middle-class ones to employ physical forms of punishment and to insist on outward behavioral conformity, whereas middle-class parents often use the threat of withdrawing love as a sanction and tend to stress the internalization of proper standards instead of simply demanding conformity in behavior. As a result, the middle-class child may react to frustration or conflict with guilt feelings and turn any consequent aggression inward, whereas the lower-class child is much more likely to define any conflict-ridden situation as a kind of behavioral combat, and to lash out at the presumed adversary. On the basis of such social-psychological mechanisms, then, we can begin to make some sense of the class-pattern variations in suicide and homicide rates that I mentioned earlier, and more generally of the existence of a violence-oriented subculture in at least some segments of lower-class society.[15]

Of course it should be emphasized that many lower-class persons do not engage in frequent acts of violence, and that even those who do, do not act violently all the time. Rather the point is simply that in some segments of our society cultural patterns exist that make violent response an appropriate form of behavior in a fairly wide variety of situations. In such situations, the guilt feelings that would follow resort to violence among many middle-class citizens may not be present; violence "can become a part of the life style, the theme of solving difficult problems or problem situations." Furthermore, in such a cultural milieu, failure to live up to expectations involving acceptance of violent solutions may work to a person's social disadvantage. "The juvenile who fails to live up to the conflict gang's requirements is pushed outside the group. The adult male who does not defend his honor or his female companion will be socially emasculated. The 'coward' is forced to move out of the territory, to find new friends and make new alliances." [16]

Such subcultural influences—even if they are not always as strong and inevitably constraining as some of these statements suggest—go a long way toward explaining social patterns of violence in our society. One is left, of course, with the problem of explaining the subculture itself—which from a technical standpoint is not such an easy

---

[15] For a discussion of the relevance of differential socialization to patterns of violence, see Lewis A. Coser, *Continuities in the Study of Social Conflict* (New York: The Free Press, 1967), pp. 62–65.

[16] Wolfgang and Ferracuti, *op. cit.*, pp. 161, 160.

task. The child-rearing analyses help us to understand the development of some of the values conducive to violence; to fully explain those practices, in turn, we would have to explore some very complex aspects of social class phenomena and family structure—which it is not possible to attempt in this book. But one readily senses that more than the impact of childhood discipline is involved here. In his analysis of delinquency, referred to above, Albert Cohen suggested that the crucial condition for the emergence of any new subculture is the existence of a number of individuals, interacting with each other, who share "similar problems of adjustment." It is easy to see that lower-class males (particularly lower-class Negro males) in modern American society have such problems in plenty, and that the objective conditions of their lives are so demoralizing and limiting that acts of interpersonal aggression may be a ready, and to some extent even a reasonable, response to such conditions.

A number of these conditions have been mentioned already, and some will be outlined in more detail below. If the concept of "relative deprivation" is helpful in explaining generally high crime rates among the poor, it is even more directly to the point when we consider violent offenses in particular. As we have noted, "success" by violence can be achieved even by those whose opportunities for more respectable forms of achievement are severly restricted. (This view may hold up somewhat better with respect to the relatively systematic violence that characterizes the fighting gang than it does with respect to discrete situational acts of violence among friends and relatives. But even in the latter context, relative deprivation may partially explain the behavior.) As Lewis Coser suggests, "Since Negroes are assigned lowest position in all three major dimensions of the American status system—ethnicity, class, and education—and since their mobility chances are nil in the first and minimal in the second and third, it stands to reason that achievement in the area of interpersonal violence might be seen as a channel leading to self-regard and self-enhancement—at least as long as conflict with the dominant white majority seems socially unavailable as a means of collective action." [17]

A related theme among lower-class males, and especially black lower-class males, has been that of a compulsive masculinity, not unlike the *machismo* emphasis found in various (largely impoverished)

[17] Coser, *Continuities in the Study of Social Conflict*, p. 80.

Latin American cultures. The relation between limited opportunity for occupational and other legitimate achievement and the need to compulsively demonstrate one's manhood is fairly obvious. In this regard the female-dominated Negro household, together with the widespread unemployment and job instability of black Americans, has special significance. In addition, one should not overlook the powerful effect a "nothing to lose" attitude—which one would expect to be prevalent in such sectors of our society—may have on resort to violence. When a person sees himself as having little or no prospect for the future, he may well be inclined to lash out violently at any convenient target without much regard for the consequences. Of course it may be true that some members of the lower classes, and some Negro Americans, nowadays see their prospects as improving a bit. But in the absence of a rapid realization of such expectations, a vague improvement in future prospects will not serve to dampen the socially produced inclination to violence. In fact, according to the logic of the relative deprivation thesis, a rise in expectations may actually increase resort to violence.

Certainly the situation of blacks in the United States today—embodying a strong public assertion of rights that previously were not openly claimed, and a concomitant heightening of personal expectations—carries a startling potential for violence, to the extent that the expectations remain unmatched by positive responses from the dominant white society. The civil (racial) disorders of recent years should have served to warn of this danger. Far from being a manifestation of the basic lawlessness of Negroes, they should be seen as an *alternative to* (and indication of the enormous potential for) serious acts of individual criminality among the downtrodden in modern America. As Michael Harrington recently has written:

If the slums were abolished within 5 to 10 years there would likely be a marked decrease in the commonplace homicides, rapes and assaults which the poor are driven to inflict upon one another. If the turbulent change in American society could be democratically subjected to social control there would perhaps be less incitement to paranoia [the reference here was to the recent political assassinations]. And if the nation actually honored its promises the disillusionment which brings people to riot could be wiped out.[18]

[18] Michael Harrington, "Is America By Nature a Violent Society?" p. 112.

Civil Disorders and Crime

In concrete political terms, the American response to the serious racial disorders of the past few years has been highly equivocal. A good example of this equivocation was provided by the McCone Commission's Report on the Watts riot in Los Angeles in the summer of 1965.[19] As a number of perceptive critics pointed out, the Report's references to the violence as a "spasm," "an insensate rage," and "senseless" revealed a striking lack of sensitivity to the true nature and meaning of the riot. In fact, there was a notable absence of indiscriminate violence; targets were carefully selected (or as carefully as possible under the conditions prevailing in such a disorder)—with identifiable Negro-owned establishments being spared, and also some white businesses that were known to have dealt fairly with Negroes. Very few incidents of personal assault were involved in the disorders—by far the larger number of arrests was for looting. As Bayard Rustin commented, many of the participants were simply "members of a deprived group who seized a chance to possess things that all the dinning affluence of Los Angeles had never given them." He went on to note:

There were innumerable touching examples of this behavior. One married couple in their sixties was seen carrying a couch to their home, and when its weight became too much for them, they sat down and rested on it until they could pick it up again. Langston Hughes tells of another woman who was dragging a sofa through the streets and who stopped at each intersection and waited for the traffic light to turn green. A third woman went out with her children to get a kitchen set, and after bringing it home, she discovered they needed one more chair in order to feed the whole family together; they went back to get the chair and all of them were arrested.[20]

Rustin suggests, furthermore, that many of the rioters also viewed the uprising as a kind of "manifesto," which could convey their deeply felt grievances and would symbolize their unwillingness to accept prevailing conditions. From this standpoint, the revolt had substantial roots in the Watts community, and was not merely the work of a few rabble rousers or outside agitators. On this matter, the McCone re-

[19] For a review of the Report's findings and critical evaluation, see Robert Blauner, "Whitewash Over Watts," *Trans-action*, March–April, 1966; and Bayard Rustin, "The Watts 'Manifesto' and the McCone Report," *Commentary*, March, 1966.

[20] Rustin, *op. cit.*, p. 30.

port was less than candid, making the assertion merely that no more than about 2 per cent of Los Angeles Negroes (which would not have been the proper base against which to assess the rate of participation anyway) were actively involved in the riot. Other observers questioned the criteria of involvement employed and found strong general support for the rioters. Thus sociologist Robert Blauner stated that "there seems to have been at least some participation from all segments of the black community," citing both interviews and feature stories in the press and on television (in which Watts Negroes were more likely than not to justify the rioting) and systematic opinion surveys of area residents (which likewise revealed strong general support for the disturbance).

The McCone Commission demonstrated a somewhat superficial understanding of the causes of the rioting, and placed an inordinate stress on the threat to "law and order" implied by such disorders. Although it recognized the disadvantaged position of Watts Negroes, and presented some worthy (if rather conventional) recommendations for increasing job opportunities and the quality of education in the area, there appeared in the report little indication that the Commission appreciated the depth and pervasiveness of the despair and frustration existing among Watts residents, or the symbolic function of the riots as a repudiation of the white exploiters. Thus, even though the Commission recognized that police-community relations were not what they might be, its overriding concern with the danger of eroding police authority and "respect for law" prevented it from directly confronting the issues raised by what virtually all residents of Watts considered to be a highly oppressive army of occupation. (The normally offensive dose of brutality, harassment, and indignities had in this case been exacerbated by the statements and behavior of then Chief William Parker, who referred to Negro rioters as "monkeys," and whom Rustin described as being unaware "that he is prejudiced, and being both naïve and zealous about law and order, [he is] given to a dangerous fanaticism.") Similarly, while the Commission realized that the living conditions of Watts residents were not good, it stopped short of recognizing that Watts was a stifling ghetto—albeit a slightly less stifling one than Harlem.

The pervasive alienation of Watts Negroes from the dominant values and institutions of the white society, symbolized by the nearby affluent areas of Los Angeles, was, as Robert Blauner has emphasized, clearly indicated by the rioters' behavior. "The sacredness of private

property, that unconsciously accepted bulwark of our social arrangements, was rejected; Negroes who looted, apparently without guilt,
generally remarked that they were taking things that 'really belong'
to them anyway. The society's bases of legitimacy and its loci of authority were attacked." [21] Generally speaking, then, in terms of both
the motivation underlying the disorders and the modes of behavior
exhibited in them, they were far from being "senseless" outbursts of
blind rage. On the contrary, this was an example of what Lewis Coser
has termed "realistic conflict." Rather than being simply an amorphous
expression of underlying tensions, the revolt arose from the frustration
of specific demands, was aimed at the sources of the frustration, and
was intended as a means of promoting specific goals. Not the least
of its functions was that of symbolic communication. As Coser states:

> What seems to have occurred at Watts was an effort of an active minor-
> ity within the Negro ghetto, supported by a mass of nonparticipants, to
> announce their unwillingness to continue accepting indignity and frustra-
> tion without fighting back. In particular, they were communicating their
> desperation through violent acts since no other channels of communication
> seemed open to them.[22]

In the light of these facts, it was highly disappointing that the
McCone Commission should have done nothing more than produce a
report that, in Blauner's terms, contained almost nothing "that is new
or that gives consideration to the unique conditions of Los Angeles
life and politics," that made virtually no effort "to view the outbreak
from the point of view of the Negro poor," and that played up the
role of militant leadership in encouraging the riots while de-emphasiz-
ing the breadth of support and participation among the ordinary
citizenry.

A much more open facing of the nature and underlying causes of
such racial disorders was produced by the Kerner Commission, whose
report—on the rioting in various U.S. cities during the summer of
1967—I mentioned and quoted from earlier. Because this report seems
especially relevant to our consideration of the relation between poverty
and American crime, a fairly detailed summary of the Commission's
conclusions may be in order.

As one of the epigraphs to this chapter indicates, the Commission
acknowledged that the background of the rioting could be found in

---

[21] Blauner, *op. cit.*, p. 9.
[22] Coser, *Continuities in the Study of Social Conflict*, p. 103.

the highly disadvantaged living conditions of Negroes in the areas concerned, the unresponsiveness of public authority to their plight, and the consequent "reservoir" of deeply felt grievance and frustration. At the outset, then, the Commission recognized that disorder "did not typically erupt without pre-existing causes, as a result of a single 'triggering' or 'precipitating' incident." Rather it developed out of "an increasingly disturbed social atmosphere," in which "tension-heightening incidents" gradually built up over a period of weeks or months and came to be related in the minds of community residents with more generalized and underlying grievances.[23]

While the specific content of grievances was found to vary slightly from city to city, "a typical pattern of deeply held grievances which were widely shared" in the Negro community emerged. Based on various investigations, including more than 1,200 interviews conducted not long after the disorders, the Commission uncovered the following categories of major grievances, which it ranked in terms of overall relative intensity:

Most intensely felt grievances:
 1. Police practices
 2. Unemployment and underemployment
 3. Inadequate housing

Second level of intensity:
 4. Inadequate education
 5. Poor recreation facilities and programs
 6. Ineffectiveness of the political structure and grievance mechanisms

Third level:
 7. Disrespectful white attitudes
 8. Discriminatory administration of justice
 9. Inadequacy of federal programs
 10. Inadequacy of municipal services
 11. Discriminatory consumer and credit practices
 12. Inadequate welfare programs[24]

The Commission pointed out that, in one form or another, police practices represented "a significant grievance in virtually all cities and

---

[23] *Report of the National Advisory Commission on Civil Disorders,* p. 111 (hereafter this will be referred to as "Kerner Report").

[24] *Ibid.,* pp. 143–44.

[were] often one of the most serious complaints." This category included complaints about physical or verbal abuse, lack of adequate
channels for lodging complaints against police, discriminatory policies
within police forces, and inadequate police protection for Negro citizens.

Significantly, the Commission clearly refuted the popular view
that participants in the riots were outsiders, criminals, or other unrepresentative types. On the contrary, the typical rioter was "a teen-
ager or young adult, a lifelong resident of the city in which he rioted,
a high school drop-out—but somewhat better educated than his Negro neighbor—and almost invariably underemployed or employed
in a menial job. He was proud of his race, extremely hostile to both
whites and middle-class Negroes and, though informed about politics,
highly distrustful of the political system and of political leaders." [25]
This refutation of the "riffraff theory" of riot participation was lent
further support in a special study sponsored by the Commission—the
final report of which was released in July of 1968. Based mainly on
systematic analysis of participation in six major riot cities (Cincinnati, Dayton, Detroit, Grand Rapids, Newark and New Haven), and
using "the age-eligible Negro population in the riot area, the neighborhood that experienced the rioting—not the city, nor even the
poverty area—as the appropriate base figure," this report concluded
that on the average about 18 per cent of the riot area residents took
part in the disorders.[26] As this study also confirmed, most of the rioters
were neither "outsiders" nor teen-agers. With respect to the activity
of "criminal" elements, the report makes an especially important comment:

Although from 40 to 90 per cent of the arrestees [who, according to this
report, probably comprised only about one-fifth of all riot participants] had
prior criminal records, the criminal element was not found to be overrepresented. For criminologists estimate that from 50 to 90 per cent of the Negro
males in the urban ghetto have criminal records. Thus to label most rioters
as criminals is simply to brand the majority of Negro males in the urban
ghettos as criminals.[27]

Indeed, as Bayard Rustin pointed out in his analysis of the Watts
riots, "Most Negroes, at one time or another, have been picked up and

[25] *Ibid.*, p. 111.
[26] As reported in *New York Times*, July 28, 1968, pp. 1, 48.
[27] *Ibid.*, p. 48.

placed in jail." Rustin reports that he himself had been arrested twice in Harlem on charges that were without adequate legal basis and were dismissed when the judge recognized him (a prospect, he notes, that does not exist for most Negro suspects).

The Kerner Commission found level of schooling to be closely associated with participating in the riots; area residents with some high school education were more likely to riot than those who had only completed grade school (although the majority of the rioters were not high school graduates). Counterrioters, "who risked injury and arrest to walk the streets urging rioters to 'cool it,'" were considerably better educated (and had substantially higher incomes than either the rioters or the uninvolved residents; the Commission notes that the people who made these efforts were already well along on the path to middle-class membership). As in the Watts riot, the 1967 disturbances primarily involved offenses against property. Over 30 per cent of the arrests were for breaking and entering—"crimes directed against white property rather than against individual whites"—while only 2.4 per cent of arrests were for assault and 0.1 per cent for homicide. In fact, as sociologist Morris Janowitz has pointed out, there seems in general to have been "a metamorphosis from 'communal' to 'commodity' riots." Overwhelmingly the damage done has been to property (primarily to private white-owned and operated retail business establishments—in Newark alone, over a thousand such establishments suffered damage to buildings, loss of inventory, or both). And as Janowitz further comments, "The deaths and casualties resulted mainly from the use of force against the Negro population by police and National Guard units. Some direct and active participation by white civilians may take place in such a riot, as was the case in Detroit . . . but this is a minor element." [28] The Commission pointed out too that not all of the property damage was purposeful or was directly caused by the rioters. Some resulted from official control efforts, and some from fires that got out of control—extending well beyond the rioters' "targets."

It was not possible for the Commission to determine whether the strong feelings of racial pride found among self-reported rioters in surveys made in Detroit and Newark antedated the rioting or were produced by it. At the very least the disorders themselves probably

[28] Morris Janowitz, *Social Control of Escalated Riots* (Chicago: University of Chicago, Center for Policy Study, 1968), pp. 10–11.

reinforced any pre-existing black consciousness. The Commission quoted a Detroit rioter as follows:

Interviewer: You said you were feeling good when you followed the crowd?

Respondent: I was feeling proud, man, at the fact that I was a Negro. I felt like I was a first-class citizen. I didn't feel ashamed of my race because of what they did.[29]

While the Commission, in its brief overview of the "basic causes" of the riots, acknowledged the role of "inflammatory rhetoric of black racists and militants" in fostering the disturbances, it is significant that in the same passage it commented that strident appeals to violence were "first heard from white racists." Similarly, in discussing the legitimation of violence as a factor underlying the riots it stated:

A climate that tends toward the approval and encouragement of violence as a form of protest has been created by white terrorism against nonviolent protest, including instances of abuse and even murder of some civil rights workers in the South; by the open defiance of law and federal authority by state and local officials resisting desegregation; and by some protest groups engaging in civil disobedience who turn their backs on nonviolence . . . and resort to violence to attempt to compel alteration of laws and policies with which they disagree. This condition has been reinforced by a general erosion of respect for authority in American society and reduced effectiveness of social standards and community restraints on violence and crime. This in turn has largely resulted from rapid urbanization and the dramatic reduction in the average age of the total population.[30]

The order in which the Commission presented these factors contributing to a violence-legitimating atmosphere, and the reasonable inference that the erosion of "respect for authority" is in part due to the terrorism noted in the beginning of the statement, are noteworthy. When taken together with the Commission's general stress on the factor of white racism and the deep-seated feelings of frustration and powerlessness among ghetto-dwellers contributing to the disturbances, the focus of its indictment is clear. The major responsibility for the riots lies not with black power leaders and organizations or with irresponsible hoodlums, but with the institutions of the dominant white

[29] Kerner Report, p. 133. For a discussion of similar reactions to the Watts riot (by nonparticipating Negroes) see Eldridge Cleaver, *Soul on Ice* (New York: McGraw-Hill Book Company, 1968), pp. 26–27.
[30] *Ibid.*, pp. 204–5.

society. This point is underlined by the Commission's portrayal of ghetto living conditions. I shall return to this material shortly, but let me for the moment cite some of the broad patterns of disadvantage the Commission mentioned as underlying the riot situations.[31]

In all the cities surveyed, Negroes had completed fewer years of schooling than whites and proportionately few Negroes had attended high school. A larger proportion of Negroes than of whites was in the labor force, yet Negroes were twice as likely as whites to be unemployed. Negroes who were employed were more than three times as likely as whites to be in unskilled and service jobs. In every city covered by the studies, Negroes earned less than whites. Negro income averaged only about 70 per cent of white income, and Negroes were more than twice as likely as whites to have an income placing them below the "poverty line." A smaller proportion of Negro children than of white children below 18 years of age lived with both parents. But it is noteworthy that "family responsibility" appeared strongly related to opportunity structures. Thus, "In cities where the proportion of Negro men in better-than-menial jobs was higher, median Negro family income was higher, and the proportion of children under 18 living with both parents was also higher. Both family income and family structure showed greater weakness in cities where job opportunities were more restricted to unskilled jobs." Fewer Negroes than whites owned their own homes. Negro renters paid the same rents as whites, but these rents represented a higher share of their incomes. And even though housing was relatively more costly for Negroes, their housing was "three times as likely to be overcrowded and substandard as dwellings occupied by whites."

The Commission's discussion of the riot process is notable for its willingness to break with the simplistic conception under which the initial socially dangerous acts are invariably attributed to the rioters, and action by official agents is viewed simply as legitimate response to such troublemaking. As I have already indicated, the Kerner Report stressed the "reservoir" of grievance and the disturbed social "atmosphere" out of which the disturbances arose in the first place. According to the Commission, a combination of "prior incidents" and these more generalized community states "contributed to a cumulative process of mounting tension that spilled over into violence when the final incident occurred." Quite properly the Commission concentrated

[31] *Ibid.*, pp. 136–37.

more directly on the general conditions and cumulative sequences of disturbing incidents than on the specific precipitating acts that sparked the rioting in particular cities. Of the various "prior incidents" that led up to the disturbances, many involved the actions of officialdom. Thus some 40 per cent were identified as involving allegedly abusive or discriminatory acts by the police. Sometimes such incidents stretched back a considerable period of time, as in the following example cited as the first of five "prior" incidents relevant to the summer 1967 disturbance in Newark:

1965: A Newark policeman shot and killed an 18-year-old Negro boy. After the policeman had stated that he had fallen and his gun had discharged accidentally, he later claimed that the youth had assaulted another officer and was shot as he fled. At a hearing it was decided that the patrolman had not used excessive force. The patrolman remained on duty, and his occasional assignment to Negro areas was a continuing source of irritation in the Negro community.[32]

The Commission described approximately 14 per cent of "prior incidents" as involving "official city actions"—such as an incident in Cincinnati two months before the disturbance, in which Negro representatives sought to appear before the city council to discuss summer recreation funds and only one spokesman was allowed to speak briefly "on the ground that the group had not followed the proper procedure for placing the issue on the agenda." Eight prior incidents were found to center around alleged discrimination in the administration of justice—such as setting of excessive bond for civil rights demonstrators.

Noting in particular the "deep hostility between police and ghetto-dwellers as a primary cause of the disorders," the Commission stressed the need to take all possible steps "to allay grievances that flow from a sense of injustice and increased tension and turmoil," while at the same time recognizing that police reform by itself can hardly solve all the ghetto-dweller's problems. In part because of the symbolic role of the police as representatives of society's authority, this was an area the Commission felt required special attention. Accordingly, it made a number of specific policy recommendations relating to police organization and practice—largely along lines indicated earlier in recommendations presented by the President's Commission on Law Enforcement. The proposals covered both the general role and activity

[32] *Ibid.,* pp. 118–19.

of the police and the more specific problems involved in attempting to control civil disorders.[33] It is only possible here to suggest very briefly the nature of these recommendations; obviously a comprehensive analysis of the role of the police in relation to America's crime problems would require a book unto itself, and is beyond the scope of this work.[34] We shall consider some additional aspects of police practice in Chapter 6—where proposals for noncriminal approaches to "unnecessary crimes" will be seen to have direct bearing on both the disposition of police resources and the nature of police attitudes and behavior.

The Kerner Commission emphasized that any police misconduct (physical brutality, verbal abuse and harassment, discourtesy) may directly contribute to the danger of civil disorder, and more generally must be considered unacceptable in a democratic society. It recommended that officers with bad reputations among ghetto-dwellers be immediately reassigned to other areas, that careful screening procedures be developed for selection of police to be assigned to minority-group areas, and that special incentives be used to attract outstanding officers to such duty. Furthermore, the Commission proposed that a clear policy of equal law enforcement for the ghetto be stated and enforced within police departments, which should also re-examine the general problem of making the most efficient use of existing personnel. "Communities may have to pay for more and better policing for the entire community as well as for the ghetto." Means of lodging complaints should be made easier. Policy guidelines should be established, covering at a minimum: "issuance of orders to citizens regarding their movements or activities," the handling of minor disputes, criteria to be employed in deciding whether to arrest for specific crimes, the selection and use of investigative techniques, procedures for safeguarding constitutional rights of persons engaging in lawful demonstrations, use of physical force in law enforcement situations, and "the proper manner of address for contacts with any citizen." Such guidelines, according to the Commission, "should not be solely a police responsibil-

---

[33] *Ibid.*, Chaps. 11–13; and see President's Commission on Law Enforcement and Administration of Justice, *Task Force Report: The Police.*

[34] For some additional useful perspectives, see Jerome Skolnick, *Justice Without Trial* (New York: John Wiley & Sons, Inc., 1966), David Bordua, ed., *The Police* (New York: John Wiley & Sons, Inc., 1967), and James Q. Wilson, *Varieties of Police Behavior* (Cambridge: Harvard University Press, 1968).

ity. It is the duty of mayors and other elected and appointed officials to take the initiative, to participate fully in the drafting, and to ensure that the guidelines are carried out in practice."

With respect to investigative techniques, the Kerner Commission noted:

Problems concerning use of field interrogations and "stop-and-frisk" techniques are especially critical. Crime Commission studies and evidence before this Commission demonstrate that these techniques have the potential for becoming a major source of friction between police and minority groups. We also recognize that police regard them as important methods of preventing and investigating crime. Although we do not advocate use or adoption of any particular investigative method, we believe that any such method should be covered by guidelines drafted to minimize friction with the community.[35]

Police departments should establish strong internal investigative units to ensure compliance with these various guidelines, as well as a "fair and effective means" of handling citizen complaints. A "community service officer program" also should be adopted, aimed at improving communication with the Negro community and providing more effective police service within it. Such a program should be given major financial support by the federal government.

In the area of riot control, the Commission called for a policy emphasizing prevention and moderation. Police officers should be made more fully aware of the potentially inflammatory conditions in the ghetto areas, and act with great circumspection to avoid incidents which might rapidly escalate into a full-fledged disturbance. An extensive program of training in riot control techniques should be undertaken, with special attention to the importance of using the minimum amount of force necessary under specific circumstances, and to the possibilities for use of nonlethal weapons. The Commission emphasized that strict discipline of any riot control force is "a crucial factor," and also that open channels of communication between the ghetto-dweller and local and state government provide an important means of keeping provocative incidents from escalating. Civil disorders, the Commission asserted, are "fundamental governmental problems, not simply police matters." Hence it is a major responsibility of municipal and state executives to maintain "close personal contact with the ghetto."

[35] Kerner Report, pp. 313–14.

Above all, the Commission cited the extreme danger of overreacting to incipient disturbance. For example, it noted that during the 1967 disorders, the rumors of widespread sniping that spread rapidly in many of the riot-torn cities were often subsequently found to have been inaccurate. In fact, "most reported sniping incidents were demonstrated to be gunfire by either police or National Guardsmen." More generally:

The climate of fear and expectation of violence created by such exaggerated, sometimes totally erroneous, reports demonstrates the serious risks of overreaction and excessive use of force. In particular, the Commission is deeply concerned that, in their anxiety to control disorders, some law enforcement agencies may resort to indiscriminate, repressive use of force against wholly innocent elements of the Negro community. The injustice of such conduct—and its abrasive effects—would be incalculable.[36]

This concern is one that was also stressed by the President's Crime Commission, and that has been mentioned in various independent analyses of the riots. Morris Janowitz, calling for development of a "constabulatory function" in riot control (involving a special metropolitan-regional police system), has emphasized the need for de-escalation of recent weapon usage and stockpiling. Riot control policies should be geared to a pattern of "selective response and a concern with the minimum application of force. The response of some police departments to engage in widespread arming of their personnel with rifles or to plan to procure armored personnel vehicles does not appear to be appropriate." [37] (As Janowitz goes on to note, the relevance of gun control legislation—to the prevention of escalated riots, as well as to the prevention of assassinations and other discrete shootings—is clear.)

The Kerner Commission also considered the role of the news media in relation to the summer 1967 disorders. While citing occasional lapses in which badly exaggerated or mistaken reports were disseminated by the media—and warning of the considerable dangers that may follow from such lapses—the Commission found media coverage of the riots to have been generally calm and factual in nature, rather than emotional and rumor-laden. It noted, however, the widespread distrust of the media existing in the Negro community (which tends to view them as part of the "white power structure"), and sug-

[36] *Ibid.*, p. 335.
[37] Janowitz, *op. cit.*, p. 26.

gested both the establishment of a central information office that could organize and disseminate accurate information during such disturbances, and the development by the media of improved guidelines governing coverage of such situations and better channels of communication between the media and local officials. Overall, and very much in line with the comments I have made earlier regarding the significance of mass communications in generating crime problems, the Commission stated its conclusion that it is not riot reporting as such, but rather the more general "failure to report adequately on race relations and ghetto problems and to bring more Negroes into journalism" about which we should be most concerned. With respect to the former, it would appear that recent racial disorders in the United States have served some positive function—for at least the television industry has responded with a great many (often quite well-prepared) programs and series of programs on the place and problems of the Negro in American society.

The Crime of American Poverty

Undoubtedly one of the most important parts of the Kerner Commission's work involved calling attention to the widespread poverty underlying the 1967 riots, and making public policy recommendations for ameliorating the deplorable conditions of life in the urban ghetto.

Over ten years ago, in his best-selling *The Affluent Society*, John Kenneth Galbraith commented that while poverty may be anticipated in developing countries such as India, its survival in the United States was indeed remarkable. "We ignore it," he wrote, "because we share with all societies at all times the capacity for not seeing what we do not wish to see." Galbraith referred to a "myopic preoccupation with production and material investment" that had diverted Americans from "the more urgent questions of how we are employing our resources and, in particular, from the greater need and opportunity for investing in persons." [38]

Six years ago, in his now classic *The Other America*, Michael Harrington asserted that there were between 40 and 50 million "invisible

[38] John Kenneth Galbraith, *The Affluent Society* (Boston: Houghton Mifflin Company, 1958), pp. 332–33.

poor" in the United States. Discussing a variety of official and unofficial estimates of the extent of poverty—and noting the inevitable element of judgment and interpretation involved in establishing the "poverty level" for income—Harrington insisted that "Give or take 10,000,000 the American poor are one of the greatest scandals of a society that has the ability to provide a decent life for every man, woman, and child." [39]

Approximately five years ago the federal government initiated the much vaunted "war against poverty." And yet today we are clearly a very long way from eradicating poverty in the United States. An enormous number of American citizens have inadequate incomes and live under conditions which the Kerner Commission recognized to be intolerable. There is a growing belief that existing public welfare programs, even as they expand, are patently inadequate. There need be no more explicit testimony to the disenchantment of the urban poor than the very disorders that brought the Kerner Commission into being. Despite the occasional statements by conservative spokesmen, demanding that the poor "stand on their own feet" and shoulder their part of the burden—to cite just a few of the time-ridden and meaningless clichés—it is becoming widely recognized that millions of Americans are in fact enmeshed in a vicious circle of poverty and related problems from which they cannot, by their own actions, extricate themselves.

According to recent Bureau of the Census data on consumer income, the officially recognized poverty situation in the United States (as of the end of 1966) had the following dimensions:

In 1966, 29.7 million, or 15 per cent of all persons, were below the poverty level [based on poverty thresholds for nonfarm households ranging from $1,560 for a female unrelated individual 65 or older to an average of $5,440 for a family of seven or more]. This represented a significant decrease in the incidence of poverty since 1965 when about 17 per cent of the population was classified as poor. Although nonwhite persons comprised only 12 per cent of the population in both 1965 and 1966, nonwhite persons constituted more than 32 per cent of those classified as poor. As compared to a white person, a nonwhite person was almost four times as likely to be poor in both 1965 and 1966.

. . . The incidence of poverty for white persons declined from 18 per cent to 12 per cent between 1959 and 1966, a decrease of one-third. At the

[39] Michael Harrington, *The Other America* (Baltimore: Penguin Books Inc., 1962, 1963), p. 189.

same time the incidence of poverty for nonwhites declined from 55 per cent to 41 percent, a reduction of only one-fourth.

The proportion of nonwhites among the poor has increased since 1959. Nonwhites accounted for 32 per cent of all poor persons in 1966 as contrasted with 28 per cent in 1959. During the same period, the nonwhite proportion of the total population increased from 11 per cent to 12 per cent. Between 1959 and 1966, the number of poor in the nonwhite population declined from 11 million to 10 million, whereas the corresponding figure for the white population dropped from 28 million to 20 million.[40]

That the government admits the existence in our supposedly affluent society of some 30 million poor people is surely a sobering thought.

Citing another government report—an October, 1967 compilation of data on the social and economic conditions of Negroes in the United States—the Kerner Commission pointed out the especially pronounced poverty of black urban ghetto-dwellers. This report had documented that while incomes of both Negroes and whites had been rising rapidly, the median family income of Negroes was in 1966 only 58 per cent that of whites. It also showed that the proportions of Negroes in upper-income categories (families receiving incomes of $7000 or more), and of Negroes employed in skilled and high-paying jobs, rose substantially between 1960 and 1966. Years of education completed by Negroes also showed a rapid rise. However, the report indicated that a great many Negroes at the lowest income levels were making virtually no significant economic progress. About 10 per cent of all Negroes "have lived all their lives in rural areas with very limited opportunities for improvement in education, employment, housing, or income." Another 10 per cent—representing more than 2 million persons—live in the slum neighborhoods of the central cities. In these areas, conditions tend to be "stagnant or deteriorating," as suggested by special censuses taken in Cleveland and Los Angeles:

Outside of the poor neighborhoods in Cleveland, Negro families made major gains between 1960 and 1965. Average incomes rose, the incidence of poverty and the number of broken families were reduced.

But in the poorest neighborhoods, all of these social indicators showed decline.

In Hough, which is one of the worst of the poor neighborhoods, the incidence of poverty increased, the proportion of broken homes increased,

---

[40] U.S. Bureau of the Census, *Current Population Reports,* Series P-60, No. 53, "Income in 1966 of Families and Persons in the United States" (Washington, D.C.: U.S. Government Printing Office, 1967), p. 4.

and the male unemployment rate was virtually unchanged. A similar study was made in various neighborhoods in South Los Angeles after the riot in Watts several years ago, and showed much the same pattern.[41]

Focusing on the critical significance of employment, the Kerner Commission indicated that even though Negro unemployment rates have declined appreciably in the post-World War II period, they are still double those for whites. "In 1967, approximately 3.0 million persons were unemployed during an average week, of whom about 638,-000 or 21 per cent, were nonwhites. When corrected for undercounting, total nonwhite unemployment was approximately 712,000 or 8 per cent of the nonwhite labor force." Of those Negroes who are employed, there continues to be a heavy concentration in the unskilled and low-paying job categories, and many are "underemployed" (for example, having only part-time employment). The Commission cited 1966 Department of Labor surveys in low-income neighborhoods of nine large cities, which showed that the "subemployment" rate (including both unemployment and underemployment) in these areas was about 32.7 per cent—or almost nine times greater than the unemployment rate for all U.S. workers. The impact of such a condition is, of course, far-reaching. As we have already seen, there seems to be a very close relation between employment opportunities and family stability. Furthermore, in fatherless families where the mother is forced to work, and where inadequate child care facilities are available, it is natural that children should spend a great deal of time on the streets—thus readily encountering crime-generating influences. The general social psychological impact of unemployment on the Negro male himself is obviously also highly significant as a factor potentially affecting crime involvement.

The grossly unsatisfactory conditions in the ghetto schools were discussed briefly in an earlier chapter. We have also seen that the housing in riot areas was disproportionately substandard—a fact which can, of course, be generalized to all urban ghetto neighborhoods. The horror of ghetto housing conditions is partly conveyed by a recent, effectively understated article in *The New Yorker* discussing the "war on rats" in New York City.[42] An interview with the director of the

---

[41] U.S. Bureau of Labor Statistics and U.S. Bureau of the Census, *BLS Report*, No. 332; *Current Population Reports*, Series P-23, No. 24, "Social and Economic Conditions of Negroes in the United States, October 1967" (Washington, D.C.: U.S. Government Printing Office, 1967), p. ix.

[42] "The War on Rats," *The New Yorker*, August 3, 1968, pp. 23–26.

New York City Health Department's Bureau of Pest Control revealed that the number of *reported* rat bites in the city had been running from almost 800 in 1959 to almost 450 in 1967, some four years after the Bureau began its work. Noting that his Bureau's operating budget was a million and a half dollars, the official claimed that if it had 5 million a year, it could do the job—that is, "really put a significant dent in the rat population of the city." Public Health Service estimates placed this population at about one rat per person, but as the official pointed out the rat population is heavily concentrated in the ghettos (a fact underscored by the concentration of blue and red pins—marking the locations of buildings certified as rat-infested and buildings in which cases of rat bite had been reported—on large maps of the city prominently displayed in the Bureau's main office). He asserted that the total number of rat-infested buildings in Harlem probably comes to several thousand. As he pointed out, the dangers of fever and disfigurement are overshadowed by the psychological effect of having to live with rats. And yet for most ghetto-dwellers there is no real alternative. Ghetto residents cannot run away from the rats. "They have to stay, and we have to help them make it bearable."

More generally, the millions of poor people in America are subject to deplorable health conditions and blatantly inadequate medical care. Michael Harrington's earlier depiction of some of the interlocking factors was succinct yet comprehensive:

Here is one of the most familiar forms of the vicious circle of poverty. The poor get sick more than anyone else in the society. That is because they live in slums, jammed together under unhygienic conditions; they have inadequate diets, and cannot get decent medical care. When they become sick, they are sick longer than any other group in the society. Because they are sick more often and longer than anyone else, they lose wages and work, and find it difficult to hold a steady job. And because of this, they cannot pay for good housing, for a nutritious diet, for doctors. At any given point in the circle, particularly when there is a major illness, their prospect is to move to an even lower level and to begin the cycle, round and round, toward even more suffering.[43]

A good reflection of these conditions (as they have come to be concentrated among black Americans) is found in the following statistics cited by the Kerner Commission: maternal mortality rates are four times as high for nonwhite mothers as for white mothers; infant

[43] Harrington, *The Other America*, p. 23.

mortality rates for babies under one month old are 58 per cent higher among nonwhites than among whites, and for babies between one month and one year old the nonwhite rates are almost three times as high; life expectancy for nonwhite Americans was, in 1965, almost seven years lower than for white Americans. While the medical situation of the rural poor is especially frightful, the low level of facilities and treatment and of active efforts to make professional contact with the poor in the urban slums also remains a disgrace. As Elinor Langer has noted, the highly touted expertise of modern American medicine is largely reserved for the rich; "the rest of the population finds even adequate services hard to come by." She cites the following findings from a health survey of a Boston public housing project:

. . . among individuals over 65, 25 per cent had chronic bronchitis, 20 per cent had chronic nervous disorders, 12 per cent were blind or had visual defects, and [that] 40 per cent of these were not receiving treatment. In New York, former Health Commissioner George James has estimated that 13,000 poor people died last year because adequate professional care was not available.[44]

That the United States, almost alone among modern democratic societies, has not yet enacted a comprehensive program of free medical care (the recently developed Medicare scheme falls far short of that goal) illustrates how vested economic interests—in this case represented by the long-time lobbying of the American Medical Association —help to determine the shape of social problems. By its effect on the health conditions of the poor, such pressure group activity also indirectly influences the nature and extent of crime in our society.

Another, often overlooked area in which the conditions of poverty undoubtedly affect the crime situation involves the inadequate recourse poor people have to proper legal assistance. We have already noted class differentials in the administration of criminal justice, and the strong hostility existing between ghetto-dwellers and the police— which may have broader significance in shaping attitudes toward the legal system as a whole and indeed toward all the dominant forces of society. But the problems of the poor in relation to the legal system extend well beyond the area of criminal law. As many studies now have documented, poor people tend to have a woefully inadequate understanding of their legal rights, to be unaware of the existence of

[44] Elinor Langer, "The Shame of American Medicine," *The New York Review,* May 26, 1966, p. 6.

legal procedures by which they might protect these rights, to have little information about how to contact lawyers (whom they tend to distrust anyway), and to receive little or no effective legal service from private lawyers they do manage to reach.[45] Were adequate legal services made available to them, the poor would be in a vastly improved position to deal with the many problems they face daily in the areas of family law, landlord-tenant relations, welfare administration, and in connection with their behavior as consumers.

Although the Kerner Commission's discussion of consumer exploitation was fairly brief, it did note that the rioters often focused on retail establishments they considered especially exploitative. The Commission also reported that "it is clear that many residents of disadvantaged Negro neighborhoods believe they suffer constant abuses by local merchants." Recognizing the considerable dependence of the poor on installment-buying transactions, the Commission pointed out that many merchants in the ghettos engage in a variety of exploitative techniques—"high-pressure salesmanship, bait advertising, misrepresentation of prices, substitution of used goods for promised new ones, failure to notify consumers of legal actions against them, refusal to repair or replace substandard goods, exorbitant prices or credit charges, and use of shoddy merchandise." [46] That low-income purchasers find such practices the norm rather than the exception has been substantially documented by a systematic survey of lower-class families in New York City reported on by sociologist David Caplovitz in his book *The Poor Pay More*. As Caplovitz also discovered:

Many consumers have almost no idea of the complex set of legal conditions embodied in the contracts they sign. The penalties that can be brought to bear on them, such as the loss of possessions already paid for, the payment of interest on money owed, the payment of lawyer and court fees, are matters that some families become rudely aware of only when—for whatever reasons—they miss their payments.[47]

The Kerner Report cited too the frequent claims of ghetto residents that they pay higher food prices than residents of better neighbor-

[45] See Jerome Carlin, Jan Howard, and Sheldon Messinger, *Civil Justice and the Poor* (New York: Russell Sage Foundation, 1968). For a brief overview see also Edwin M. Schur, *Law and Society: A Sociological View* (New York: Random House, Inc., 1968), pp. 95–106.

[46] Kerner Report, p. 276.

[47] David Caplovitz, *The Poor Pay More* (New York: The Free Press, 1963), p. 155.

hoods, and yet receive inferior quality meat and produce. Even though a number of factors other than exploitation may partly explain such differentials (for example, restricted mobility of low-income purchasers, high operating costs of ghetto stores, etc.), "it is probable that genuinely exploitative pricing practices exist in some areas." At any rate, the Commission recognized that the belief in exploitative food pricing was an important factor contributing to antiwhite feeling in the ghettos. In a number of slum neighborhoods, residents recently have created cooperative markets to combat the exploitative pricing to which they are convinced they have been subjected. Conventional legal aid programs have not been adequate—either in scope or in militancy—to vigorously assist the poor in coping with their legal difficulties and in fighting such exploitation. The recently established "legal services" programs—supported by the federal Office of Economic Opportunity and featuring "neighborhood law offices" and other similar devices aimed at providing easy access to knowledgeable counsel who will actively advance the poor person's cause—may begin to secure some of the ghetto-dweller's legal rights (and, indirectly, produce a change in the direction of more favorable attitudes toward the American legal system).

Similarly, conventional public welfare programs are increasingly denounced for their inadequate coverage, as well as for their restrictive regulations, punitive and humiliating procedures, and their generally patronizing approach to the poor. The attitude informing these programs has largely been that welfare is a privilege, not a right, and that the person on welfare should be grateful for whatever he gets, however difficult we make it for him to get it. Welfare recipients should be prepared to undergo sharp questioning and routine examination of their living places to determine the extent of their eligibility for welfare support. Women on relief have even been expected to submit to surprise "midnight raids" of their apartments—aimed at determining whether a man might be present, which would bring into question the woman's continued eligibility. Bureaucratic procedures are often so elaborate that it is next to impossible for the person on welfare to know just how to proceed so as to obtain that to which he is entitled under the law. Subsidies rendered under these programs are, to say the least, minimal.

In *The Poorhouse State*, Richard Elman comments on the amount available for food for a family of four under the typical New York City welfare budget (in 1966):

To feed itself on $25.62 weekly a family will have to be sparing with fresh milk or butter; fresh eggs, fruits, and vegetables will also have to be considered luxuries. The average American is said to consume 160 pounds of meat annually, but this family would eat beans to supply its major protein dosages. They would learn to substitute peanut butter for chicken (as one manual that I read recommended) and government surplus cornstarch for potatoes. Rice and the various cereals would be consumed in large quantities. They would—if truly frugal—reboil their coffee grounds and mix their stale bread with government-surplus molasses to make pudding.[48]

As Elman suggests, "A typical welfare budget is designed to deprive. It standardizes bare subsistence in a country in which luxuries have become necessities." In fact most welfare budgets set such frugal standards, and are administered so punitively, that they almost "clamor to be violated." It is hardly surprising, then, if the welfare system often becomes a kind of combat between the supposedly benevolent administrators and social workers and the welfare recipients they are supposed to be helping.

Realizing the patent inadequacy of this system and the widespread demoralization it produces, Richard Cloward and Frances Fox Piven of the Columbia University School of Social Work proposed, in May, 1966, a "strategy to end poverty"—in which such enormous pressure would be brought to bear on the welfare system that its inability to provide for the real needs of the poor would become obvious and more direct federal action ("major economic reforms at the national level," including a guaranteed annual income) would become necessary. "In order to generate a crisis," Cloward and Piven argued, "the poor must obtain benefits which they have forfeited. Until now, they have been inhibited from asserting claims by self-protective devices within the welfare system: its capacity to limit information, to intimidate applicants, to demoralize recipients, and arbitrarily to deny lawful claims." [49] A massive education campaign could, they insisted, make poor people aware of their legal rights; organizers could become advocates bringing or threatening to bring legal action to enforce such rights; and organized demonstrations could "create a climate of militancy that will overcome the invidious and immobilizing attitudes which many poten-

[48] Richard M. Elman, *The Poorhouse State* (New York: Delta Books, 1966, 1968), p. 56.
[49] Richard A. Cloward and Frances Fox Piven, "A Strategy to End Poverty," *The Nation*, May 2, 1966, p. 512. For a novelist's powerful portrayal of the welfare system see Sol Yurick, *The Bag* (New York: Trident Press, 1968).

tial recipients hold toward being 'on welfare.'" Along the lines suggested in this manifesto, and in part encouraged by it, welfare recipients in various cities have during the past few years begun to organize and to demonstrate against the inadequacies of local welfare programs. Whether these somewhat sporadic developments will coalesce, to produce an effective nation-wide "welfare revolt," or even a "welfare caucus" that could wield real political power, remains to be seen. But we are at least safe in assuming that discontent about the welfare system represents an important element in the more general discontent of the poor in our society, and as such is not without significance in relation to the crime situation.

There has been much discussion and debate among specialists concerning the extent to which poverty in modern American society constitutes a distinct and compelling "subculture" (just as there has been a similar debate focusing on the precise nature of the cultural context of delinquency). But there is no dispute among the experts as to the fact that millions of American citizens are living under conditions to which we should not willingly subject any human being. Preliminary findings in a Congressional investigation of hunger in the United States—in progress at the time this is written—are once again forcefully documenting this outrageous fact.[50] The persistence of dire poverty, together with the continuing and patent racial discrimination in our society, has created a situation in which—unless there is a drastic alteration of public policies—a strong likelihood exists, as the Kerner Commission noted, of "major disorders, worse, possibly, than those already experienced." It was with consciousness of both the appalling nature of our present situation and these grim prospects for the future that the Commission proposed a massive, greatly accelerated effort to eradicate poverty in the United States.

The Commission called for a comprehensive national manpower policy, under which major goals would include the creation of new jobs, widespread and improved job recruitment and vocational training, and stimulation of both public and private investment geared toward those ends. Under programs recommended by the Commission, one million new jobs would be created in the public sector over a three-year period, and another one million in the private sector (with a large-scale use of tax credits as incentives to private employers—a device which "should also be provided for the location and renovation

[50] See *New York Times,* February 23, 1969, p. 6E.

of plants and other business facilities in urban and rural 'poverty areas' "). Special (financial) encouragement should also be given to Negro ownership of businesses in ghetto areas.

Also recommended by the Kerner Commission were extensive efforts to improve our school system—along lines I indicated earlier. The major aims in this sphere would be to eliminate de facto school segregation, provide quality education for ghetto schools, improve community-school relations, and expand opportunities for both higher education and vocational training. To these ends, major financial support must be provided by the federal government. Noting that federal expenditures for education, training, and related services had increased from $4.7 billion in fiscal 1964 to $12.3 billion in fiscal 1969, the Commission stated that the existing network of federal educational programs "provides a sound and comprehensive basis for meeting the interrelated needs of disadvantaged students. We need now to strengthen that base . . . and to build upon it by providing greatly increased federal funds for the education of the disadvantaged."

The Commission also urged "drastic reforms" of our public welfare system, a system it described as contributing materially "to the tensions and social disorganization that have led to civil disorders." Pointing to the widespread dissatisfaction with the system, and citing a 1965 estimate that 50 per cent of persons eligible to receive assistance under welfare programs (nationally) were not on the welfare rolls, the Commission proposed various changes in regulations, designed to extend coverage and reduce restrictive practices of various sorts. But its major recommendation in this area was simply that "the federal government should absorb a far greater share of the financial burden than presently." Thus it proposed specific ways for providing uniformly more adequate levels of assistance in particular welfare programs (such as Aid to Families of Dependent Children), and also suggested as part of national long-term strategy that very serious consideration be given to "the development of a national system of income supplementation to provide a basic floor of economic and social security for all Americans." The latter program would be aimed at providing, "for those who can work or who do work, any necessary supplements in such a way as to develop incentives for fuller employment"; and, "for those who cannot work and for mothers who decide to remain with their children, a system that provides a minimum standard of decent living and to aid in saving children from the prison of poverty that has held their parents."

Finally, the Kerner Commission recognized that today, "after more than three decades of fragmented and grossly underfunded federal housing programs, decent housing remains a chronic problem for the disadvantaged urban household." Nearly two-thirds of nonwhite families in the central cities, it noted, live in neighborhoods characterized by substandard housing and general urban blight. Nor is bad housing limited to Negroes. In 1966, over 4 million of the nearly 6 million occupied substandard housing units were occupied by whites. Calling for the expansion "on a massive basis" of the supply of housing suitable for low-income families, the Commission recommended provision of "600,000 low- and moderate-income housing units next year, and 6 million units over the next five years." It also urged expanded and modified below-interest rate and rent supplement programs, and an ownership supplement program; "direct federal write-down of interest rates on market rate loans to private construction firms for moderate-rent housing"; an expanded and more diversified public housing program; an expanded Model Cities Program; a greatly expanded but reoriented (to the needs of poor people) program of urban renewal; reform of obsolete building codes; passage of a "national, comprehensive and enforceable" open-occupancy law; and reorientation of federal housing programs to place more low- and moderate-income housing outside of ghetto areas.

Recommendations of the Kerner Commission, in sum, add up to a massive no-holds-barred reconstructing of the basic conditions of urban living in the United States. Although there is no way to prove it, there is every reason to believe that measures coming anywhere close to full implementation of this program would significantly reduce America's crime problems—as well as making this country a halfway liveable place for millions of its now denied citizens. The probable impact of such changes on legitimate opportunity structures, on the self-images of disadvantaged slum-dwellers, and on general patterns of alienation, would have to be enormous. Unfortunately, at the time this is written, there still are no signs of a clear national commitment to the kind of action needed to ameliorate the basic conditions of American poverty. Measures enacted over the last year or two do not come close to meeting the specifications of the Kerner Report, the Johnson administration never really expressed its unequivocal support of the Commission's work, and in the 1968 election campaign the platform of neither major party demanded without qualification enactment of the policies the Commission recommended. A report entitled "One Year Later," released in February 1969 by two private organizations concerned with urban problems, has emphasized the nation's failure to enact policies based on the Kerner proposals, and has warned of the grave dangers such complacency entails.[51]

The War on Poverty, the War in Vietnam, and the "War" on Crime

As I have stressed, the violence unleashed in the 1967 racial disorders does not represent a general tendency toward lawlessness that is seducing more and more Americans. Rather it is a sign of perhaps unparalleled disaffection in the body politic, and a partial indication of the vast reservoir of crime-generating frustration and demoralization present in American society today. In such situations violence should serve as a useful danger signal that, as Lewis Coser notes, "cannot fail to be perceived by men in power and authority otherwise not noted for peculiar sensitivity to social ills." [52] Unhappily, as Coser goes on to state, it does not necessarily follow that they will in fact respond "with types of social therapy that will effectively remove the sources of infection."

The military struggle in Vietnam undoubtedly has impaired our efforts to control crime. While direct and indirect exposure to modern warfare could be having the dangerous effect of indirectly legitimating violence as a solution to human problems, even more significant—as I stated earlier—are the alienation-promoting and economic aspects of the current international conflict. Unpopular international involvements, such as that in Vietnam, can only serve to reinforce existing domestic tendencies toward alienation and hostility, particularly among our youth. For the black American, the Government's vigorous prosecution of such wars, while it appears incapable of preserving human rights and meeting basic needs at home, only exacerbates his already-growing contempt for this nation's professed values and basic institutions. The economic impact of the war—in absorbing enormous funds and considerable energy that could instead be used to combat crime-producing social conditions—can hardly be questioned.

Quite apart from financial limitations imposed by the war, and

[51] See *New York Times*, February 23, 1969, p. 1.
[52] Coser, *Continuities in the Study of Social Conflict*, p. 83.

despite the fact that few leaders can any longer ignore the close relation between poverty, discrimination, and America's high crime rates, there appears to be deplorably little inclination to take the political action needed to fight poverty and hence crime. Ideological preference for the "get tough" orientation to crime problems may partly account for this, but probably unwillingness to support such a broadly based (and extremely costly) program of federal intervention as was called for in the Kerner Report also underlies the resistance. Even in their efforts to strengthen law enforcement programs—an area of policy in which the more punitive-minded of our politicians often can join with more liberal reformers in proposing government expenditures —a tremendous emphasis has been placed on the preservation of local autonomy. At its heart, the reluctance to mount an all-out attack on poverty may reflect a persisting fear of central planning. If this is so, then the prospects for reducing crime are indeed grim. For the kinds of steps needed to produce this result require extensive planning and massive funding, both at the federal level. It is in such a fact, and the apparent unwillingness of many American political figures to face up to it, that the essentially political nature of crime becomes readily apparent.

5

"RESPECTABLE" CRIME

Many of the problems of "white-collar crime" and of relaxed public morality, of high-priced vice and of fading personal integrity, are problems of *structural* immorality. They are not merely the problem of the small character twisted by the bad milieu. And many people are at least vaguely aware that this is so. As news of higher immoralities breaks, they often say, "Well, another one got caught today," thereby implying that the cases disclosed are not odd events involving occasional characters but symptoms of a widespread condition. There is good probative evidence that they are right.

C. Wright Mills, *The Power Elite*

To most "informed" middle-class Americans, serious crime seems overwhelmingly a problem of lower-class behavior. Certainly this assumption is borne out by the official statistics, and as we have seen it may also be factually the case that—because of socioeconomic pressures and related attitude structures—a high proportion of the more visible and more vocally condemned varieties of "street crime" is concentrated among individuals located on the lower rungs of the socioeconomic ladder. But as we have also noted, developing a comprehensive and accurate picture of the social distribution of all criminal behavior is a complicated undertaking, and furthermore it is one in which the assessor's own value judgments (or, in the broadest sense, "political" choices) can hardly ever be kept completely out of the picture. Unfortunate as it may be, our "official" comprehension of how criminals are situated in our society tends to reflect the distribution of attitudes and power in that society more than it does the real distribution of criminal behavior.

Even with respect to the crimes considered thus far there is, as I have suggested in several places, an element of deceptiveness in the official data relating social class and crime. Not the least disturbing aspect of this situation is the quite evident vicious-circle process by which middle-class suspects or defendants—when they do come to light—are given preferential treatment on the grounds that they are not really "criminal types." (The modern tendency in sentencing—to take into account not merely the nature of the act committed but the broad pattern of the defendant's life and the "prospects" for his future behavior—allows the "respectable" citizen caught in criminal acts a degree of immunity not available to his supposedly less respectable colleagues in crime.) But the dimensions of "respectable crime" extend well beyond these favored offenders. Many middle- and upper-class citizens engage in the borderline criminal offenses considered in the next chapter—crimes with respect to which, and whatever the social class membership of the individuals involved, levels of public visibility and effective enforcement are extremely low. And, perhaps most significant of all, are the aforementioned "white-collar crimes" —occupational and related offenses committed by persons of high socioeconomic status—to which we now turn. It is largely because Americans have displayed a relatively tolerant attitude toward these crimes that criminal behavior appears so heavily concentrated among the lower classes. The consequences of such leniency—in terms both of direct and indirect economic costs to the citizenry and of a more diffuse contribution to the undermining of standards of public morality—are substantial and adverse. As I stated earlier, from the standpoint of policy the issue regarding white-collar offenses is not so much a technical one of whether they *are* crimes; rather we need to confront directly the question whether (and to what extent) they *should be* treated as acts of serious criminality. American society has paid a high price for having answered this question (by and large) in the negative.

Nonprofessional Fraud

If we adopt this orientation, then the major objection advanced by critics of the "white-collar crime" concept—that such offenders are not defined either by themselves or by the public as criminals—no longer can be seen as foreclosing consideration of such law violations. On the contrary, the issue becomes precisely that of whether those definitions should be allowed to stand.

There is some indication that in recent years official reaction to white-collar criminality has slightly hardened. The federal prosecution in 1961 of twenty-nine corporations and forty-five top-level executives in the electrical industry for having conspired illegally to fix prices, rig bids, and divide markets (on equipment valued at $1,750,000,000 annually) was not only the biggest criminal case in the history of the Sherman Antitrust Act, but also a landmark in the application of significant criminal sanctions for involvement in acts of white-collar crime.[1] Fines totalling $1,924,500 were levied against the corporate defendants, but even more significant were the thirty-day jail terms imposed on seven of the executives (four of whom were vice-presidents, two division managers, and one a sales manager) and the suspended jail sentences given to twenty-seven other individual defendants. As various observers have noted, even the half-million-dollar fine levied against General Electric would have little real impact on that corporate collossus (the extremely costly settlement of the many damage suits brought by customers in the wake of these prosecutions did, in this instance, constitute a significant financial impact); jail sentences for specific executives, however, were something else again. It had been extremely rare in the past for such sentences to be imposed (let alone actually served) on individual white-collar criminals of such stature.

The other side of this case (one giving less cause for optimism among those who would favor systematic action against corporate crime) is seen in the rationalizations of their behavior presented by various of the defendants, in the fact that following conviction and serving of sentence most of the offenders were back at their old jobs (General Electric being unique among the corporate defendants in the extent to which it systematically "cleaned house"), and in the general recognition that the impact of the prosecutions on overall levels of corporate morality and legality would probably be a quite limited one.

There was ample evidence that the defendants knew their collusive action to fix prices and share business was in some sense improper:

[1] See Richard Austin Smith, "The Incredible Electrical Conspiracy," *Fortune*, April, 1961, reprinted in M. Wolfgang, *et al.*, ed., *The Sociology of Crime and Delinquency* (New York: John Wiley & Sons, Inc., 1962), pp. 357–72; also Gilbert Geis, "White Collar Crime and the Heavy Electrical Equipment Antitrust Cases of 1961," in Geis, ed., *White-Collar Criminal* (New York: Atherton Press, 1968), pp. 139–51.

The conspiracies had their own lingo and their own standard operating procedures. The attendance list was known as the "Christmas-card list," meetings as "choir practices." Companies had code numbers—G.E. 1, Westinghouse 2, Allis-Chalmers 3, Federal Pacific 7—which were used in conjunction with first names when calling a conspirator at home for price information ("This is Bob, what is 7's bid?"). At the hotel meeting it was S.O.P. not to list one's employer when registering and not to have breakfast with fellow conspirators in the dining room. The G.E. men observed two additional precautions: never to be the ones who kept the records and never to tell G.E.'s lawyers anything.[2]

Indeed some of the defendants openly admitted knowledge of some impropriety, yet at the same time tried to argue away its full legal implications. Their acts, it was claimed, may have been technically illegal but not really deserving of the label crime; or, alternatively, such acts were admitted to technically violate the criminal law, yet were held not to be really unethical because they were alleged to have some positive social consequences. Furthermore, defendants insisted that price-fixing was virtually a way of life in their industry, that this was made clear to them when they first took up their jobs, and that they were under subtle or not so subtle pressure from superiors to engage in such behavior.

In the absence of a continuous pattern of vigorous prosecution in diverse industries following the electrical cases, it seemed unlikely that this one instance of nonpreferential sanctioning of executives—even though it touched a good many individuals—would substantially deter legally questionable corporate behavior in American society. Very likely some individuals were severely jolted by the shock of seeing their colleagues imprisoned; in such cases the convictions may well have had some real deterrent effect. Yet just as the predominant reaction of the defendants was not sincere acceptance of guilt but rather a sense of being the "fall guys" for what was standard (and hence, legitimate) business practice, so too the most likely overall outcome appeared to be "business as usual."

Business as usual undoubtedly encompasses a broad range of persisting white-collar crime. We have no adequate statistics concerning the current extensiveness and economic cost to society of major regulatory offenses of this sort—violations of laws such as those in the areas of antitrust, food and drug control, securities regulation, labor

[2] Austin, *op. cit.,* p. 362.

relations, and conflicts of interest. But it is difficult to believe that the amount of such crime is not enormous. Of course, it may be argued that such matters should not be subject to proscription by the criminal law at all—that this is another of the areas in which our society has succumbed to overlegislation and overregulation. We are familiar with the fairly well-elaborated philosophy that actively opposes governmental intervention in the economy, as seen for example in the writings and public statements of such conservative spokesmen as Barry Goldwater. The very fact that such an argument is made, and that this philosophy has a good deal of public support (especially perhaps in business circles), strongly suggests that the attitudinal structures necessary to inhibit violation of such statutes (or, to put it more positively, to encourage adherence to their provisions) exist in only weak or compromised form—at least in certain segments of our society.

While it may be going too far to suggest that many white-collar offenses represent conscious challenges to, or protests against, restrictions many consider to be "bad law" (a kind of businessman's civil disobedience), it is quite clear that a considerable amount of group and attitudinal support is present for behavior that skirts along the border of, and at times oversteps, such regulatory proscriptions. One must also recognize that the institutional structure of big business itself contains elements conducive to this kind of law violation. In a recent study of lawyers' ethical dilemmas it was found that conformity to and deviance from ethical norms were closely related to the distribution within the bar of financial strains and of opportunities to obtain clientele, as well as to more specific client and colleague pressures and attitudes, the modes of organization of law practice, and the level and nature of lawyer contacts with courts and government agencies.[3] Similarly in the business world a variety of structural features—including internal corporate authority structures and power struggles, differential pressures on executives to achieve corporate goals by whatever means, structured avenues to success within particular industries, the history of the corporation's and the industry's relations with government agencies and with major clients (often the government itself), and even the social and attitudinal features of the local community within which a particular corporate operation is located —probably have important bearing on the nature and extent of white-collar criminality.

[3] Jerome E. Carlin, *Lawyers' Ethics: A Survey of the New York City Bar* (New York: Russell Sage Foundation, 1966).

A perceptive analyst of white-collar crime has pointed out that it is precisely the ambiguous nature of these offenses that makes them sociologically interesting; that the controversy over such laws "gives us a clue to important norm conflicts, clashing group interests, and maybe incipient social change." [4] Offenses by businessmen and corporations illustrate nicely what I have called the political nature of American crime problems. In the absence of a full consensus concerning the moral standards that should guide business practice in our society, the activities and relative power positions of competing interest groups (as they bear on legislation and the enforcement of legislation) will in large measure determine the extent to which white-collar criminality is exposed and subjected to meaningful negative sanctions. At the moment such violations remain grossly underreported and underprosecuted. In addition to suggesting the continuing power of business interests as such, this fact also reflects the persisting dominance of business *values* throughout our society—a point to which I shall return shortly.

White-collar crime is not merely a matter of major corporate delictions. On the contrary, it consists of an extremely wide variety of behaviors displayed at all levels in the business world, in diverse occupational settings, and throughout numerous spheres of American life. In grouping white-collar offenses and related types of crime under the category "nonprofessional fraud," I have sought to focus on a key element that permeates this area of law violation—that of misrepresentation, breach of trust, lack of fair dealing. While technical distinctions may be drawn between these several concepts (and other similar ones), in a more general sense all of these behaviors involve as a central theme the attempt to "put something over"—on the government, the public, competitors, one's employers, or other selected individuals. The fraud involved in such situations is "nonprofessional" because it is not the violator's major means of earning a living. We are not essentially concerned here with professional defrauders—even though in some instances the fraudulent behavior may be sufficiently habitual that the line between professional and nonprofessional becomes blurred —but rather with otherwise "respectable" citizens, going about their everyday business, at some point in the course of which they resort to one or another variety of (criminal) fraudulent behavior.

The nature of the perceived "victim" represents an important ele-

[4] Vilhelm Aubert, "White Collar Crime and Social Structure," *American Journal of Sociology,* 58 (November, 1952), 266.

ment influencing the ease or difficulty with which individuals engage in criminal acts. One of the major factors underlying the rationalization of major corporate regulatory offenses is the ease with which the offender can convince himself that in acting against the government he is not "hurting" any specific individual, or alternatively that if the government itself be viewed as a victim, it is a victim that deserves what it gets.

Without doubt similar mechanisms facilitate widespread violation of income tax laws and regulations, at both the corporate and the individual levels. We are all familiar with the great American game of tax avoidance, because middle-income individual taxpayers often play it with as much verve as do major corporations. It is true that legalistic distinctions can be drawn between avoidance and evasion. In his 1960 book *The Operators* (in which he claimed that, "Never in our history has the practice of fraud been so dignified by constant use and acceptance"), Frank Gibney succinctly summarized the matter as follows:

> Tax evasion is a criminal offense against society punishable by large fines and jail terms. Tax *avoidance* is merely the case of a citizen taking advantage of his right to pay as little tax as is legally required of him. ("Minimizing" one's tax is the euphemism currently used.) The federal courts have consistently guaranteed this right of the taxpayer to do as much dodging as possible within the limits of the law. "There is nothing sinister," Judge Learned Hand once said, "in so arranging one's affairs as to keep taxes as low as possible. Everybody does so, rich or poor; and all do right, for nobody owes any public duty to pay more than the law demands." [5]

As Gibney goes on to point out, this would be fine if everyone were able to appreciate and apply this distinction with ease, and if the complexity of the tax laws were not such as to invite a continuous search for loopholes. Clearly for most individuals, and even for major corporations with high-powered legal and accountancy staffs and advisors, the borderline between legitimate minimizing and illegal manipulation is extremely hazy. Gibney even quotes a veteran Internal Revenue Service lawyer as admitting that "avoidance is nonfraudulent evasion."

As in the case of corporate regulatory crimes, we have to recognize that individual immorality is an insufficient explanation of such law

[5] Frank Gibney, *The Operators* (New York: Harper & Row, Publishers, 1960), pp. 217–18.

violation. Again institutional factors are involved—in this case the fact that we have structured the "game" of taxpaying in such a way that substantial fraud became almost inevitable. By creating a plethora of deductions, exemptions, write-offs, special tax rates, and so on, the system itself summons forth elaborate efforts at minimizing and ingenious attempts to "dodge" liability, which must frequently skirt the edge of illegality. When the individual citizen of moderate income plays the game, the social cost of his petty defalcations (falsifying an exemption, padding a deduction) is not likely to be great—although certainly across the board these individual infringements do add up. In the case of big business, a great deal more is at stake. As C. Wright Mills noted in *The Power Elite*, "For virtually every law taxing big money, there is a way those with big money can avoid it or minimize it." [6] Thus there have developed various familiar "tax gimmicks," such as manipulation of capital gains and losses, creation of private trusts and foundations, exploitation of oil "depletion allowances," deferred payment salaries for top executives, routine and substantial padding of expense accounts, and many others. At the corporate level, analysis of tax implications has become so important that, according to Gibney, "taxes are now the *motivating* factor in thousands of business maneuvers. The very words 'tax considerations' have acquired a magic ring." [7] The same author cites Internal Revenue Service figures for 1958 of approximately one and a half million dollars in back taxes and penalties—based, of course, on the usual selective examination of returns. And he reports statisticians as having calculated that "honest payment by everybody liable to income tax would enable the government *to decrease the general tax burden by 40 per cent.*" [8]

This last figure suggests rather graphically the largely unrecognized or passed over, yet very real, cost to the individual citizen of tax crimes. With respect to some of the common regulatory offenses discussed earlier, the citizenry feels the impact in an even more diffuse and indirect way—by being subjected to monopolistic manipulation, unnecessarily high prices, and so on. Each type of white-collar crime does inflict some form of major social cost on society, whether this comes readily to public attention or not. Hence the view frequently adopted by white-collar offenders that nobody is really being hurt by

[6] C. Wright Mills, *The Power Elite* (New York: Oxford University Press, Inc., 1957), p. 155.
[7] Gibney, *op. cit.*, p. 221.
[8] *Ibid.*, p. 201.

their behavior must be seen in *objective* terms as a convenient form of self-deception. Of course, we should keep in mind that in many instances "view" is too strong a word here. Rather than making a conscious decision to violate the law, the individual is behaving in ways strongly encouraged by certain prevailing attitude and value patterns (of which more below), and also, as I have just indicated, such behavior is shaped by the structural features of our highly institutionalized "tax game."

An area in which the social costs of white-collar crime have received a fair bit of public airing, and in which it has become increasingly difficult for both the offender and the "victim" not to appreciate the real harms attending violation, is that of food and drug regulation —especially cases bordering on or constituting "medical" fraud. Discernible costs from such offenses are of various kinds. Recent Congressional investigations, together with muckraking efforts by some well-informed journalists, have charged the American drug industry with stifling possible lines of medical progress, with maintaining excessively high drug prices, and as a result earning unconscionably high profits. Related practices laid to the industry have included questionable drug advertising (with an unnecessary and costly emphasis on drug trade names rather than generic names), price-administering, and other activities aimed at limiting competition.[9] While many of the societal costs in this area are thus strictly financial ones, even more alarming are the prevalence of deceptive drug claims and the dangers involved in release to the open market of new and inadequately tested drugs (as well, of course, as drugs known to have potential harmful effects or side-effects that are inadequately indicated).[10]

Although there have been attempts to control such practices through regulatory statutes and administrative action, there has also been substantial resistance to governmental activity in this area. As sociologist Bernard Barber has pointed out, it has usually required some kind of crisis situation to propel the frequently voiced reform proposals into actual legislation. Thus he notes that the Pure Food and Drug Act of 1906, the first major control bill, was itself passed as a result of the exposure of conditions in the meat industry. The Food, Drug and Cosmetic Act of 1938 (which gave the Food and Drug

[9] For a succinct summary see Bernard Barber, *Drugs and Society* (New York: Russell Sage Foundation, 1967), pp. 117–33.

[10] A thorough treatment of such matters may be found in James Harvey Young, *The Medical Messiah* (Princeton: Princeton University Press, 1967).

Administration the power to test and hence control the introduction to the market of new drugs) was passed in the wake of another crisis —in which over one hundred people died following the early marketing of a particular form of one of the first "miracle" drugs. And the Kefauver-Harris Bill of 1962, which strengthened the Administration's testing and licensing powers yet further, followed the thalidomide tragedy—in which thousands of deformed babies were born of mothers who had taken that tranquilizer early in pregnancy.[11] With respect to administering such statutes, Barber states:

> The Food and Drug Administration has had great difficulties in exercising the control that legislation has assigned to it, namely, the control over accurate labeling, safety, and efficacy. It has had trouble recruiting good staff, in keeping up with its work load, and in keeping its staff from resigning to work for better pay in the drug industry. It has been under pressure from legislators, other government agencies, from the drug industry, the medical profession, and from the general public.[12]

It is significant—as an illustration of the structural and value-related aspects of this phenomenon—that medical fraud in our society ranges from deceptive practices in the marketing of drugs by major (and largely "respectable") pharmaceutical concerns to fraudulent propagation of "miracle" cures and "quack" remedies by individual (illicit) entrepreneurs. This wide range of practices, then, includes nonprofessional or incidental fraud, and also some instances in which the fraud itself becomes the operator's profession. If the broad social costs of the latter seem less impressive than those incurred through legitimate industry's activities, the immediate interpersonal costs—in terms of preying on the frustrations and wishful thinking of many ordinary American citizens—may be quite striking indeed. From fraudulent diet remedies to meaningless cancer "cures," from all-purpose "medical compounds" to various "royal jelly" preparations alleged to accomplish everything from curing heart disease to restoring sexual potency, from supposed hair restorers to bust developers—the repertoire of medical quackery to which Americans have persistently been exposed (and by which thousands of unfortunate people have heartlessly been deceived) is virtually endless.[13]

[11] Barber, *op. cit.*, pp. 130–31.
[12] *Ibid.*, pp. 131–32.
[13] See Young, *op. cit.*, for extensive documentation; also Gibney, *op. cit.*, Chap. 3. An early survey was made by T. Swann Harding, *The Popular Practice of Fraud* (New York: Longmans, Green & Co., 1935).

Of course such depredations scarcely represent a new development, nor one that is uniquely American. Frustrated, suffering, or doomed individuals will always harbor hopes for "some way out," and perhaps there will always be an unscrupulous character willing to take advantage of their vulnerability. Yet Americans seem almost peculiarly susceptible to this form of fraud, perhaps in part because of the dominant theme of optimism that has permeated our value system. In concluding his recent and comprehensive survey of medical fraud, James Harvey Young noted that despite significant regulatory gains, quackery remains "a major social problem." While pointing out that some forms of pseudo-medical deception are bound to be with us always, Young did however express guarded optimism that the level of such criminality might be receding. "Ever stronger federal regulation, more rigorous state laws better enforced, education more appropriately aimed than in the past, an increasing adequacy of sound medical care for a larger portion of the population, these forces might be expected eventually to reduce in some measure quackery's enormous toll in wasted dollars and frustrated hopes for health." [14]

Equally pervasive at all levels of our society—and hence, once again, suggesting that the criminality in question involves a great deal more than the unscrupulousness of particular individuals—are numerous other types of consumer fraud. On the one hand we have the various more or less sophisticated forms of fraud (can we call them anything less?) perpetrated by big business through national advertising. As our laws and regulations and their administration now stand, the amount of fraudulent advertising that is patently illegal is perhaps very small. Yet any sensitive observer of the American scene recognizes that modern mass advertising at its heart represents a kind of institutionalization of deception and misrepresentation. Indeed many perceptive social critics insist it is nothing less than an enormous swindle—albeit a somewhat genteel one. We are all too familiar with advertising's appeal to the emotions, its play on (and to some extent creation of) status anxieties, its continuous use of techniques of symbol-manipulation that in other contexts would be called the devices of "propaganda," its relentless insistence on the individual's ever-expanding consumption "needs"—whether related to real need and usefulness or not. American advertising has perfected, perhaps to a degree not yet attained elsewhere, great skill in "creating" commodity obsolescence. It has also

[14] Young, *op. cit.*, p. 433.

made ingenious (though basically exploitative) use of some psychological and social scientific knowledge about man's basic impulses as a grounding for advertising and marketing campaigns—through the so-called "motivation research" that Vance Packard vigorously exposed in his book *The Hidden Persuaders*.[15] Overall, it has demonstrated a thoroughgoing commitment to and promotion of the values of "conspicuous consumption" and "pecuniary emulation" so trenchantly commented upon by Thorstein Veblen in his classic *Theory of the Leisure Class*.[16]

To what extent can we indict advertising as a component of what is commonly termed "white-collar crime?" Although many advertising appeals and campaigns come very close to constituting downright frauds in their own right, it seems to me that the greater significance of advertising for an understanding of the crime problem lies in its more subtle effects on American values. Not only does deceptive advertising spill over at its edges into instances of clearly illegal fraud (as, for example, in medical quackery advertisements), but the cumulative impact of advertising is to nurture a disposition both to engage in and to succumb to fraudulent practices and appeals—perpetrated by whatever specific techniques, having whatever specific content, occurring incidentally or systematically, in all institutional realms and at all social levels of our society. Of course we know that spokesmen for advertising interests will insist that advertising merely reflects American values, it does not create them. (And other significant arguments will be advanced in its behalf: that it has expanded consumer choice, led to a competitive improvement in products, facilitated mass distribution, and so on.) Advertisers will even cite sociological findings I mentioned in an earlier chapter, suggesting that the mass media have primarily a reinforcement effect, and hence do not directly form or shape values and behavior.

While this may to some extent be true of any specific advertising campaign in the short run, when we consider the long-term effect of advertising as a whole (in which certain major themes have clearly predominated, regardless of the products involved) the claim appears disingenuous in the extreme. Mass advertising promotes a philosophy of behavior and of man's nature which cannot help but exert indirect

[15] Vance Packard, *The Hidden Persuaders* (New York: David McKay Co., Inc., 1957).
[16] Thorstein Veblen, *The Theory of the Leisure Class* (New York: Random House, Inc., Modern Library, 1934).

influence on the value patterns and dominant activities of our society. In his lively critique of American life *Culture Against Man,* anthropologist Jules Henry has nicely summarized the "pecuniary conception of man" that "advertising as a philosophical system" displays:

Insatiably desiring, infinitely plastic, totally passive, and always a little bit sleepy; unpredictably labile and disloyal (to products); basically woolyminded and nonobsessive about traditional truth; relaxed and undemanding with respect to the canons of traditional philosophy, indifferent to its values, and easily moved to buy whatever at the moment seems to help his underlying personal inadequacies—this is pecuniary philosophy's conception of man and woman in our culture.

As Henry goes on to comment, the obvious flaw in this contemptuous view is that it sees man as expendable, "for without man there could be no products—a matter of elementary pecuniary biology." [17]

Surely the far-reaching ramifications of this philosophical outlook are integrally tied up with the pervasive phenomenon of fraud in American life. I shall return to this and related value patterns in further discussion below. Let me simply emphasize here that the seemingly diverse types of fraudulent behavior exhibited in our society are properly viewed as exhibiting some important common elements. Whether the offense involves income tax evasion by an individual or misrepresentation in the prospectus for a stock offering, improper labeling of drugs or collusive agreement to overprice in a particular industrial market, a philosophy of contempt for and manipulation of individuals at least subtly colors the behavior. Similarly the perpetual exposure of the public to high-pressure sales techniques, hyperbole in advertising, and mass depersonalizing of seller-consumer relations, induces a kind of narcotization to fraud in which the citizenry becomes largely inured to deceptive practice, conditioned to uncritical responses to appeals and deals, with each potential "victim" of fraud himself prepared to capitalize on whatever fraudulent opportunities present themselves. There is, then, a mass susceptibility to fraud, a collective leaning toward a "putting something over" outlook—for which advertising, along with other major agencies of value shaping and reinforcement, bears at least some degree of responsibility.

[17] Jules Henry, *Culture Against Man* (New York: Random House, Inc., Vintage Books, 1963), pp. 79, 80.

At roughly the other end of a continuum of fraudulent practices we find the crass exploitation of the individual consumer by the lone merchant—of the sort Caplovitz uncovered in such magnitude in *The Poor Pay More.* Again, as in the case of the smaller-scale medical frauds, the social costs are primarily personal and immediate ones— inflicted largely on the already deprived segments of the population. In such cases ignorance on the consumer's part, more than his personal avarice, plays heavily into the hands of the exploiter. General cultural pressure—to adopt particular patterns of consumption, particular attitudes toward social status and status symbols, and the like—does enter into the picture here too.

Embezzlement

An important category of crime by "respectables" that is closely related to the traditional white-collar offenses is that of embezzlement, or theft by employees—who violate their positions of trust by converting their employers' money to their own use. Such thefts occur at all levels of business, are perpetrated through a variety of techniques (often entailing substantial alteration of financial documents), and involve widely varying amounts of money—ranging from the major theft of bank funds by the trusted vice president, to the persistent pocketing of small sums by clerks in retail establishments.

Once again, unfortunately, available official statistics cannot come even close to indicating the true scope of the problem. Embezzlements are notoriously underrecorded; according to some estimates no more than 1 per cent of all cases of trust violation result in criminal actions. The concern's interest in avoiding adverse publicity, its possible sympathy for the situation of a long-time employee, and its frequent unwillingness to expend the effort needed for prosecution, militate against formal legal action in such cases. As a classic study of theft noted:

It is well known, also, that a large number of cases of embezzlement never reach the courts because agreements for repayment have been made. Indeed, probation is frequently granted for the purpose of allowing and securing restitution. States' attorneys and criminal courts spend a large part of their time arranging such settlements in cases of fraud, embezzlement and other types of theft. The social attitudes which make possible such legal phenomena need only be set beside those which refer to crimes of violence, to be appreciated.[18]

According to a management consultant who has made a special study of employee theft, "the losses to American business through embezzlement, missing inventory, manipulation and falsification of records . . . which incidentally do not include such items as padded overtime, theft of company secrets, and customer ill will, exceed four million dollars a day, every working day of the week, every week of the year." [19] Other specialists estimate that the total amount stolen by employees in any one year may be twice as great as the total loss from burglaries, armed robberies, auto thefts, and pickpocketing. It has even been suggested that "With the rapid and extensive increase in white-collar crime and the abasement of our ethics of fair play and honesty, we are inexorably heading toward that final denouement, a nation of embezzlers." [20]

The process by which a long-time and highly trusted employee— particularly one fairly high up in the firm's organizational structure —engages in a major breach of trust must be a complex one. Here again, the traditional explanations of crime—poverty, mental illness, and so on—do not seem very helpful. Most persons convicted of sizeable embezzlements come from middle-class backgrounds; and it was their presumed respectability, responsibility, and stability that earned for them such positions of trust in the first place. Only very rarely do such persons have any involvement in delinquency or crime prior to their acts of embezzling. And it is most unlikely that they will have entered into the trusted employment in question with the express aim of committing these crimes.

Donald Cressey, the leading sociological student of embezzlement, interviewed a great many convicted embezzlers in prison, in the hope of finding out just what it was in their situations and minds that led them into such acts. He was convinced that it was less important to catalogue in detail the personal and social characteristics of these offenders, which did not appear to have great bearing on their crimes, than to understand in some depth the social-psychological processes by which highly "respectable" persons turn to embezzlement. After

[18] Jerome Hall, *Theft, Law and Society* (Boston: Little, Brown And Company, 1935), p. 309.
[19] Norman Jaspan with Hillel Black, *The Thief in the White Collar* (Philadelphia: J. B. Lippincott Co., 1960), p. 234.
[20] *Ibid.*, p. 15.

considering and revising various plausible hypotheses in the light of his extensive interview data, Cressey finally came up with the following formulation:

> Trusted persons become trust violators when they conceive of themselves as having a financial problem which is nonshareable, are aware that this problem can be secretly resolved by violation of the position of financial trust, and are able to apply to their own conduct in that situation verbalizations which enable them to adjust their conceptions of themselves as trusted persons with their conceptions of themselves as users of the entrusted funds or property.[21]

As we can easily see, there are three major elements involved here. The first, existence of a pressing financial problem that the individual conceives of as nonshareable, suggests the importance of the offender's having come to feel that other avenues of help are not open to him. It is not so much the objective severity of the problem that is crucial, but rather how the individual himself defines his situation. A difficulty that one person sees as highly disturbing and which he finds himself unable to communicate to others (for reasons of pride, for example), another person may handle more openly and with much greater ease.

A second key element is that of "opportunity" referred to earlier. Not only must the individual be in a situation where objective opportunity for theft is present, but he must also recognize that opportunity. In most of the occupational situations giving rise to embezzlement the existence of such opportunities is patent, and the fact that they are at times exploited is well known to the employee—the very practice of "bonding" supposedly trusted employees makes this feature of the situation glaringly evident to them. Typically too, specialized skills other than those ordinarily used in the daily routine need not be learned. As one embezzler told Cressey, "In my case I did not use any techniques which any ordinary accountant in my position could not have used; they are known by all accountants, just like the abortion technique is know by all doctors." [22]

For a general understanding of embezzlement in American society, it is probably the third element—the individual's conceptualization and verbalization of the trust violation in such a way that it can be reconciled with his conception of himself as a basically honest person—that

---

[21] Donald P. Cressey, *Other People's Money* (New York: The Free Press, 1953), p. 30.
[22] *Ibid.*, p. 82.

is most significant. A common way of thinking about such a phenomenon would be to term it "rationalization." However that term usually connotes an after-the-fact justification. Research into the embezzlement process has revealed that what is involved is really not such an *ex post facto* rationalizing. On the contrary, it appears that such justifications have been internalized by the individuals *before* they commit their acts of embezzlement; it is exposure to and awareness of them that permits the otherwise respectable person to engage in trust violation. As Cressey has put it in a more recent article:

> Vocabularies of motive are not something invented by embezzlers (or anyone else) on the spur of the moment. Before they can be taken over by an individual, these verbalizations exist as group definitions in which the behavior in question, even crime, is in a sense *appropriate*. There are any number of popular ideologies that sanction crime in our culture: "Honesty is the best policy, but business is business"; "It is all right to steal a loaf of bread when you are starving"; "All people steal when they get in a tight spot." Once these verbalizations have been assimilated and internalized by individuals, they take a form such as: "I'm only going to use the money temporarily, so I am borrowing, not stealing," or "I have tried to live an honest life but I've had nothing but troubles, so to hell with it." [23]

Cressey's analysis clearly has its limitations. It does not enable us to predict which individuals are going to engage in embezzlement, and the formulation would probably be very difficult to test in a statistical sense. Perhaps there is some systematic patterning that underlies the response of specific kinds of persons to specific kinds of problems as being nonshareable. Nonetheless, this formulation does give us a meaningful sense of the sorts of processes that probably are necessary if embezzlement is to result. And, particularly important, it highlights the cultural grounding of this form of crime. That justifications for breach of financial trust exist in our culture does not, of course, mean that individuals are in fact quite justified in committing acts of embezzlement. It does strongly suggest, however, that a "rotten apple" approach to the problem will not suffice. For embezzlement to be significantly curbed, modification of powerful value themes of American culture will be required: it will not do simply to concentrate on better screening of prospective employees and more careful supervision of their activities (helpful as such efforts might be).

[23] Cressey, "The Respectable Criminal," *Trans-action*, March–April, 1965.

Also relevant to the embezzlement problem is the factor of perception of a "victim," which I mentioned earler. At least one study has shown that public attitudes toward stealing vary according to the nature of the (hypothetical) organization against which the theft might be directed. Respondents in this study said they would steal with least reluctance from a large business firm, with somewhat more reluctance from government agencies, and with still more from small businesses.[24] Presumably this reflected some kind of ordering as to the seriousness of the victimization in such cases—although concern about dangers of being caught may also influence attitudes toward stealing. Here again we see evidence of the cultural underpinnings of crime. These findings do not simply reveal personal viewpoints that have been arrived at by particular individuals in isolation, but rather reflect a patterning of attitudes in line with the value priorities given emphasis in our society.

Nonprofessional Forgery and Shoplifting

We might also include under the category of "respectable" crime certain other kinds of theft by amateurs, such as nonprofessional check forgery and amateur shoplifting. Naïve check forgery (by individuals having no previous criminal record or involvement) is an offense usually committed by persons who evidence a "distaste or sense of repugnance toward forms of crime other than forgery." Indeed, forgers "come from a class of persons we would ordinarily not expect to yield recruits to the criminal population," the forgery representing "behavior which is out of character or 'other than usual' for the persons involved."[25] Edwin Lemert, the leading sociological student of forgery, also found that a cumulative process of tensions leading to feelings of social isolation usually characterized the situation in which "well-educated, often gifted, and certainly otherwise law-abiding persons" turned to this crime. Among the forgers he studied, Lemert found, for example, a high rate of severe marital problems and dis-

---

[24] See Erwin O. Smigel, "Public Attitudes Toward Stealing as Related to the Size of the Victim Organization," *American Sociological Review*, 21 (June, 1956), 320–27.

[25] Edwin M. Lemert, "An Isolation and Closure Theory of Naïve Check Forgery," in Lemert, *Human Deviance, Social Problems, and Social Control* (Englewood Cliffs, N.J.: Prentice-Hall, Inc., 1967), p. 102.

ruptions. But whatever forces drove the individual into a position of isolation, they seemed to result in a kind of "dialectical" process in which he found himself in pressing need of money (whether for gambling, to meet debts, to "live it up," or whatever) and at the same time experienced an ever-intensifying sense of being isolated.

Forgery became, for these individuals, a way of achieving "closure" in such a high-tension situation. Its extremely low visibility, and the ambiguous public reaction to passing bad checks (though forgery is technically a major crime, informally we do not tend to consider it so serious—and indeed the line between intentional forgery and a mistake is sometimes hard to establish), help to make forgery a promising "solution" for such individuals. Furthermore, forgery is very easy to commit. When Lemert asked a class of college students to explain how they would obtain and pass a bad check if circumstances required such behavior, they indicated a wide range of ingenious techniques—very similar to those actually employed by the forgers he had studied—and only one student out of the twenty-five questioned was unable to suggest a plausible technique.

While it appears, then, that this offense often reflects situational factors creating extreme tension for the particular individuals, there are also more general cultural aspects of the behavior. As I just pointed out, the public condemnation of forgery is far from being uniform and vigorous. Lemert suggests, too, that the precautions taken by business to guard against the passing of bad checks may even serve as a "challenge to contrive workable evasions of the protective devices." Even more crucially, at least some of the pressures driving individuals into forgery offenses reflect the dominant values in our culture:

. . . for some of the check forgers ordinary expenditure behavior in our society took a desperate kind of meaning. Indulgence in clothes, automobiles, housing, and expensive leisure time pursuits seemed to fulfill intricate, specialized socio-psychological functions over and beyond the satisfactions people ordinarily or "modally" receive from buying such things. These people "get the bug," as one detective put it; they become fixated upon some object and spend most if not all of their waking moments scheming how to obtain it. Such fixating, in part a response to high-pressure advertising and selling methods, is, we urge, more commonly the reaction of the socially isolated person.[26]

[26] *Ibid.*, p. 107.

Nonprofessional shoplifting is another form of criminal behavior extremely prevalent among otherwise respectable Americans.[27] It is widely recognized that an enormous amount of petty shoplifting goes undetected. And many of the cases that are detected are never even reported to the police. According to some estimates, as much as one and a half million dollars worth of goods may be taken by shoplifters from American retailers each year. Store protection specialists report that most of these losses can be attributed to the acts of "snitches" (amateurs) rather than to the work of professional "boosters." Research has shown that amateur shoplifters represent close to a cross sample of the general population in terms of socioeconomic status, and that women shoplifters greatly outnumber men. Amateur shoplifters steal for their own use, rather than seeking to convert the goods for profit; many of these petty thefts by females represent attempts to garner items they are unable to buy because of limited shopping budgets. Although these women do not think of themselves as criminals at the time they commit their offenses, they are often quick to admit the theft when they are apprehended, and usually (as mentioned in an earlier chapter) they are so jolted by the experience that their violations then cease. There is some evidence of seasonal variation in shoplifting—one study showing especially high rates for the months of October through December (a time of special budgetary strain).

Most nonprofessional shoplifting, then, can probably be attributed to individual feelings of deprivation—not of a really pressing sort, but rather distress over inaccessibility of relatively minor items. These feelings themselves, however, can only be appreciated by taking account of the broader cultural context. The view that the department store is not really "hurt" by such theft, the satisfaction Americans often find in individually "putting something over" on any large institutional unit, and the effects of status-striving pressures on American consumption patterns all may be implicated in this type of criminality.

Confidence Games

In the strictest sense confidence games do not involve "respectable crime" since ordinarily they are perpetrated by professional

[27] See Mary Owen Cameron, *The Booster and the Snitch* (New York: The Free Press, 1964). For a brief summary of findings on shoplifting, see Gibbons, *Society, Crime and Criminal Careers*, pp. 287–94.

swindlers. They deserve inclusion in the present discussion, however, for at least two reasons. To be successful a confidence game requires the participation of one or more "respectables" who are themselves prepared to engage in illegal or at least morally questionable behavior. Secondly, it is quite apparent that professional and nonprofessional fraud are indirectly related to each other by virtue of broad cultural themes in American life from which they both derive substantial support. These themes bear both on the inclination to defraud others and on the susceptibility to being defrauded.

While there is a variety of standard confidence games (of both the relatively elaborate "big con" and the more limited "short con" types), all these swindles have certain common basic principles and procedures.[28] Con games always require locating a sucker (known in the swindler's argot as the "mark") who is willing to profit through a dishonest deal; establishing some degree of rapport (a relation of "confidence") with him; and then gaining access to his funds—of which he is eventually relieved. Because of the extent to which he is "taken in" by the swindler, the mark never realizes (until it is too late) that he is the object of, rather than a conspirator destined to benefit from, the swindle. David Maurer, a leading student of confidence games, describes the key process nicely:

A confidence man prospers only because of the fundamental dishonesty of his victim. In his operations, he must first inspire a firm belief in his own integrity. Second, he brings into play powerful and well-nigh irresistible forces to excite the cupidity of the mark. Then he allows the victim to make large sums of money by means of dealings which are explained to him as being dishonest and hence a "sure thing." As the lust for large and easy profits is fanned into a hot flame, the mark puts all his scruples behind him. He closes out his bank account, liquidates his property, borrows from his friends, embezzles from his employer or his clients. In the mad frenzy of cheating someone else, he is unaware of the fact that he is the real victim, carefully selected and fattened for the kill. Thus arises the trite but nonetheless sage maxim: "You can't cheat an honest man." [29]

Precisely because the victim of the confidence game was himself trying to gain dishonestly, he is most unlikely to lodge a complaint with

[28] The following comments are based in part on my earlier article, "Sociological Analysis of Confidence Swindling," *Journal of Criminal Law, Criminology, and Police Science,* 48 (October, 1957), 296–304. The classic study of con games is David W. Maurer, *The Big Con* (New York: Signet Books, 1940, 1962). See also Sutherland, *The Professional Thief.*

[29] Maurer, *op. cit.,* pp. 13–14.

the police. As a result—and quite apart from either the "fix" that some-times may protect the big-time professional swindler, or the statutory intricacies that may in some jurisdictions make effective prosecution of con men difficult—the con game carries considerable immunity from control by law enforcement agencies. It has been estimated that no more than 5 to 10 per cent of the victims of confidence swindles even report the offense to the police, and of course a substantial proportion of such reports in turn fail to result in convictions. Specialists are con-vinced, however, that con games and related frauds constitute one of the largest categories of crime in our society. Maurer suggests that confidence games may have produced "more illicit profit for the opera-tors and for the law than all other forms of professional crime (except-ing violations of the prohibition law and illicit gambling) over the same period of time." [30]

How can we account for the apparently widespread susceptibility to these nefarious schemes? Ignorance is hardly a sufficient explanation, for the best marks are often persons of considerable education who have achieved significant occupational success. Actually, individuals of all sorts in our society seem to yield readily to the swindler's wiles, and it is unlikely that this victim-proneness is dying out. A recent news account of con games known to the police in Boston referred to such swindling as a "growing and dangerous menace" in that city. A detec-tive was quoted as saying that "people just don't seem to learn that you can't get something for nothing. Barnum was wrong when he said there's a sucker born every minute. They're born every half-minute here in Boston." [31]

Vulnerability to con games can be explained on at least two levels— one centering on the very nature of the personal interaction involved, and the other placing such swindling in the broad cultural context of modern American society. It is significant, to begin with, that the con game is, in a very real sense, a *game* (and perhaps noteworthy that confidence rackets are called "games," whereas other criminal offenses are designated in much more somber terms). As the classic social theo-rist Georg Simmel stated:

All the forms of interaction or sociation among men—the wish to outdo, exchange, formation of parties, the desire to wrest something from the other, the hazards of accidental meetings and separations, the change

[30] *Ibid.*, p. 15.
[31] *Boston Globe*, September 8, 1968, p. 20.

between enmity and cooperation, the overpowering by ruse and revenge—
in the seriousness of reality, all of these are imbued with purposive con-
tents. In the game, they lead their own lives; they are propelled exclusively
by their own attraction. For even where the game involves a monetary
stake . . . to the person who really enjoys it, its attraction rather lies in the
dynamics and hazards of the sociologically significant forms of activity
themselves. The more profound, double sense of "social game" is that not
only the game is played in a society (as its external medium) but that, with
its help, people actually "play" "society." [32]

At least some of the appeal confidence swindling intrinsically holds for
the participants may be attributable to this "games" aspect. The notion
that in all his social relations the individual is continuously engaged
in a process of "presentation of self"—that subtle awareness of and response to the image one is projecting and the reactions of others to it,
emphasized in the writings of sociologist Erving Goffman[33] finds illustration in the con game situation. Indeed, as Maurer points out, "Big-
time confidence games are in reality only carefully rehearsed plays in
which every member of the cast *except the mark* knows his part perfectly." [34] Playing such roles successfully requires a great deal of skill
and subtlety in interpersonal behavior, and hence may provide the
effective swindler with a considerable sense of accomplishment. Then
too, as one observer has commented, "Above all, every deception, every
imposture is an assumption of power. The person deceived is reduced
in stature, symbolically nullified, while the imposter is temporarily
powerful, even greater than if he were the real thing." [35]

If the inherent attractions for the con man (that complement the
basic goal of financial return) are readily apparent, there may be
equally powerful, if not quite so obvious, satisfactions accruing to the
mark. He too may be spurred on by power considerations; after all,
he seeks basically to "take advantage" of a supposed third party. And
in some instances the mark gets so carried away with the assumed
possibilities of the situation that inwardly he starts plotting to divest
the (unrealized) swindler of his share of the proceeds from the "deal."

[32] Kurt H. Wolff, ed., *The Sociology of Georg Simmel* (New York: The Free
Press, 1950), pp. 49–50.
[33] See Erving Goffman, *The Presentation of Self in Everyday Life* (New York:
Doubleday Anchor Books, 1959).
[34] Maurer, *op. cit.*, p. 91.
[35] Alexander Klein, ed., *Grand Deception* (New York: J. B. Lippincott Co.,
1955), p. 13.

In effect the actual victim enters into what might be called a spurious coalition with the swindler directed against an imaginary victim. The extent to which the mark tends to get "caught up in" this situation indicates not merely his dishonesty and greed, but probably as well that the satisfactions inherent in besting others in the intricate "game" of social interaction are centrally involved. At virtually every stage of the swindling process, in fact, the stratagems and difficulties that characterize all social relations are in evidence. Thus Goffman, in a perceptive analysis of the process of "cooling the mark out" (reconciling the victim to his loss and getting him out of the way), has shown that this feature of con games is in fact prototypical of a more general feature of social behavior—in which other losers (whether they be failing students, doomed patients, or the objects of misrepresentative sales pitches) are similarly "cooled out." [36]

But confidence swindling also presents features that are especially calculated, in terms of American institutions and values, to offer strong appeal and satisfaction for the parties to the game. The con man is generally recognized to be at or near the top of the underworld's status hierarchy. In part this is due to the sheer skill his job involves, and his ability to score without recourse to the use of weapons and threat of violence employed by professional "heavies." At the same time, the high esteem in which the successful swindler is held may also reflect the fact that his occupational techniques are ones that specifically receive strong social approval under dominant American values. Various observers have commented on the close relation between confidence swindling and salesmanship. As Maurer states, con men, in a sense, "only carry to an ultimate and very logical conclusion certain trends which are often inherent in various forms of legitimate business." [37] To a great extent our society is built upon the values of salesmanship in the broadest sense, with the manipulation of ideas and above all of people largely supplanting the craftsmen's creative skill as a highly prized quality of work. We revere the individual's ability to "sell a bill of goods," to "put across" his personality, to induce the confidence of others, to operate smoothly in social situations. These qualities are the very hallmark of the experienced swindler, con men having "cultivated the social side more than any other criminal group. They are able to fit in unobtru-

---

[36] Erving Goffman, "On Cooling the Mark Out: Some Aspects of Adaptation to Failure," *Psychiatry*, 15 (November, 1962), 451–63.

[37] Maurer, *op. cit.*, p. 150.

sively on any social level . . . Although their culture is not very deep, it is surprisingly wide and versatile." [38]

The close relation between con games and common business practice and values also helps to account for the apparently continuous supply of appropriate "marks." It is perhaps not surprising to find professional con men agreeing that businessmen make the best marks, and there seems to be strong feeling among them that American businessmen are particularly susceptible (although such swindling is of course far from being a uniquely American phenomenon). Maurer suggests that the American credo of rugged individualism and self-made success plays right into the swindler's hand. Because of this ideology the successful businessman tends to credit himself with unusually good business judgment and risk-taking ability, and these beliefs serve to clinch the circle of susceptibility, once the con man creates initial interest in the "deal." The considerable emphasis on risk-taking in our society may also help to make American businessmen likely marks. As anthropologist Geoffrey Gorer has commented, gambling is "a respected and important component in many business ventures . . . . Like the gambler 'for fun' the American businessman is generally prepared to take proportionately far greater risks than his European equivalent." [39] Further facilitating the work of the con man is the characteristically easygoing gregariousness of Americans—which renders possible and plausible the swindler's approach to a complete stranger, in which he suggests an underhanded but (supposedly) mutually beneficial scheme.

A Society of Frauds?

No thinking American can doubt that fraudulent behavior is commonplace in our society. Deception and predatory economic behavior are not restricted to any particular sector of American life. On the contrary, fraud cuts across various institutional realms in such a way that we are forced to see it as a significant characteristic of our entire social system. Advertising fraud, consumer fraud, medical fraud, welfare and charity frauds, con games big and small, forgeries, embezzlements, violations of securities laws and copyright regulations—all

[38] *Ibid.,* p. 155.
[39] Geoffrey Gorer, *The American People* (New York: W. W. Norton & Company, Inc., 1948), p. 178.

these and more represent symptoms of an underlying systematic disorder. And, as I have pointed out, most of these substantive types of fraud themselves exist on several different levels of society, and in several different forms—with the dividing lines between legal and illegal, and within the illegal category between professional and nonprofessional, exhibiting an extremely hazy quality.

What is at least as disturbing as the widespread prevalence of fraud is the ambiguous and largely apathetic public reaction to it. The split between our public rhetoric and ideology of honesty and fair dealing, on the one hand, and our private morality of "anything goes," on the other, is evident, yet it seems to be a discrepancy about which nobody really wants to do very much. Americans have become alarmingly inured to the practice of fraud, perhaps to the extent of having concluded that it is an inevitable concomitant of their way of life, of which only the most disgruntled troublemakers would complain.

Each exposé of a particular form of institutionalized immorality is followed, after not very much time, by a return to passive acquiescence and individual willingness to "play the game." How many of us think twice about the TV-quiz show and disk-jockey payola scandals that supposedly shocked the entire country in the late 1950's? Yet the practices revealed in those inquiries represented something close to a high point in an industry's contempt for the public, and were clearly symptomatic of the far-reaching nature of attitudes favorable to fraud in our society. Noting that the "contestants" who engaged in collusive quiz-show deceptions were mostly well-educated white-collar workers and professionals, Meyer Weinberg has suggested that their behavior may have reflected their expertise in handling and managing other people.

They did not find it difficult to enter into rigging for this, too, was nothing but a gigantic "handling" operation. Those who manipulate others make handles of themselves. Rigging was a highly profitable way of allowing one's self to be used for another's gain. The fact that it was so well paid was its cardinal justification. Was it, after all, less moral than the deliberately stalling letters a sales correspondent might write to a complaining customer? Or, less moral than a public relations adviser who helps arrange the emotions of people? Or, less moral than a professor who publishes books all but written by his graduate students? [40]

[40] Meyer Weinberg, *TV in America: The Morality of Hard Cash* (New York: Ballantine Books, 1962), p. 222.

Even though some of the contestants were fairly certain that these "business" principles were wrong, all of them, Weinberg insists, had absorbed the principles and acted under their influence.

Despite tightened Federal Communication Commission control, some official recognition that much of the commercial television output is "a vast wasteland" (the famous 1961 speech by Commissioner Newton Minow), and growing interest in and (limited) support of public broadcasting schemes, we may well wonder whether the impact of these scandals on television practice was really a very potent one. Certainly the casual viewer gets the impression that, just as in the case of the electrical conspiracy, there was a rapid reversion to "business as usual." Likewise, major revelations of political corruption, of the rigging of sports events, and other similar frauds, seem to come and go over the years—for a moment giving rise to fervent exclamations of shock and dismay, but producing little meaningful change in underlying institutions and practices.

A few years ago Jessica Mitford's *The American Way of Death* appeared—a remarkable, well-documented, and biting attack on what is perhaps the apotheosis of sharp sales practice in our society, the conduct of the American funeral industry.[41] Although it achieved both critical acclaim and best-sellerdom, it is unlikely that this revealing and sensible effort appreciably influenced actual practice. Perhaps a major exception to this general tendency has been the reasonably successful effort to get the American automobile industry to institute much needed safety features in their new model cars (not exactly a reduction in "fraud," unless in the very broadest sense), which seems to have been generated largely by Ralph Nader's powerful study *Unsafe at any Speed*.[42] In this instance—and in all other instances where public concern about fraud and related practices has been translated into official action—reform occurred only after explicitly political pressure was exerted; usually this has occurred through widely publicized hearings convened by Congressional committees or regulatory agencies.

[41] Jessica Mitford, *The American Way of Death* (New York: Simon and Schuster, Inc., 1963).
[42] Ralph Nader, *Unsafe at any Speed* (New York: Grossman, 1965). See also Jeffrey O'Connell and Arthur Myers, *Safety Last* (New York: Random House, Inc., 1968).

American Values and Fraud

It would seem to be in this very broad area of fraudulent behavior, rather than in that of interpersonal violence about which the public is so greatly exercised, that underlying values of modern American life most directly promote and shape criminality. In part what may be involved here is a stratum of "subterranean values"— values that are "in conflict or in competition with other deeply held values but which are still recognized and accepted by many." Such value contradictions may sometimes reflect a clash of subcultures or interest groups, but the situation may be even more complicated than that. These contradictions "may also exist within a single individual and give rise to profound feelings of ambivalence in many areas of life. In this sense, subterranean values are akin to private as opposed to public morality. They are values that the individual holds to and believes in but that are also recognized as being not quite *comme il faut.*" [43]

As Matza and Sykes go on to point out, the search for kicks, the drive toward "big-time spending," and the emphasis on "rep" that seem significant in the causation of much delinquency and crime "have immediate counterparts in the value system of the law-abiding," as indeed does a "taste for violence." Dual cultural traditions, then, may pull the individual in opposite directions, a point Sutherland also had in mind when he noted that a modern society invariably contained both definitions favorable to the law and definitions favorable to law violation. In the area of business values especially, as I have emphasized, this kind of duality is glaringly evident. Although business transactions ostensibly are to be governed by principles of honesty, mutuality of benefit, public accountability, and even some concern for the public interest, in fact the operative values all too often support secretive and deceptive efforts to maximize self-advantage without much regard for the other parties involved or for the general good.

Of course, this undercurrent of values conducive to business crimes and related offenses is not surprising, given the extensive influence of the "business spirit" in our society. Indeed, certain of the values that

[43] David Matza and Gresham Sykes, "Juvenile Delinquency and Subterranean Values," *American Sociological Review*, 26 (October, 1961), 716.

help promote criminality in America are far from being subterranean in character. Thus, sociologist Donald Taft has cited the following "characteristics of American society" as having possible significance in the causation of crime: "its dynamic quality, complexity, materialism, growing impersonality, individualism, insistence upon the importance of status, restricted group loyalties, survivals of frontier traditions, race discrimination, lack of scientific orientation in the social field, tolerance of political corruption, general faith in law, disrespect for some law, and acceptance of quasi-criminal exploitation." [44] While this list is something of a hodgepodge (including some subterranean values, some more dominant ones, and also a few behaviors that are more a result of certain values than values in their own right), the first few items—dynamism, complexity, materialism, impersonality, and individualism—may be especially noteworthy. These are clearly dominant values or characteristics of American life, and they seem in some sense to have very real bearing on at least some types of criminality.

As I pointed out in an earlier chapter, sociologists are reluctant to accept the idea that a society's major values or dominant characteristics "cause" crime. Because of their very dominance or socially approved nature, these elements also underlie a great deal of acceptable, sometimes highly desired behavior. And in either case, to consider them as major causal factors is difficult—because of the many other factors and processes intervening "between" the values and the acts. In any case, reference to such values clearly will not enable us to predict which individuals will commit crimes and which won't, since the very same values promote both law violation and law-abidingness.

At the same time, we can hardly ignore the fact that the general quality of American life significantly shapes and colors crime problems. It is true that the values promoting fraud are not uniquely American, nor is the institutional framework within which fraud thrives. To some extent, the impersonality, instrumentalism, and competitiveness that help to generate fraud are intrinsic to the nature of modern urbanized society. Sociologists frequently draw the basic distinction between the "primary relations" (intimate, spontaneous, diffuse, and guided by mutuality of ends) that tend to dominate social interaction in small homogeneous communities, and the "secondary relations" (segmentalized, impersonal, instrumental) that more typically charac-

[44] Taft and England, *Criminology,* p. 275.

terize complex societies. The inclination to try to "take advantage of" the other party is, in a sense, built into the structure of social relations in our kind of social order. Indeed, it is precisely for this reason that the so-called formal mechanisms of social control, including law, must play such an important role in modern society.

It is also true, as I have noted, that the values that promote these kinds of crime are not unique to capitalism. Socialist regimes have found it quite impossible to eliminate all impulses toward accumulation of property, competition, even "profit." Nor have such regimes always found themselves able to do away entirely with such devices as competitive advertising—even where the competitors may be state owned and controlled. Despite these points, it is difficult not to conclude that American society has embraced an ideology of what might be termed capitalism with a vengeance—a reverence for the values of individualism, competition, and profit of such intensity as to provide incentives to crime that go well beyond a level that must be considered inevitable in a modern complex society, even a basically capitalist one.

In such a situation, in which these crime-encouraging values and characteristics are diffused throughout diverse realms of the social system, one cannot help but be struck by the interrelatedness of numerous practices that otherwise might be viewed as discrete items of behavior. The early French criminologist Gabriel Tarde contended that "All the important acts of social life are carried out under the domination of example," and stated further: "Criminality always being . . . a phenomenon of imitative propagation . . . the aim is to discover . . . which among these various spreadings of example which are called instruction, religion, politics, commerce, industry, are the ones that foster, and which the ones that impede, the expansion of crime." [45] Although most modern social psychologists would consider "imitation" a grossly unsophisticated concept for explaining human behavior, few would dispute the contention that values and practices "spread" from one unit of society to another—in fact, the attempt to spell out the complex processes by which this may occur lies at the very heart of social psychology.

As we have seen, major explanations of crime concentrate heavily on the significance of socialization processes and reference groups,

---

[45] Gabriel Tarde, *Penal Philosophy,* tr. Howell (Boston: Little, Brown And Company, 1912), p. 362.

as well as on such factors as socioeconomic status, felt deprivation, and opportunity. Taft has argued that "pattern setting by prestiged groups" is an important element of the American crime situation, insisting that the level of morality displayed by lawyers and judges, politicians, business and labor leaders, sports celebrities, and members of other prestigious subgroups has a special influence in shaping the "moral tone" of our society.[46] While it would not be easy to formulate this notion in terms offering a rigorous and testable theory of crime causation, in a more general sense it seems to have some validity. Certainly it is reasonable to think that the middle-level bank executive who embezzles has in some degree been influenced by revelations of upper-level defalcations, the professional con man by a realization that "everyone has his racket," the corporate offender by the belief that even government officials are corrupt. Surely this is what we mean when we say that "definitions favorable to law violation" exist and circulate within a society. That such definitions are so widespread makes clear why the rather glib distinction commonly drawn between "criminals" and the law-abiding is so difficult to maintain. And this existence of diffuse, almost omnipresent, crime-encouraging definitions seems also to present almost insurmountable obstacles for the would-be reformer.

Can We Curb Swindling?

It is commonly asserted, by those who feel great concern about this situation, that what is needed is a "return to morality." The emphasis usually is placed upon the reform of individuals; if each individual will only behave morally, then the entire situation will change. Without doubt, such an assertion is correct. But the problem remains: how can such modifications be effected? As some of the earlier discussion should have made clear, sociologists recognize that the motivation and behavior of man is deeply rooted in his culture and the institutional arrangements of his society. Accordingly, while it may not be a forlorn hope that at least some of the Americans now engaging in fraudulent practices might "pull themselves up by their bootstraps" and personally begin to act in a more "moral" fashion, a broadly based reduction in fraud requires a systematic program of reform that goes beyond the level of individuals.

[46] Taft and England, op. cit., Chap. 2.

Because that is true, and given the extent to which fraudulent behavior is deeply rooted in our present values and institutions, it is without doubt unrealistic to expect that we can eliminate it wholesale. That does not mean, however, that nothing can be done. If the American citizen really wants to, he can mount and support political and other actions that will begin to attack directly some of the institutionalized sources of fraud in our society. Presumably some of the needed reforms could be accomplished through self-regulation and internal controls on the part of particular industries and organizations. Structural change within an organization may eliminate some of the pressures and opportunities leading individuals at various levels within it to engage in certain kinds of fraudulent behavior. And of course self-imposed restraint—in competitive activities, advertising, and the like—could lead to substantial reform. It seems likely, however, that in this latter area strong government prodding, if not control, will be needed.

Sometimes it is argued that new laws will not help. Probably it is true that some fraud has been engendered by the very proliferation and complexity of our legal and regulatory provisions. Yet the failure of regulation has mainly come about through indifferent enforcement and the refusal to plug up "loopholes," rather than simply because there are too many laws. Nor is the frequent assertion that laws cannot change men's values and attitudes persuasive. Proper enforcement of laws in this area could rather quickly affect *behavior,* and studies even show that such behavioral change may later be accompanied by important changes in outlook. Furthermore, we should recognize that the area of white-collar crime and "respectable" fraud may be one of those in which the deterrent effect of criminal law is particularly strong. It is rather ironic that Americans persistently argue for stronger law enforcement aimed at offenses against which (because of the underlying pressures and situations driving people to the crime) the criminal law may have little deterrent effect, whereas here (where the offender usually has much to lose through severe sanctioning, and is often in a position to rationally assess the gains and costs of violation) little pressure for vigorous enforcement is exerted.[47]

Quite simply, a strong case can be made for clamping down on white-collar crime and related offenses. The direct cost of such crime

[47] This point has recently been made by sociologist William Chambliss, "Types of Deviance and Effectiveness of Legal Sanctions," *Wisconsin Law Review* (1967), pp. 703–19.

to society is substantial, the indirect cost in terms of promoting a climate of fraud may also be great, and these are offenses that can in some considerable measure effectively be curbed by criminal law. It should similarly be possible to reduce the number of major tax "loopholes" and perhaps modify and simplify the system of deductions and exemptions in such a way as to reduce both the invitation to and opportunity for tax dodging. Perhaps one of the most central reforms would be to exert much stricter governmental control (where self-regulation proves impossible) over deceptive advertising and sales practices. We are beginning to see action of this sort, through "truth in packaging" provisions and the like, but a great deal more needs to be done. If my analysis is correct, then the content of everyday advertising must be seen to have a special significance with respect to the prevalence of fraud in modern American life. The widespread acceptance of deception and misrepresentation as a basic feature of advertising promotes on a broad scale both the inclination to perpetrate fraud and the receptiveness to fraud—and hence must be radically altered. Just how far this process can go, given the nature of our competitive economy, and precisely what forms it should take, are matters that call for a specialized knowledge I do not have. There seems little doubt, however, that substantial restriction of the most blatant forms of deception could—well within the bounds of a viable capitalism—make for a major reduction in the institutionalized encouragement to fraud.

This is the kind of suggestion that, remarkably, is all too rare in discussions of crime. To say that we should combat crime by controls on advertising may seem to "the man in the street" barely relevant to those aspects of American crime that are generating the greatest public and official attention and concern. But here we confront one major area of crime that does seem at least potentially manageable, and that may have very broad ramifications affecting the moral tenor of our legal system and our society at large. That "respectable crime" has been an object of selective inattention in American life is itself one of the major crimes of our society.

6

UNNECESSARY CRIMES: THE PERILS OF OVERLEGISLATING

> We have made considerable efforts to discover what sort of person the offender is and why he has broken the law, and we rack our brains to find out what to do with him. This, however, is not enough. Hardly ever do we pause for a moment to examine critically the contents of that very law the existence of which alone makes it possible for the individual to offend against it.
>
> Hermann Mannheim, *Criminal Justice and Social Reconstruction*

If it is urgent that some existing criminal laws (such as those relating to white-collar crime) be more rigorously enforced, it is equally important for us to recognize that criminal sanctions are not necessarily appropriate to every effort at social control. When we attempt to employ the criminal law to regulate private morality, to enforce dominant conceptions of good taste, or to ensure political orthodoxy, we begin to run into very serious difficulties. Grave questions may be raised about both the propriety and the effectiveness of such efforts, and disinterested observers may well conclude that the social costs of seeking criminal law "solutions" in these areas greatly outweigh any social benefits that might result.

Philosophers of law and sociologists have long emphasized the limited effectiveness of criminal laws that do not have strong support in the society's dominant social norms. The eminent British philosopher Jeremy Bentham, in a statement the relevance of which remains strong today, asserted:

With what chance of success . . . would a legislator go about to extirpate drunkenness and fornication by dint of legal punishment? Not all the tortures which ingenuity could invent would compass it: and, before he had made any progress worth regarding, such a mass of evil would be produced by the punishment, as would exceed, a thousandfold, the utmost possible mischief of the offence.[1]

In similar vein, the American jurist Roscoe Pound wrote a famous essay on "The Limits of Effective Legal Action," [2] and sociologist William Graham Sumner advanced his well-known argument that the *mores* always precede and take precedence over mere laws.[3]

Nonetheless, as the quotation from Mannheim suggests, specialists in criminology have typically adopted a rather narrow perspective in which they focused inordinately on individual causation (and individual treatment)—along lines mentioned in earlier sections of this book. They have tended not to actively raise questions about what the substance of the criminal law should be, but rather to more or less take the existing laws as "given." Recently, however, two lines of inquiry and analysis—one developed by legal philosophers and legislative draftsmen, the other by sociologists—have jointly served to encourage a more active and critical scrutiny of the substantive provisions of the criminal law. A landmark in this trend, although the thrust of its basic argument was gradually built up through the earlier writings of certain criminal law specialists, was the 1957 report of the British governmental Committee on Homosexual Offences and Prostitution—usually known as the Wolfenden Committee, after its chairman.

The most controversial recommendation in this report asserted that private and consensual homosexual behavior on the part of adults should no longer be considered a criminal offense (a provision which has since been enacted by Parliament, and also has been recommended in this country under the Model Penal Code drafted by the American Law Institute). But perhaps even more significant than its specific recommendations was the general view of the functions of the criminal law expressed by the Committee. Criminal sanctions, it urged, should be used to maintain public order and decency, to protect individuals from offensive and injurious behavior and from exploitation and corruption—especially those who might have some special vulnerability. Beyond what might be necessary to carry out those pur-

---

[1] Jeremy Bentham, *An Introduction to the Principles of Morals and Legislation* (New York: Hafner Publishing Co., Inc., 1948), p. 320.

[2] Roscoe Pound, "The Limits of Effective Legal Action," *International Journal of Ethics*, 27 (January, 1917), 150–67.

[3] William Graham Sumner, *Folkways* (New York: Mentor Books, 1960).

poses, the criminal law should not interfere with the private lives of citizens. Moral repugnance alone, the Committee argued, does not provide a sufficient basis for invoking criminal sanctions: "Unless a deliberate attempt is to be made by society, acting through the agency of the law, to equate the sphere of crime with that of sin, there must remain a realm of private morality and immorality which is, in brief and crude terms, not the law's business. To say this is not to condone or encourage private immorality." [4]

A sharp rejoinder to this philosophy of the criminal law was developed by British jurist Patrick Devlin, who asserted that "the criminal law as we know it is based upon moral principle. In a number of crimes its function is simply to enforce a moral principle and nothing else." According to Devlin, "The suppression of vice is as much the law's business as the suppression of subversive activities; it is no more possible to define a sphere of private morality than it is to define one of private subversive activity." [5] Partly in reaction to Devlin's argument, H. L. A. Hart, a leading British legal philosopher, has defended the Wolfenden Committee's conception of the role of the criminal law—placing (as the Committee in effect did) the burden of justifying applications of the law squarely on those who would seek to impose such control over the behavior of individuals. Condemning an overeager recourse to attempts at legal control, Hart called upon basic principles of individual liberty as support for the Committee's approach:

. . . a right to be protected from the distress which is inseparable from the bare knowledge that others are acting in ways you think wrong, cannot be acknowledged by anyone who recognises individual liberty as a value. For the extension of the utilitarian principle that coercion may be used to protect men from harm, so as to include their protection from this form of distress, cannot stop there. If distress incident to the belief that others are doing wrong is harm, so also is the distress incident to the belief that others are doing what you do not want them to do. To punish people for causing this form of distress would be tantamount to punishing them simply because others object to what they do; and the only liberty that could

[4] Committee on Homosexual Offences and Prostitution, *Report,* Home Office, Cmnd. 247 (London: Her Majesty's Stationery Office, 1957), pp. 9–10, 24.

[5] Patrick Devlin, *The Enforcement of Morals* (London: Oxford University Press, 1965), pp. 7, 13–14. (The statement under discussion here was first presented by Devlin in an address before the British Academy, delivered in March of 1959.)

coexist with this extension of the utilitarian principle is liberty to do those things to which no one seriously objects.[6]

Hart also questioned whether legal proscription of consensual homosexual acts would either effectively curb the offending behavior or even help to support the general morality of society, and he noted the considerable human suffering such interference with private lives might produce.

Along with this jurisprudential controversy, which has been couched largely in rather abstract philosophical and legal terms, the growing sociological concern with societal reactions to deviance (discussed briefly in Chapter 3) has directed attention to both the substance and the administration of criminal law. While sociologists have long been aware of the phenomenon of "patterned evasion of norms" [7]—situations in which there is widespread deviation from a professed norm, and hence a kind of institutionalized ambivalence regarding the behavior in question—they are now beginning to look even more directly at the sociolegal problems that lie along the "borderland of criminal justice," [8] problems which until a few years ago were being examined only by a few specialists in criminal law.

Scholars in several disciplines—as well as practitioners in such fields as law, police work, medicine, social work, and psychiatry—are beginning to speak out against the American tendency to make anything and everything a crime. There is increasing recognition that the attempt to "solve," through resort to the criminal law, problems that might more appropriately be dealt with through informal controls, expanded social services, or management by the healing professions, often invites trouble and produces new or greatly expanded social problems. And there is also some feeling among students of these matters that at least some of the behaviors we now treat as criminal might better be simply left alone; that in some areas of human behavior a greater tolerance of diversity, rather than special efforts at control—by whatever means—would constitute the wisest "policy."

[6] H. L. A. Hart, *Law, Liberty and Morality* (Stanford: Stanford University Press, 1963), pp. 46–47.

[7] See Robin Williams, *American Society: A Sociological Interpretation,* 2nd ed. (New York: Alfred A. Knopf, Inc., 1960), Chap. 10.

[8] Francis A. Allen, *The Borderland of Criminal Justice* (Chicago: University of Chicago Press, 1964). An important study in this area, published as this book was going to press, is Herbert Packer, *The Limits of the Criminal Sanction* (Stanford: Stanford University Press, 1968).

Crimes Without Victims[9]

In one sense, every criminal law can be expected to fall short of absolute deterrence, for as Edwin Sutherland properly noted, "When the mores are adequate, laws are unnecessary; when the mores are inadequate, the laws are ineffective." [10] But sometimes criminal laws are so blatantly ineffective and unenforceable that they are of special sociological significance—because of the value inconsistencies or conflicts of interest they indicate—and also of special policy significance, in that they may suggest an unwise (even positively harmful) disposition of the relatively scarce resources of law enforcement and the administration of justice. I have used the term "crimes without victims" to refer to one particular category of such glaringly unenforceable law—that in which we have attempted to legally proscribe the willing exchange of socially disapproved but widely demanded goods or services. Although my book of that title dealt at length with only three such "offenses"—abortion, homosexuality, and drug addiction—a number of other kinds of behavior, including prostitution, gambling, and various additional sexual offenses, would fall into this category as well.

Perhaps the crucial common characteristic of these behaviors is that in each case the "crime" involves—we might even say "consists of"—a consensual transaction or exchange. Certainly one aspect of "victimless" offenses is that there is not, in the usual sense, a direct and clear harm inflicted by one person against another. On the contrary, the offending behavior involves the providing to one person by another of something that is greatly desired. It is true that we could debate at some length the issue of whether there really is no "victim" in each of these situations. Thus one might argue that the addict is victimized by the drug peddler, that the fetus is a victim in the case of abortion, that the prostitute is being victimized, and so on. But there is another sense in which these situations are victimless, one that is equally significant and less debatable. Whether or not we should determine that somehow particular individuals are in fact victimized (re-

<hr>

[9] This section sets forth some of the main points I developed in my book *Crimes Without Victims* (Englewood Cliffs, N.J.: Prentice-Hall, Inc., 1965). I have also drawn on a briefer (unpublished) discussion of this topic I presented at Brown University, Department of Sociology and Anthropology Colloquium, April, 1966.

[10] Sutherland and Cressey, *op. cit.,* p. 11.

gardless of how they themselves view the situation), the fact remains that because of the transactional nature of the "offense," there is no victim in the conventional sense of a citizen complainant who will seek to initiate prosecution and give needed evidence to law enforcement authorities. The customer ordinarily does not bring a complaint against the prostitute, or vice versa; the addict does not urge prosecution of the peddler who supplies him with drugs; the aborted woman does not usually want to see the abortionist who finally complied with her wish to have her pregnancy terminated "brought to justice."

This absence of complainants lies at the heart of the unenforceability of these laws, and very strongly colors the entire enforcement process. It places enforcement authorities in a particularly difficult, indeed highly untenable situation, often driving them to adopt harshly punitive or ethically (and legally) questionable enforcement techniques. Avenues for obtaining evidence in these areas are extremely limited. For example, in the case of abortion, major leads usually occur only when women die or are hospitalized because of complications from the illegal operation. Even then, a long and expensive process of surveillance eventuating in a raid (which must be carefully timed) will be necessary if the prosecutor is to come into court with evidence adequate to support his charges. This suggests the general issue of whether the costly use of police resources is justified, given the other kinds of crime about which the public feels (perhaps more properly) great concern. In virtually all of these borderline offense areas, the preparation of adequate evidence for prosecution involves a substantial use of police personnel. In one narcotics case, it was reported that five detectives spent a month in Greenwich Village disguised as beatniks— one was even said to have gained quite a reputation as a poet—and over one hundred policemen and policewomen were involved in the resulting arrests.

Because of the central problem of obtaining evidence, techniques that come close to (or constitute) entrapment are widely used in these situations. We all know that it is common practice to use plainclothesmen to impersonate potential "customers" of the prostitute and "prospects" for the homosexual. While the formal legal defense of entrapment may help protect innocent bystanders from inadvertently being trapped into compromising behavior, the adverse social consequences of these practices remain considerable. They require law enforcement officers to engage in ethically questionable and highly undignified behavior. The effects on the self-concepts of the deviating individuals themselves may be undesirable. And, more broadly, if engaged in on a wide enough basis they may help to create an acceptance of systematic spying in certain sectors of our social life, a result that should be of great concern to us on both moral and constitutional grounds. A recent comprehensive inquiry into the enforcement of laws on homosexuality in the Los Angeles area revealed the almost continuous use of extremely elaborate methods of hidden observation for surveillance of public toilets and other suspected homosexual meeting places—techniques which, of course, invade the privacy of many completely "innocent" persons as well as of some homosexuals.[11]

Another very common practice in the enforcement of borderline crime laws is the use of underworld informers. A major illustration of this is found in narcotics law enforcement. As Alfred Lindesmith has pointed out, the addict's extreme dependence on drugs makes him especially vulnerable to pressures to inform:

The "stool pigeon" is usually inducted into this activity by pressure of various sorts depending upon circumstances and the resistance offered. An inexperienced addict may give way at once when threatened with arrest, or in the face of a prison sentence and the promise that if he cooperates he will receive a short sentence, be placed on probation, or perhaps released. The police sometimes offer an addict leniency if he agrees to turn in one or more peddlers. The most effective reward of all is that the informer may be allowed to continue his habit, at least temporarily. Persons who show unusual ability may make informing a career and use it to maintain their habits over a period of years. Usually, however, the active career of a "stooly" is brief because he soon comes to be known.[12]

There is considerable professional disagreement concerning the propriety of such methods. According to two experienced law enforcement officials, "No modern policeman who properly uses informers needs to be apologetic about them. The apology should come from the officer who fails to use this device to protect his community."[13] But critics point out that this technique compels law enforcers themselves to support or even engage in criminal behavior, that there is

[11] "Adult Homosexual Behavior and the Law," *UCLA Law Review*, 13 (1966), 643–831.
[12] Alfred R. Lindesmith, *The Addict and the Law* (Bloomington: Indiana University Press, 1965), p. 47. For further information about the operation of the informer system as a police technique, see Skolnick, *Justice Without Trial, op. cit.*, Chaps. 6 and 7.
[13] Malachi Harney and J. C. Cross, *The Informer in Law Enforcement* (Springfield, Ill.: Charles C Thomas, Publisher, 1960), pp. 17–18.

considerable danger of informers "framing" suspects, and that using evidence obtained from anonymous informers violates the defendant's right to full knowledge and confrontation of evidence and witnesses on which his prosecution is based. It is difficult to exaggerate the extent to which such methods, highly questionable in terms of the basic principles of a democratic society, are employed in the attempt to control private consensual "offenses." According to Lindesmith, "The use of addict 'stool pigeons' is so common that it is sometimes an embarrassment to the police. It tends to create a class of law violater who is to a degree and for varying periods of time exempt from the penalties of the law. Because of the secrecy shrouding the informer, the police sometimes arrest each other's stool pigeons and the latter sometimes try to make buys from each other. Arrested addicts sometimes indignantly ask to be released on the grounds that they are working for the police." [14]

These are not the only questionable police practices that abound in the area of crimes without victims and other borderline offenses. It is significant that many of the most important U.S. Supreme Court rulings concerned with alleged infringements of suspects' constitutional safeguards (such as those against improper arrest, illegal search and seizure, and self-incrimination) have involved efforts to enforce such laws. Many of the issues surrounding wiretapping and other types of electronic surveillance, for example, have arisen out of enforcement activities in the areas of gambling and political ("national security") crime—the latter constituting another highly questionable kind of borderline offense. Other extreme methods to which police may be driven in these scarce-evidence enforcement areas are illustrated by the notorious behavior that resulted in the Supreme Court's 1952 decision in the case of *Rochin v. California*. There, officers who suspected the defendant of dealing in narcotics broke into his room, and during a struggle the suspect swallowed some narcotics that had been resting on a bedtable. He was rushed to a hospital, where despite his protests his stomach was pumped, and the morphine that was recovered in this manner was introduced in court as evidence against him. Speaking for the Supreme Court, which unanimously reversed his conviction, Justice Frankfurter stated:

> . . . the proceedings by which this conviction was obtained do more than offend some fastidious squeamishness or private sentimentalism about combatting crime too energetically. This is conduct that shocks the con-

[14] Lindesmith, *The Addict and the Law*, p. 49.

science . . . this course of proceeding by agents of government to obtain evidence is bound to offend even hardened sensibilities. They are methods too close to the rack and the screw to permit of constitutional differentiation.[15]

It is widely recognized by disinterested students of crime that whatever drastic methods are employed, law enforcement efforts in the victimless crime area are bound to meet with very limited success. The basic effect of repressive laws of this sort seems to be simply to divert the demand from legal to illegal channels, and to place the illicit supplier in a particularly strong economic position. Law professor Herbert Packer has suggestively referred to a kind of "crime tariff" that goes into operation in such situations. He points out that "Regardless of what we think we are trying to do, if we make it illegal to traffic in commodities for which there is an inelastic demand, the actual effect is to secure a kind of monopoly profit to the entrepreneur who is willing to break the law." [16] While the various kinds of illicit traffic may vary considerably in degree of organization and monopolistic concentration, at the very least, as economist Thomas Schelling notes, "any successful black marketeer enjoys a 'protected' market in the same way that a domestic industry is protected by a tariff, or butter by a law against margarine. The black marketeer gets automatic protection, through the law itself, from all competitors unwilling to pursue a criminal career. The laws give a kind of franchise to those who are willing to break the law." [17] The nature and ramifications of this process are well illustrated by the economic traffic in illegal abortions. As an early study of the abortion problem noted, restrictive legislation set in motion "an endless circle":

> The ready willingness of women to visit an abortionist brought him immense profits. A fraction of these profits made it possible to cause an abortion with a greater degree of safety to the woman and a smaller chance of exposure of either the woman or the doctor. This led to a further appeal to women who wished to bring an abrupt termination to their pregnancies. And so the chain was complete.[18]

[15] *Rochin v. Calif.*, 342 U.S. 165, 172 (1952).
[16] See Herbert Packer, "The Crime Tariff," *American Scholar*, 33 (1964), 551–57; also Packer and R. J. Gampell, "Therapeutic Abortion," *Stanford Law Review*, 11 (May, 1959), 417–55.
[17] Thomas C. Schelling, "Economic Analysis and Organized Crime," in President's Commission on Law Enforcement and Administration of Justice, *Task Force Report: Organized Crime*, p. 117.
[18] Abraham Rongy, *Abortion: Legal or Illegal?* (New York: Vanguard Press, Inc., 1933), p. 117.

Related to this is the process criminologist Edwin Sutherland termed competitive development of enforcement and antienforcement techniques. The classic illustration is the competition between manufacturers of safes and professional safe-crackers, exhibiting a spiral of continuous efforts by each side to outdo the other. The same sort of thing happens with respect to crimes without victims; efforts to curb drug smuggling lead to ingenious new smuggling techniques, enforcement activity directed against call girls and abortionists is thwarted by the use of elaborate "codes" in arranging encounters with customers and patients, and so on.

Enforcement officials have long since given up on any attempt to eliminate these borderline offenses. Police activity in these areas is usually sporadic and perfunctory, and can best be described as reflecting a policy of harassment and regulation—rather than one aimed at significant reduction of the behaviors in question. We are familiar with the occasional exposés of "abortion mills" and "dope rings," which to some extent appear in response to pressures on the police to indicate they are making some effort to "control" these problems. The routine and relatively meaningless nominal fining of prostitutes, who promptly return to their "beat"—a practice so common that streetwalkers consider it simply a routine aspect of their work situation—is also well known. The harassment of homosexual bars and other meeting places, and the occasional well-publicized "crackdown" on homosexuals in a particular metropolitan area, are likewise hardly calculated to have any real effect in curbing homosexual behavior. Most specialists in enforcement, as well as academic students of these problems, realize that as long as the demand for the proscribed goods and services is strong enough—and remains unsatisfied through legal channels— some method of meeting that demand illicitly will always be found, whatever obstacles one tries to erect.

As we have already seen, public policies concerning crimes without victims have a distinct and direct influence on enforcement practices. They also exert a considerable and largely undesirable influence on the attitudes of law enforcement personnel. Placing on the police the burden of dealing with these borderline offenses holds out considerable opportunity for and incentive to police corruption. The frequently ambivalent public attitude toward these supposedly offending behaviors, the fact that the acts in question usually occur in private— which means that enforcement officers have a great deal of discretion in "deciding" whether a particular incident shall come to public light and be officially defined as an "offense"—and the extreme reluctance of certain borderline offenders to have their behavior made public (for example, the otherwise "respectable" homosexual), are all factors working in this direction. Furthermore it is understandable that in this area of enforcement activity police demoralization is high. Despite the fact that effective enforcement of these laws is virtually impossible, officials are often subjected to public pressure and criticism for failing to establish efficient control over the proscribed behaviors. Given the cross pressures on law enforcers, the generally recognized ambivalence toward the "offenses," and the probability of low police morale, one hardly finds surprising the conclusion of the task force report on police of the President's Crime Commission: "A considerable number of the most serious and persistent kinds of unethical conduct are connected with failure to enforce laws that are not in accord with community norms." [19]

If our borderline crime policies present unique problems for law enforcement authorities, they also exert a pronounced influence on the behavior and outlooks of the deviating individuals they are meant to control. As I pointed out earlier, the absence of a deterrent effect does not mean that a legal policy is without any social effect whatsoever. Analysis of the process of "labeling criminals," referred to in Chapter 3, suggests that both deviant "careers" and deviant "self-images" are significantly shaped by the official (and unofficial) social reactions to the deviant behavior. The impact on the individual of what I have termed the "criminalization of deviance" varies considerably among the different kinds of victimless crime. How severe this impact is will depend largely on the extent to which the legal proscription of his behavior drives him into various related activities of an instrumental or supportive nature. The more the deviating individual is forced, under legal and social pressure, to act like a criminal and to band together with his own "kind," the more likely it will be that he becomes conscious of his "criminality"—which in turn pushes him into still further expanded patterns of deviant behavior. Both the nature of the initial deviance, and the nature of the enforcement pressure, are significant in shaping this process. When the proscribed acts can without difficulty be well integrated with an otherwise conforming way of life, the individual is probably not much affected by the formal labeling of his behavior as "criminal." Thus, the man in the street who plays the

[19] President's Commission on Law Enforcement and Administration of Justice, *Task Force Report: The Police*, pp. 211–12.

"numbers" can hardly care less that gambling is a crime—even though the commission of such gambling "offenses" may become for him a routine long-term pattern of behavior. Ordinarily he need not get involved in any "secondary deviance" in order to sustain this pattern— although, of course, the financial pressures generated by more substantial gambling are another story.

The example of the abortion seeking woman is a bit more complicated.[20] In part because her criminal involvement is (ordinarily) non-repetitive, it seems unlikely that she would develop any view of herself as a criminal; and there is no sustained pattern of behavior that would promote a special "subculture" of similarly situated women. At the same time, the severe restrictions our society has placed on the granting of legal ("therapeutic") hospital abortions subject such women to dangers and situations that are likely to have some adverse psychological impact. There are some very real physical dangers attending many illegal operations—dangers which would not ordinarily be present in a hospital abortion, and mere knowledge of which probably adds greatly to the emotional impact of the abortion experience. Beyond the danger of medical complications, for most women in our society the immediate social situation of obtaining an illegal abortion is an extremely unpleasant one. No matter how professional and well organized an abortionist is, a certain element of sordidness invariably attaches to the encounter with him—if only because of the need for secrecy that is always a feature of such situations. We do not really have much systematic data concerning the social-psychological impact on abortion seekers of our having designated abortion a crime. The evidence we do have suggests that few aborted women seriously regret their decisions to terminate pregnancy, and many (of those lucky enough to locate skilled operators) even view the abortionist with some respect and gratitude. Much of this evidence stems, however, from studies in which women of relatively high socioeconomic status—those most likely to obtain competent and relatively safe abortions—were overrepresented. We should be careful, too, lest we assume from the apparent infrequency of serious psychological after-effects that subtle and long-term consequences of our having "criminalized" these women must be without significance.

A particularly unhappy aspect of our present abortion policies is

---

[20] See Schur, *Crimes Without Victims*, pp. 11–66; and my more recent article, "Abortion," *The Annals of the American Academy of Political and Social Science*, 376 (March, 1968), 136–47.

that they discriminate harshly against women of low socioeconomic status. (This factor of socioeconomic differentials is present, in one form or another, in several of the other borderline crime areas as well —since the ability to obtain desired illegal goods and services often depends on the adequacy of the customer's financial resources.) The social class factor apparently influences access to both legal and illegal abortion opportunities. Under our present system of hospital abortion boards, presenting a request for a therapeutic abortion is a fairly complicated task. Many lower-class women have little knowledge of these procedures, or even of the grounds on which they might seek legal termination of a pregnancy. But these factors alone seem inadequate to explain the striking socioeconomic differentials in the actual performance of hospital abortions. Although therapeutic abortions are granted infrequently (the estimated national total is now around 8,000 a year), studies show that the overwhelming majority of those that are performed involve white middle-class women.

In the absence of access to legal abortion facilities, a woman's economic and social standing becomes even more crucial in shaping the abortion experience. To some extent this is a matter of simple economics; it is well known that the quality of illegal abortions varies directly with the price paid, and of course as quality goes down, the risk goes up. (In this connection, it is suggestive that the proportion of maternal deaths attributed to abortion in New York City is twice as high for nonwhites and Puerto Ricans as for white women.) The lower-class woman suffers not only from being unable to pay for an adequate illegal abortion, but also because she usually doesn't have access to accurate information about where to obtain such an operation. Women in this situation are probably among those most likely at some point to attempt a self-induced abortion, often by methods that may be extremely dangerous.

Alarm about the thriving business in illegal abortions, recognition of the unenforceability of existing statutes, and concern with the dangers, indignities, and extreme unpleasantness to which abortion seeking women are exposed, have in recent years spearheaded a growing pressure for changes in American abortion laws. In most states abortion has been a crime unless "necessary to preserve the life of the mother"—an exception which, given modern medical advances, has not been very meaningful. Because of this restrictiveness most of the abortions in this country (estimated to run between 200,000 and 1,200,000 annually) have been illegal ones. Increasingly, medical and legal organizations and other groups of prominent citizens are joining the individual critics who have long condemned American abortion policies. Particularly influential has been the recommendation of the American Law Institute that abortion by a licensed physician should be legal if there is "substantial risk that continuance of the pregnancy would gravely imperil the physical or mental health of the mother or that the child would be born with grave physical or mental defect," and also in cases of pregnancy resulting from rape, incest, or "other felonious assault" (including illicit intercourse with a girl below the age of sixteen).[21]

A nation-wide survey of public opinion (conducted by the National Opinion Research Center in December, 1965) revealed strong support for abortion laws patterned along the lines of this recommendation, although respondents were unwilling to go beyond it and approve abortion on broader social and economic grounds. When the representative sample of 1,484 adult Americans were asked whether they would approve of legal abortion in each of six sets of circumstances, percentages approving were as follows: If the woman's own health is seriously endangered by the pregnancy, 71 per cent; if she became pregnant as a result of rape, 56 per cent; if there is a strong chance of serious defect in the baby, 55 per cent; if the family has a very low income and cannot afford any more children, 21 per cent; if she is not married and does not want to marry the man, 18 per cent; if she is married and does not want any more children, 15 per cent. Although none of the circumstances cited would morally justify interruption of pregnancy according to Roman Catholic doctrine, close to half of the Catholic men and women questioned in the survey favored allowing legal abortion in the first three instances.[22]

Despite the Church's continuing insistence that all direct and intentional abortions (even "therapeutic" ones) constitute immoral taking of life—and the considerable amount of political pressure that has been brought to bear in support of this position—there seems to be a distinct trend toward legislative reform along the lines of the American Law Institute's proposal. In the last few years, several states—the most publicized being California and Colorado—have modified their abortion statutes. A special study commission in New York recom-

[21] American Law Institute, *Model Penal Code*, Proposed Official Draft (Philadelphia: American Law Institute, 1962), pp. 189–90.
[22] See Alice S. Rossi, "Abortion Laws and their Victims," *Trans-action*, September-October, 1966.

mended (in the spring of 1968) revamping that state's abortion policies, but legislative support of this proposal was (again, as in several
past attempts) inadequate to push through the reform bill that had
been introduced. Many specialists, however, insist that even reform
patterned on the ALI recommendation will be inadequate. This would
only cover the most glaring indications for abortion, and would leave
unaided women (married and unmarried) who—for a wide variety of
social and economic reasons—have determined that their pregnancies
should be interrupted. Furthermore, under most of these reform laws,
the abortion seeker would still have to go through various bureaucratic procedures (abortion committee, etc.) before being accredited
for a legal operation. Nothing short of abortion "on demand," these
critics insist, will eliminate the indignity and the abridgment of personal freedom built into the present system. For these reasons, a substantial national movement for complete repeal of abortion laws
(rather than piecemeal reform) is now developing. Other analysts feel
that the reform proposals (which usually cover at least the woman's
physical and mental health) could effect some real change, if a broad
enough interpretation were given to the term "mental health." To
date, however, experience under the "reform" laws has been discouraging. No state in this country has yet adopted the very broad reform recently enacted in Great Britain—where risk to "the physical
or mental health of any existing children" (this has been referred to as
the "social clause") is now included among the indications for legal
termination of pregnancy.[23]

In the case of another borderline crime area, that of homosexuality,
we find a somewhat different configuration of effects of criminalization
on the deviating individuals.[24] Even if legal and social stigmatization
of the homosexual were reduced, it seems likely that such persons
would continue to be very much aware that they are deviants, and
also probable that a reasonably distinct and to some extent organized
homosexual subculture would persist. At the same time, the fact that
even private homosexual behavior has been formally designated a
crime, and the persistent legal harassment of homosexual gathering
places, cannot help but exacerbate the homosexual's negative self-

[23] See *New York Times*, October 26, 1967, p. 1.
[24] See *Crimes Without Victims*, pp. 67–119. I am also drawing on an unpublished paper I prepared as a member of the National Institute of Mental Health
Task Force on Homosexuality, titled "Sociocultural Factors in Homosexual Behavior."

conceptions and the entrenchment of special forms of adaptation. Legal stigma adds to social stigma, and probably intensifies the need most homosexuals feel to conceal their condition much of the time. One British homosexual has described the pressure to exercise concealment as follows:

> I was forced to be deceitful, living one life during my working hours and another when I was free. I had two sets of friends; almost, one might say, two faces. At the back of my mind there was always a nagging fear that my two worlds might suddenly collide. . . .[25]

Although some homosexuals may be able to "pass" in the "straight" world without feeling great stress, it would seem that for one with any substantial standing in the general community (for example, in the occupational and associational realms), the anxieties would be considerable. It is true that some confirmed homosexuals may choose not to practice concealment, but often this will be at the price of foregoing extensive involvement in at least some sectors of the larger social world. In particular the choice between openly acknowledging and concealing homosexuality will greatly influence occupational opportunity. The admitted homosexual will often be welcome only in certain occupational spheres that traditionally have been tolerant of homosexuals. A special aspect of this problem has been the practice of certain government agencies (and the armed forces) to formally exclude homosexuals from employment—on the grounds either that they represent bad "security risks," or that they lower morale, constitute an unhealthy influence through some supposed process of "contagion," and the like. With the possible exception of a special vulnerability to blackmail that could render homosexuals a slightly greater risk than heterosexuals in top-secret government positions, these claims have not been substantiated. Indeed many specialists believe they tell us more about the fear of homosexuality among "normals," than about the likely consequences of alternative employment policies.

Vulnerability to blackmail and to other kinds of exploitation is another feature of the homosexual's situation that is heightened by the legal proscription of his preference in sexual behavior. Despite the fact that the laws against homosexuality have been enforced in a sporadic and nonrigorous manner, the individual homosexual finds himself in an extremely precarious position in relation to the law and to enforcement officials. I have already noted the pattern of systematic harass-

[25] Peter Wildeblood, *Against the Law* (London: Penguin Books, 1955), p. 37.

ment, the use of *agents provocateurs* (vice squad decoys), and the utilization of elaborate spying techniques. These become very real elements in the homosexual's day-to-day existence, and the possibility of being exposed and prosecuted must be ever present in his thinking and a strong influence on his behavior. There have been many involved and often successful efforts by professional as well as amateur thieves to compromise and extort money from homosexuals—a type of "secondary crime" that seems largely created by our present laws regarding their behavior. Nor is it surprising that some police officers have also engaged in direct exploitation of homosexuals. More generally, and despite increased efforts by some enlightened enforcement officials to encourage homosexuals to register complaints when appropriate, the homosexual feels himself to be largely without recourse to any real protection of the law. As such he becomes particularly vulnerable to theft and violence, as well as to blackmail.

Over the past five or ten years there has been an apparent increase both in the number of scarcely concealed homosexual social organizations and in the development of largely homosexual organizations geared to public education, legal protection, and reform of policies dealing with homosexuality. We might expect the social organizations to form even in the absence of legal repression, but the other development (the so-called "homophile" movement) seems directly related to the homosexual's legal situation. These organizations may serve an important morale-building function, as well as providing individual homosexuals with necessary legal and other assistance. They also, however, disseminate various ideologies concerning "homosexuality as a way of life," "the social value of homosexuality," and so on—ideologies that can be expected to have a considerable (and not always desirable) impact on the attitudes of homosexuals themselves and perhaps even on future social reactions and public policies toward homosexuality.

The growing pressure for legal reform of laws relating to homosexual behavior—which may not be as strong as in some of the other borderline crime areas, but is certainly not negligible—is based largely on an appreciation of the unpleasantness and vulnerability such laws create for a considerable number of our citizens. It is widely realized that these laws are unlikely to have much deterrent effect, and that criminal sanctions can at best curb public nuisances and serious harms that may at times be created by homosexuals. For this purpose, laws covering private consensual sexual behavior are not needed. Because of the nature of the "transaction" involved, this particular victimless crime does not give rise to any substantial "black market," although the activities of homosexual prostitutes may in part reflect the illegality of homosexual behavior. In short, the amount of secondary deviation and crime produced by the legal proscription is, in this instance, not terribly great. On the other hand, there is a growing conviction that these laws interfere unnecessarily with the private lives of a great many Americans who might otherwise (some do anyway) make a reasonably good adaptation in other spheres of social life, and who in any case cause no real social harm.

As these examples show, each of the victimless crime situations has some distinctive features; they vary quite a bit in the extent to which illicit traffic, secondary deviation, and adverse psychological consequences are present, as well as in the nature of the enforcement problems and other specifics. Of all the major "crimes without victims" drug addiction may be the one in which there is the most complete elaboration of secondary problems and undesirable features, in a large measure due to our having criminalized the problem. For that reason, it may be worthwhile to consider it in slightly greater detail.

Drug Addiction: A Self-Escalating Problem

Although many of the secondary effects of our attempt to treat drug addiction as a problem for the criminal law have received fairly wide publicity, there is depressingly little indication that the basic lesson implied by this experience has really been learned.[26] In recent years many professional organizations (medical, legal, etc.) and special study groups have called for reform of America's narcotics policies, but at the governmental level of actual public policymaking, there has been a distinct timidity about trying out genuinely new approaches.

[26] For general treatment of American drug problems and policies, see Lindesmith, *The Addict and the Law*; Schur, *Crimes Without Victims*, pp. 120–68; and Schur, *Narcotic Addiction in Britain and America* (Bloomington: Indiana University Press, 1962). I have also drawn on a lecture, titled "Drugs, Law, and Society," I delivered at the University of Delaware, Newark, Delaware, in February, 1968, and now published in *The Threat of Crime in America* (Newark: University of Delaware, 1969). In particular, the comments concerning treatment programs are for the most part taken directly from that lecture; used here by permission.

To some extent this hesitancy may be attributable to an execessive concern with problems of individual causation and treatment. There is a lingering hope that somehow a research "breakthrough" will produce an easy "solution" to the drug problem, despite the fact that there are no signs of any imminent revelations of this sort. At present, the various theories used to "explain" drug addiction comprise a welter of sometimes conflicting emphases adopted by specialists in diverse disciplines, making evident little more than the socio-legal-medical complexity of the drug problem. (Although this discussion focuses primarily on actual narcotic addiction—that is, true addiction to drugs such as heroin and morphine that produce physiological as well as psychological dependence—the main points about the role of policy have some relevance to other drug problems as well.)

By and large, the major explanations of drug addiction mirror the broad categories of theorizing I discussed earlier in the chapters on theories of crime causation. There is the special feature in this case that one might construe the very fact of full addiction in an individual—involving actual physical dependence on the drug with a characteristic abstinence syndrome seen on withdrawal—as constituting a "medical" condition, much as diabetes is considered a medical condition. (One psychiatrist drew this point sharply by satirically describing a hypothetical country where insulin taking was made a crime, where all insulin "addicts" therefore were driven to crime to support their habits, and where special police units were constituted to track down these addicts and combat the illicit traffic in insulin.) But the mere physiology of full addiction is not a complete explanation; we know that some independent psychological craving for the drug also is involved in addiction.

Probably the most widely accepted view of the causes of addiction has been developed by psychologists and psychiatrists, who insist it is largely a symptom of underlying psychic disturbance, and that a particular personality pattern establishes a "predisposition" to drug taking. I have already reviewed some of the problems attending such theories, and the major criticisms of them. There is also a large body of research findings on the spatial and social distribution of drug use in various large American cities, showing a pattern of very high concentration in certain slum areas, in line with other findings on crime distribution mentioned above. Some social researchers have tried to combine this kind of data with the psychological approach, to explain both the geographical concentration and the fact that only some individuals in the high drug-use areas (those predisposed because of family background factors, etc.) take up drugs. Other sociological research has explored the learning processes involved in initiation into drug use, and the ways in which subcultural involvement seems to develop. But often, in the search for a narrowly conceived causal explanation, situational and opportunity factors (one must gain access to the drug to take it), and the impact of public policy in shaping the drug situation, have been slighted.

If we concentrate somewhat less on why individuals become addicted and somewhat more on why the addiction problem is the way it is, it is impossible not to see existing drug policies as being partly responsible for the nature and extent of the problem. There are certain socially objectionable aspects of our present drug situation that cannot be attributed primarily to either the nature and effects of the drugs themselves, or to any underlying or background characteristics of the drug users. One understands these secondary features only if one considers the social consequences of the laws and enforcement policies by which we have tried to control the illicit use of drugs.

The practical effect of our narcotics laws has been to define the addict as a criminal offender. By a process of administrative regulation and broad interpretation (as well as selective attention to some judicial rulings, and a by-passing of others), federal authorities effectively converted the Harrison Act—a largely regulatory statute passed in 1914, application of which served as the prototype for subsequent drug control laws, both federal and state—into a virtual ban on medical administration of drugs to addicts. Although today it is not, strictly speaking, a crime to be addicted to opiates, under existing state and federal statutes the addict cannot legally possess the drug to which he is addicted. Similarly, although it may be legal for a doctor to prescribe limited amounts of a narcotic for an addict under certain restricted circumstances, in general the medical practitioner runs considerable legal risk in undertaking any treatment or management of cases of addiction—apart from withdrawing an addict from drugs in a hospital. The impact of this restrictive policy on the overall drug problem should have been predictable. It is hardly surprising that the absence of legal drug sources has generated a highly profitable black market. As one legal expert has stated, "It is precisely our law enforcement efforts, and nothing else, that keep the price of drugs, nearly worthless in themselves, so high as to attract an endless procession of criminal entrepreneurs to keep the traffic flowing." [27]

Because of the lack of a complaining victim, enforcement officials experience great difficulty in obtaining evidence of narcotics violations. This leads to the various special investigatory techniques—including widespread use of informers—that were mentioned earlier, but disinterested observers are in agreement that the police are unable to significantly cripple the organized and extensive networks of underworld drug distribution. Many studies have shown that the brunt of enforcement efforts is felt by the addicts and small-time pushers or peddlers. The higher-ups in the narcotics racket, criminal entrepreneurs who are themselves rarely addicted, seem relatively immune to control. It is also widely recognized that the attempt to cut off initial sources of supply by preventing smuggling of narcotics into the country can never fully succeed.

Virtually all observers—including enforcement officials—admit that the need to finance the drug habit produces a great deal of secondary crime committed by addicts. Most American addicts regularly engage in petty theft or prostitution in order to obtain the funds needed to purchase black market drugs. As the task force on drugs of the President's Crime Commission has noted, the price of such drugs fluctuates greatly, but "it is never low enough to permit the typical addict to obtain it by lawful means." The same report cites some alarming statistical projections, including the following: "Assuming that each of the heroin addicts in New York City, whose names were on file with the Bureau of Narcotics at the end of 1965, spent $15 a day for his drug, and that in each case the $15 represented the net cash proceeds after conversion of stolen property worth $50, the addicts would be responsible each year for the theft of property valued at many millions of dollars in New York City alone." [28] Considering that this estimate was limited to New York and to known addicts, the total amount of property crime by addicts may actually be very much larger. (At the time of this report, the official figure on known addicts throughout the country was approximately 53,000—with more than half said to be lo-

[27] Rufus King, Testimony, in Hearings Before the Subcommittee on Improvements in the Federal Criminal Code, U.S. Senate, Committee on the Judiciary, 84th Cong., 1st. Sess., on the causes, treatment, and rehabilitation of drug addicts (Washington, D.C.: U.S. Government Printing Office, 1956), Pt. 5, p. 1379.

[28] President's Commission on Law Enforcement and Administration of Justice, *Task Force Report: Narcotics and Drug Abuse*, p. 10.

cated in New York State, but unofficial estimates asserted that the "real" national total was at least as high as several hundred thousand.)

The task force admitted that the projections could well lead to an assumption that "addicts must be responsible for most crimes against property where addiction is widespread," but went on to caution that such an assumption has not been, and cannot easily be verified. At the same time, it cited reports from the New York City Department of Correction, indicating that almost 40 per cent of its average 1966 population (about 10,000 persons) had an admitted history of drug use. Even assuming that a good many of the persons who become addicts might have engaged in some crime had they not become addicted, it is hard not to conclude that an enormous amount of property crime is directly caused by the tremendous financial pressure involved in maintaining a narcotics habit. It is significant that in Great Britain, where the addict has usually been able to obtain his drugs legitimately and at low cost (a matter I shall return to shortly), there has been very little crime associated with addiction.

Repressive drug policies have also reinforced the development and expansion of a specialized addict subculture. Other factors, such as the enhancement of morale through being with one's own "kind," may be involved, but it seems clear that the pressures produced by antiaddiction efforts have been a major force driving addicts to band together. Except for physician-addicts and some other addicted persons who may manage to obtain drugs from legitimate sources, all American addicts must involve themselves in the complex underworld-related drug distributing system. Such addicts are necessarily thrown into contact with peddlers and pushers, and many become pushers themselves in order to help support their habits. Inevitably there is also frequent interaction with other addicts, and in general it is to the addict's advantage to immerse himself as much as possible in the drug distributing and drug consuming "world." At least in part such subcultural elaboration also has a direct antienforcement aspect—as seen in the development of neighborhood "grapevine" communications systems, mechanisms for identifying and protecting against informers, and the like.

It is important to keep in mind that the mere condition of being addicted to narcotics does not automatically place a person in any addict subculture. Research has shown, for example, that American physician-addicts do not have this subcultural involvement—precisely because they have no real need of it. The experience in Britain also suggests that degree of access to drug supplies and extent of financial resources are the key factors determining whether or not the addict becomes immersed in a specialized subculture. The British addict has usually had no need to maintain contact with other addicts or with underworld distributors, and it is probably for that reason that there has been relatively little development of addiction-centered subculture in Britain (this is true at least of the legally available opiates). In America, our drug policies have driven the addict almost completely out of "respectable" society. By defining him as a criminal, we have pushed the addict in the direction of becoming one. The human and social costs of this decision have been almost incalculable.

Unfortunately, these adverse social consequences of present policy have not been significantly offset by success in the medical treatment of cases of addiction. For some years the U.S. Public Health Service has offered a comprehensive treatment program for addicts at its hospitals in Lexington, Kentucky, and Forth Worth, Texas, and now we are seeing the establishment of specialized addiction treatment facilities in several states and major cities. Although estimates of treatment success vary according to who is doing the estimating, it is apparent that the treated addict's eventual relapse to drugs has been the rule rather than the exception. Withdrawing the addict from drugs in a hospital is not difficult, but keeping him off of drugs following release is another matter. Whatever psychotherapy is employed in the institution is, in many cases, trying to reverse behavior patterns and outlooks that have become an all-enveloping way of life—and frequently the "patient" in such a situation cannot in any complete sense be considered to have voluntarily submitted to treatment (though most institutional programs do provide treatment for both compulsorily committed individuals and "voluntary" patients).

Furthermore, most programs have been hampered by lack of adequate aftercare arrangements. It is now generally recognized that some outpatient supervision must follow treatment in an institution if the addict is to be enabled to resist the pressures he is likely to face on return to the community. One group of specialists has advocated a comprehensive community-based treatment program—in which a stage of institutional withdrawal treatment would be followed by gradual steps toward complete return to ordinary community life, under the continued supervision of a neighborhood clinic operated jointly by a hospital and a cooperating neighborhood agency. And, similarly, there has been some effort to ease the transition from institution to community through the device of a "halfway house" (one of which, for example, has been operated fairly successfully in East Los Angeles). Officials of the New York State Parole Department claim reasonable success in keeping paroled addict-offenders off drugs, under a system in which special parole officers handle reduced caseloads; spokesmen for that program insist that the element of compulsion has positive value in efforts to keep addicts abstinent.

Two rather experimental treatment efforts—which incidentally approach the problem from almost diametrically opposed perspectives—seem to me worthy of special consideration. One is the program of Synanon House,[29] in which former addicts play the major "treatment" role: first withdrawing new members from drugs (abruptly but with much interpersonal support), and then attempting gradually (through a special group discussion technique referred to as "attack therapy" and through a more general pattern of community life and work in a completely drug-free environment) to develop antidrug attitudes, social skills, and positive social values. Also central to the program is a system of graded work roles, in which the member gradually takes on positions of increased responsibility. Notwithstanding the strictness of the organization's rules and the harshness of the completely candid group discussions (which are called "small s synanons"), an extremely high level of morale seems to develop among the members of a Synanon House. While only limited statistics are available, it appears that this approach has enabled a good many former addicts to stay off drugs. Most seem to have remained (residentially or occupationally) within the Synanon organization—which has led critics to claim that this is really a "protective community" rather than a therapeutic one, and to argue that dependence on Synanon has been substituted for dependence on drugs. However true that may be, the general approach—particularly in contrast to conventional treatment institution programs—seems to have real promise as a technique for the voluntary treatment of some addicts.

A second important development in treatment has been the pioneering Methadone Maintenance Research Program,[30] directed by Drs. Vin-

---

[29] See Lewis Yablonsky, *Synanon: The Tunnel Back* (New York: The Macmillan Company, 1964); also Rita Volkman and Donald R. Cressey, "Differential Association and the Rehabilitation of Drug Addicts," *American Journal of Sociology,* 69 (September, 1963), 129–42.

[30] A readable account of the methadone research is provided by Nat Hentoff, *A Doctor Among the Addicts* (Chicago: Rand McNally & Co., 1968).

cent Dole and Marie Nyswander of Rockefeller University and now partially supported by the State of New York. In this program the addict-patients—all of whom are volunteers—are first hospitalized, withdrawn from heroin, and then switched over to the milder addictive drug methadone (which can be administered orally in an orange juice solution), the dosage being built up to a point at which they can be stabilized (and at which they experience neither craving for heroin nor any adverse effects from the methadone itself, provided the dosage is continued). In the second phase of the program the addict comes to an outpatient clinic at some time every day to obtain his "drink" of methadone. Finally, when the patient develops adequate functioning in the community at large, such visits may be less frequent—with the addict picking up a week's supply of methadone, for example. Patients in this program appear able to work satisfactorily and in general to function quite adequately when maintained on such stabilized doses of methadone. Of course, it must be recognized that the system has been used only for voluntary patients, and that careful screening procedures have been employed in their selection. Some critics insist that the entire philosophy of the program is dangerous— simply switching addicts from one drug to another. But Drs. Dole and Nyswander counter that past treatment efforts have been unwisely fixated on the perhaps unrealistic goal of complete abstinence; their goal instead is to develop reasonably normal, functioning citizens. They analogize their technique to insulin therapy for diabetes, where the disease is not cured but simply brought under control. And unlike giving liquor to the alcoholic, methadone maintenance in no way seriously impairs the individual's functioning. Whereas this maintenance approach may not work for all addicts, for some it seems to be approaching proven effectiveness.

It must be kept in mind that such efforts as the Synanon and methadone programs are only experiments. They represent extremely small-scale exceptions to the typical treatment still accorded American addicts—harassment, imprisonment, withdrawal from drugs (sometimes gradual, but often "cold turkey"), perhaps enforced "treatment" of some kind, and release with the prospect of beginning the cycle all over again. Both of these interesting experiments run counter in some respects to officially accepted policies and promises. In the case of Synanon, the apparent success of untrained former addicts in "treating" addicted individuals (outside of a hospital setting) is not easily accepted by conservative officials. Then too, the plan of a group of former addicts to live communally in a "respectable" residential neighborhood (as Synanon members have sought to do) has met with great community opposition.

The methadone program contradicts even more strikingly "established" notions about dealing with addiction. In addition to relying largely on ambulatory treatment (which the Federal Bureau of Narcotics and other official agencies have invariably condemned), methadone maintenance challenges the dominant preoccupation with complete abstinence as the sole indicator of successful treatment. Even some relatively enlightened doctors believe than any program involving provision of drugs to addicts implies "perpetuating disease" and "giving up" in the effort to cure addiction. What these practitioners ignore is that addiction is equally perpetuated under present arrangements. As the author of the New York Academy of Medicine's 1955 proposal for a network of narcotics clinics stated, "We are not saying to give the addicts more drugs. We are simply advising a different method of distribution . . . every addict gets his drug right now . . . why not let him have his minimum requirements under licensed medical supervision, rather than force him to get it by criminal activities, through criminal channels?" [31]

Many officials view the methadone program as alarmingly similar to Britain's approach to the drug problem—the relevance of which the Narcotics Bureau has long been at great pains to deny. Although the British have maintained statutory controls over possession and distribution of dangerous drugs, treatment of addiction has been considered a medical matter. While doctors have been warned to prescribe narcotics with caution, they have been permitted (within broad limits) to prescribe drugs for addicts, and "treatment" has been interpreted broadly to include ambulatory management and even extended drug maintenance when that is considered medically advisable. Under this system there has been only a limited amount of opiate addiction (probably fewer than a thousand opiate addicts in the United Kingdom), virtually no black market in opiates (since provision of drugs under the National Health Service eliminated the economic incentives for illicit trafficking), and little or no crime associated with

---

[31] Hubert S. Howe, Testimony, in Hearings Before the Subcommittee on Improvements in the Federal Criminal Code, p. 1332.

opiate addiction.[32] There has been extended debate about the meaning of the British experience, but it seems clear that the medically oriented policy there has itself helped to keep the situation within manageable limits.

In the last few years the British have reported some apparent increase in the amount of addiction and as a result they are moving in the direction of somewhat tighter control over prescribing for addicts (but without abandoning their overall medical orientation to the problem). Some American officials and news reporters have referred to these changes as somehow indicating a "failure of the British system," a claim that hardly seems warranted. Several factors (including better reporting procedures and emigration of Canadian and perhaps some American addicts to Britain) could account for the increase in known addiction cases. But, more significantly, there have been no reports of either substantial illicit traffic in opiates or of crime associated with opiate addiction. The basic logic of the British system—curtailing secondary aspects of the drug problem by keeping its management in medical hands—seems to hold up. It is reasonable to predict that if the British do move significantly in the direction of American policy, the consequences of doing so will be unhappy ones.

Recently in the United States professionals interested in the drug problem have come to feel that some kind of "medical approach" to addiction must accompany the reliance on law-enforcement measures. Unfortunately, however, the rhetoric of enlightened reform in this area has not been matched by adequate policy revision. There has been a definite move (reflected in a number of recent state laws, and also in federal legislation) toward a much heralded "civil commitment" program, but it is highly questionable whether this can really be considered a medical approach to the problem. Under this scheme selected addict-offenders are given the option of undergoing treatment while criminal charges are held in abeyance; in some versions a certified addict can be compulsorily committed for treatment, even in the absence of a specific criminal charge against him. Certainly the

[32] On British drug policies see Schur, *Narcotic Addiction in Britain and America;* Lindesmith, *The Addict and the Law,* especially Chap. 6; and Rufus King, "An Appraisal of International, British and Selected European Narcotic Drug Laws, Regulations and Policies," in *Drug Addiction: Crime or Disease.* Interim and final reports of the Joint Committee of the American Bar Association and the American Medical Association on Narcotic Drugs (Bloomington: Indiana University Press, 1961).

aim of replacing jail with medical treatment is a commendable one, and it is not surprising that liberal reformers have viewed this system as a step forward. Presumably some addicts at least would be dealt with more humanely than under previous policies. Furthermore, these programs have also usually allowed for some voluntary commitments to treatment institutions.

However, critics have cited a number of shortcomings: the element of compulsion underlying most of the commitments, the possibility of lengthy commitment of addicts who have not even been charged with crime, the prospect under these laws of longer commitment (of an addict who is charged with a crime) than would occur under regular criminal statutes, the inadequacy of available treatment facilities, and the ineffectiveness of existing treatment programs. As of this writing, constitutional challenges to the civil commitment laws are still being aired in the courts, and the New York program (one of the two largest, the other being in California) has been seriously troubled by numerous escapes and various other difficulties. If such programs could be administered strictly by medical men, in nonprisonlike institutions, and with highly flexible treatment programs, they might (if the overriding spirit of compulsion could be reduced) do some good. At the moment, however, they are being embraced officially as another weapon in a continuing "war against addiction"—in that kind of atmosphere it is most unlikely that any very effective treatment can occur. Recently a legal consultant to the narcotics task force of the President's Crime Commission stated that "as long as there is no evidence to show that existing methods for treating addiction hold out a reasonable prospect for cure, civil commitment is but a euphemism for imprisonment." [33]

Needless to say, even if a fairly effective treatment program were to emerge out of this scheme, the underlying supply-demand cycle that feeds the self-escalating drug problem would remain untouched. It is discouraging that the task force on drugs recommended no really significant modification of our present addiction laws.[34] While the accompanying research papers by outside consultants systematically explored the problems inherent in existing drug policies, the only substantive reform urged by the task force itself (and the larger Com-

---

[33] Dennis S. Aronowitz, "Civil Commitment of Narcotic Addicts and Sentencing for Narcotic Drug Offenses," in *Task Force Report: Narcotics and Drug Abuse,* p. 151.

[34] Compare the Commission's own recommendations, pp. 1–20 of the Task Force Report, with the accompanying papers by outside consultants.

mission) was to support earlier recommendations for wider flexibility in sentencing policy. Apart from this, the Commission advocated increased enforcement staffs and restated the perennial call for further research.

The Dilemma of Borderline Crime

There are many conventional and law-abiding citizens who view with great alarm any and all of these proposals for the "elimination" of borderline offenses. Isn't there something wrong, they ask, with the very idea of "legalizing vice"? Won't such "permissiveness" weaken the moral fibre of the American people, and in the long run threaten the integrity of our legal system? Is there some kind of conspiracy afoot to undermine all decent moral standards?

Because there is no clear-cut consensus about the meanings that should attach to many of these labels, it is difficult to answer such charges on their own terms. Yet the origins and aims of the reform proposals in question are neither devious nor mysterious. Nobody is out to undermine morality. The reformers are not insisting that all behavior should be considered equally acceptable or desirable. There is, however, a growing disinclination to consider every existing legal rule as sacrosanct. Some of our substantive criminal laws are being challenged because on close examination it becomes clear not only that they don't work, but also that they actually produce more social harm than good. Furthermore, critics of such laws are insisting that those who wish to impose criminal sanctions on behavior which does not involve clear interpersonal harm must justify that imposition. It is not enough to say that the law has long been on the books, for it may simply constitute a long-standing error in judgment. Nor is it adequate to maintain that the laws speak for morality, and that to modify them is to capitulate to immorality. On the contrary, as we have seen, there is good reason to argue that these laws, as they presently stand and are enforced, produce a great deal of immorality that might not otherwise exist. And their very unenforceability, widely acknowledged, tends to throw the legal system into disrepute, to label it as hypocritical.

Finally, our present laws in the victimless offense areas greatly encourage the forces of organized crime in American society. As the President's Crime Commission noted, "Organized criminal groups participate in any illegal activity that offers maximum profit at minimum risk of law-enforcement interference. They offer goods and services that millions of Americans desire even though declared illegal by their legislatures." This is no small matter, for as the Commission also pointed out, organized crime "involves thousands of criminals, working within structures as complex as those of any large corporation, subject to laws more rigidly enforced than those of legitimate governments. Its actions are not impulsive but rather the result of intricate conspiracies, carried on over many years and aimed at gaining control over whole fields of activity in order to amass huge profits." [35]

I have purposely not mentioned the question of organized crime until now, because of my conviction that—as the President's Commission itself noted—the provision of these illegal goods and services constitutes the "core" of such activity. It is true that we find organized crime operating in other areas and in other ways as well—extortion and labor racketeering, infiltration of legitimate business, and so on. And it is also true that organized crime has traditionally served diverse functions in American society—such as providing a deviant, yet often effective, ladder of social mobility for ethnic minorities, and offering an underworld counterpart of the intricate structure of conventional "big business." Hence perhaps no specific set of policy measures could completely or immediately eliminate such criminality. But in very large measure it is the profit from illicit trafficking to meet public demand that nurtures and enriches the apparatus of organized crime. Students of the problem may differ in their views about the precise form such organization takes—the debate about the existence and nature of the Mafia, or "the syndicate," is of long standing. But few specialists would deny the centrality of its supply-and-demand underpinnings. Indeed, as Donald Cressey suggests, in contrast to offenders whose behavior is strictly predatory, the organized criminal, who is likely to be "participating in crime on a rational, systematic basis," really "offers a return to the respectable members of society." [36] If we could eliminate the economic incentives girding up these various forms of illicit trafficking, we could very likely deal a serious blow to the entire apparatus of organized crime.

Notwithstanding these considerations, and despite the apparent les-

[35] President's Commission on Law Enforcement and Administration of Justice, *Task Force Report: Organized Crime*, pp. 1, 2.

[36] Donald R. Cressey, "The Functions and Structures of Criminal Syndicates," p. 29. The same author has just published a comprehensive analysis of organized crime, Donald R. Cressey, *Theft of the Nation* (New York: Harper and Row, Publishers, 1969).

sons to be learned from the Prohibition fiasco, America has persistently turned to the criminal law whenever confronted with troubling behavior or situations. As Daniel Bell has nicely put it, "in no other country have there been such spectacular attempts to curb human appetites and brand them as illicit, and nowhere else such glaring failures. From the start America was at one and the same time a frontier community where 'everything goes,' and the fair country of the Blue Laws." [37] Although the penchant for criminalizing situations that will produce black-markets has been particularly noticeable, our excessive reliance on criminal law "solutions" has extended well beyond problems of that sort.

One broad area in which such overlegislation has been especially pronounced is that of sexual behavior.[38] Indeed, so far-reaching have been these efforts at legal control that probably no sexual act other than ordinary intercourse between married (and consenting) adults in private has been left out of the repertoire of behaviors that are legally banned in one or another jurisdiction. While the attempts to outlaw abortion, homosexuality, and prostitution are among those that produce the most substantial (and adverse) social impact, our statute books are cluttered with numerous other unworkable and questionable sexual prohibitions. Laws against fornication and adultery are widely recognized as being unenforceable and, by and large, hardly any attempt is made to apply them. In many jurisdictions, provisions regarding "unnatural sex practices," or "crimes against nature" (or offenses described in similarly cryptic terms), make illegal sexual activities that are widely engaged in by married couples. The laws establishing an offense of "statutory rape"—in which intercourse with a girl below an arbitrary "age of consent" becomes criminal, even if she was in fact fully consenting or if she herself initiated the sexual encounter—are usually thought to be unwieldy and frequently to produce unjust results. Special statutes proscribe exhibitionism (indecent exposure) and voyeurism (peeping Toms), types of behavior that may be disturbing to others but which criminologists have concluded produce no real social harm.

Perhaps the most distressing effort to control sexual behavior has been the special legislation passed in many jurisdictions providing

[37] Daniel Bell, "Crime as an American Way of Life," *Antioch Review,* 13 (Summer, 1953), 132.
[38] See Morris Ploscowe, *Sex and the Law,* rev. ed. (New York: Ace Books, 1962); also Paul Gebhard, *et al., Sex Offenders* (New York: Harper and Row, Publishers, 1965). A good brief overview may be found in Gibbons, *Society, Crime, and Criminal Careers,* Chap. 15.

for the commitment and treatment of the so-called "sexual psychopath," or "abnormal sex offender." Clearly the idea behind this type of law was—at least in part—commendable. The hope was to isolate the really dangerous sex criminal so as to protect the public, and at the same time to provide such individuals with the psychiatric treatment they so badly needed. In practice, however, the offender category created by these laws became a dangerous wastebasket, into which could be thrown all varieties of sexually deviating individuals.

Just as there is no universally accepted and clearly delimited psychiatric definition of "psychopath," these laws themselves were framed in extremely vague and indefinite terms so as to cover diverse types of sexual behavior—types that are of vastly differing degrees of social dangerousness. The statutes have usually provided for indeterminate commitment, sometimes with inadequate attention to procedural safeguards in the commitment process, and without much regard for whether adequate treatment facilities or meaningful and effective treatment programs were available. Furthermore, "Because of the vagueness of the statutes, the sex-psychopath laws have been used primarily against minor sex offenders and in considerable degree *have not* been employed to isolate dangerous sex criminals." [39] It is not surprising that these laws have been very widely criticized by crime specialists, yet today they remain on the statute books in many states.

Overall, the problem seems to be that in the area of "sex crimes" our emotional responses frequently get the better of us. Certainly some atrocious acts of sexual violence are committed, and these are crimes about which we are rightly concerned. However, we must not allow ourselves to be so carried away on a tide of indignation that we ignore the important differences between varying kinds of offensive sex behavior. In particular, the distinction between violent and nonviolent offenses, and offenders, must be kept in mind. There is, for example, overwhelming evidence that most of the minor sexual offenses, such as exhibitionism and peeping, are committed by passive and sexually inadequate individuals who are most unlikely to turn to acts of violence. The typical homosexual offender is also most unlikely to produce direct interpersonal harm. Studies of forcible rape often reveal a considerable amount of ambiguity in the situation giving rise to the rape charges: the offenders often insist (and sometimes, apparently, with at least partial validity) that the woman was in fact

[39] Ploscowe, p. 214.

far from resistant. Even with respect to child-molesting, an offense that understandably gives rise to extremely strong public reaction, there is some evidence that fears have been exaggerated—many of these offenses are essentially nonviolent, and the assumption that they invariably produce severe psychic trauma in the victims is probably unwarranted.[40]

Again, this is not to say that there are no sexual crimes toward which we should feel revulsion and against which we should attempt to employ any preventive measures that seem feasible. Nor is the point merely that nonviolent sex offenses greatly outweigh violent ones—although this is the case. The major difficulty in this area is simply that we have enacted criminal legislation that goes well beyond what is necessary to cover socially harmful sexual acts. We might do well in this connection to follow the guidelines set down by the Wolfenden Committee—and to employ the criminal law in attempts to control only that sexual behavior which involves direct physical force, exploitation of minors or other vulnerable individuals, and serious threats to public order and decency. Even in these areas, the effectiveness of criminal law may well be limited; sexual activity would seem to be a type of human behavior not terribly likely to be influenced through legislation. But when private and consenting behavior is involved, it is quite clear that sex laws are without effect and almost completely unenforceable. The secondary problems that may be created through such legislation vary from offense to offense, and in some instances may not be great. Yet most laws of this sort undermine the standing of the legal system and divert a certain amount of enforcement energy into questionable tasks. Finally, when crucial distinctions are blurred to produce an all-enveloping undiscriminating campaign against "sex criminals," we are in serious danger of using the legal system itself to produce real injustice and social harm.

Of course the overreaching grasp of our criminal law has not been limited to the field of sexual behavior. As we have seen in the case of drug addiction, it extends to other types of behavior that are sometimes designated as "vice." Another good example of this is public drunkenness, which is explicitly made a criminal offense in most American jurisdictions. Noting that approximately one of every three arrests is for drunkenness, the President's Crime Commission pointed out that enforcement of these laws "places an extremely heavy load on

---

[40] For a review of research findings relating to these several types of offenses, see Gibbons, pp. 377–96.

the operations of the criminal justice system. It burdens police, clogs lower criminal courts, and crowds penal institutions throughout the United States." [41] The "revolving door" nature of law enforcement in this area is well known. Chronic drunks (usually slum-dwellers with long histories of drunkenness arrests) are picked up by the police, thrown in "the tank" to sober up in the absence of funds for bail, whisked through the lower courts without much attention to procedural niceties, possibly sentenced to a short jail term, and finally released to start the cycle once more. The legal mechanisms for processing such offenders usually provide no special facilities for treatment of alcoholism where appropriate, and show no signs of effectively curbing drunkenness. With these facts in mind, the Crime Commission reached the following conclusion: "Drunkenness should not in itself be a criminal offense. Disorderly and other criminal conduct accompanied by drunkenness should remain punishable as separate crimes. The implementation of this recommendation requires the development of adequate civil detoxification procedures." [42] If this recommendation and the accompanying proposal for creation of civil detoxification centers ("sobering up stations") were adopted—and public health facilities at which drunks could sober up and obtain further treatment on a voluntary basis were created—then clearly the burden on the courts and local jails, and to some extent on the police, would be enormously eased.

Going beyond the behaviors that are commonly termed "vice," another area in which we find the criminal law often overextended is that of political deviation. It is generally understood that totalitarian regimes will, of necessity, take action against a wide array of political "offenses" as part of their efforts to maintain power. In a democratic society, however, it is usually assumed that as a matter of principle political behavior should only be designated a crime if it constitutes a distinct threat to social order (as in the "clear and present danger" doctrine propounded in some of the classic U.S. Supreme Court decisions dealing with restrictions of free speech and assembly). Presumably this means that apart from treason or sabotage the citizen should be more or less free to think and act with reference to political issues as he sees fit. In our own society, however, one that proclaims individual liberty as a central operating principle, we have seen a long

[41] President's Commission on Law Enforcement and Administration of Justice, *Task Force Report: Drunkenness*, p. 1.

[42] *Ibid.*, p. 4.

succession of specific "political crimes" and related offenses by which legislators and law-enforcers have sought to curb political movements of which they did not approve.[43] Sometimes special laws were enacted —as in the case of the early "alien and sedition" statutes and the more recent "subversive activities" legislation—while at other times existing state laws or local ordinances were invoked, as in efforts to control and counter certain aspects of the civil rights and peace movements and related citizen protests. The recent prison sentences pronounced on five anti-Vietnam war spokesmen (whose convictions for "conspiracy" to encourage opposition to and refusal to participate in that war are now being appealed)—including the nationally renowned pediatrician-author, Dr. Benjamin Spock—are but one example of how far the concept of political crime can be stretched should governmental authorities find it expedient. Clearly the Government hopes that "making an example" of such protest leaders will have a deterrent effect on dissidents at lower levels in the peace movement. In some individual cases this may indeed occur. However, the potential ramifications of such political prosecutions on the general atmosphere relating to freedom of speech and political activity in our society are ones about which we should feel grave concern.

There is no evidence to indicate that legislation aimed at nebulously defined "subversive" activity has ever had any significant value in promoting the general welfare in a democratic society. Yet we know from the not too distant past of the "McCarthy era" that such efforts can have an insidious and quite devastating influence on the state of basic freedoms in such a society. And furthermore, the frequent recourse to lengthy and special investigative techniques (such as "undercover agents," wiretapping of suspected "subversives," etc.) in this area should alert us to the likelihood that the creation of political crimes often entails highly questionable use of limited law-enforcement resources. In general, the case seems strong for limiting political offenses to those acts that constitute a direct danger to the integrity of the political system—and not to include those that simply involve a voicing of opposition to particular policies of a specific government.

A final example of our tendency to "criminalize" too many of the

---

[43] For background on political offenses, see Thomas I. Emerson and David Haber, eds., *Political and Civil Rights in the United States*, 2nd ed., 2 vols. (Buffalo: Dennis and Co., 1958); also the classic study by Zechariah Chafee, Jr., *Free Speech in the United States* (Cambridge: Harvard University Press, 1941); and the excellent historical review by Leonard W. Levy, *Legacy of Suppression* (Cambridge: Harvard University Press, 1960).

problems confronting us lies in the area of juvenile offenses. This illustration has its special irony because when the juvenile court movement arose, at the turn of the century, one of its major aims was to shield young offenders from the stigma and other adverse consequences of being treated as criminals. Children who got into trouble with the law would be kept out of the regular jails and given necessary training or treatment in special juvenile institutions. They would not be called "criminals" and would not receive an official "record." The proceeding through which their cases were to be handled would not be the combat-like adversary procedure of the ordinary criminal trial—with its narrow focus on determining guilt or innocence—but rather an informal investigation in which the child's entire background and situation would be carefully sifted to determine what steps would be in his best interests.

Paradoxically our juvenile court system represents another overextension of the crime-defining process (even though the court hearings themselves are considered civil, rather than criminal, proceedings). Why is this so? To begin with, many of the statutes through which these courts have been assigned jurisdiction over offending acts of juveniles (the age limits vary from state to state) are loosely drawn documents. Not only do they cover acts by juveniles that would be ordinary crimes if committed by adults, but they extend the court's power to a broad range of behaviors that might be called noncriminal delinquency. Under these laws children may be adjudicated delinquent because of "ungovernability," "incorrigibility," "waywardness"—or any number of similarly nebulous "offenses," none of which comes close to satisfying the usual requirement of specificity in the definition of crimes.

Not only may the grounds for adjudication be extremely vague, but the procedures followed in the hearing of juvenile court cases have frequently fallen far short of the standards usually believed required for "due process of law." As in the case of the broad scope of the statutes, this procedural casualness was also intentional. The hearings (rather than "trial") should not, it was felt, be a battle between opposing lawyers in which "winning" the case became the major goal. Technical rules regarding admission of evidence should not be used as stratagems to rule out information that might assist in determining what steps would best serve the child's own interests. A broadly ranging social investigation of the child's situation (family background and home life, school performance, other behavior difficulties, etc.) should be used by the court in reaching this determination. (In a criminal trial, evidence of this sort would usually be admitted only in connection with sentencing, since it has no direct relevance to questions of guilt or innocence.)

In recent years, many observers have concluded that the juvenile court's efforts to individualize justice—efforts undertaken in the name of what one commentator calls the "rehabilitative ideal" [44]—have actually produced a good deal of injustice. These critics note that the attempt to decriminalize juvenile proceedings has been largely an exercise in euphemism. That there is a hearing instead of a trial, that the child is adjudicated a delinquent rather than convicted of crime, that he is sent to a training school and not a prison, does not alter the ultimately punitive nature of the process. The delinquent is stigmatized, and he is punished—whatever the intentions may be to do otherwise. Under the provisions of the juvenile court statutes a child committing a specific criminal act may often be committed for a term in excess of the "sentence" he might have received had he been proceeded against under the (adult) criminal law. Futhermore, available statistics on treatment success (for example, those on recidivism, or "repeaters") do not give much cause for optimism that the process is culminating in rehabilitation.

Given these facts, the by-passing of procedural safeguards (justified on the ground that the hearing is not criminal in nature) and the granting to juvenile courts of jurisdiction over large and vaguely defined stretches of youthful behavior, have both been called strongly into question. Criticism along procedural lines led to an important U.S. Supreme Court decision in 1967, in which denial of various procedural safeguards in an Arizona juvenile court case was held unconstitutional.[45] It is expected that this ruling will have a far-reaching effect in those jurisdictions where procedural laxity in juvenile proceedings had previously been the norm. With respect to the scope of the juvenile court's jurisdiction, perhaps the most authoritative critical comment to date has been that of the President's Crime Commission. Discussing at some length the problem of overextension into the area I have termed noncriminal delinquency, the Commission asserted that, "serious consideration should be given to complete elimination from the court's jurisdiction of conduct illegal only for a child." [46] All in all,

[44] Allen, *Borderland of Criminal Justice.*
[45] *In re: Gault,* 87 S.Ct. 1428 (1967).
[46] *Task Force Report: Juvenile Delinquency and Youth Crime,* p. 27.

it seems that we may be rapidly moving toward a system in which the quasi-criminal procedures and sanctions of the juvenile court will be invoked only where a youth commits a specific act proscribed by the regular criminal law. Determination that he did in fact commit the act will be made through a hearing in which, while efforts to protect the child from harsh stigmatization will continue to be made, crucial evidentiary and procedural safeguards will be provided. This may also involve a greater separation of adjudication and disposition (deciding what should be done with the youth once he has been held delinquent) than has been present in the past—with the broad social investigation applying mainly to the latter phase rather than being brought in at the outset.

These seemingly technical reforms may have a considerable impact on our general crime picture. We have already seen how the early "labeling" of a youngster as a troublemaker or delinquent may be a first and sometimes overwhelming step propelling him in the direction of a criminal career. It is widely recognized too that commitment to a juvenile training institution is probably as likely to promote further criminal involvement as to inhibit it—partly because of the stigma that clearly does attach to such commitment, but also because of the value patterns and associations the child inevitably encounters there. Some sociologists have also argued that the very informality of the juvenile court proceedings—and the consequent lack of uniformity and consistency in its rulings—may help to produce among the juveniles it deals with a sense of injustice and alienation and a disrespect for the legal system, which may indirectly encourage further patterns of anti-social behavior.[47] On all these grounds it would seem a step forward to develop as many informal alternatives to the juvenile court as possible (through public and private social agencies, for example), to limit the court's jurisdiction to specifically criminal acts of real seriousness, and where the court does take jurisdiction, to see to it that the child "in whose interests" it acts is provided with adequate legal guidance and protection.

[47] See David Matza, *Delinquency and Drift.*

CONCLUSION

There is no doubt that many of the common human situations leading to crime will be with us always. Furthermore, the very processes by which we single out certain of our number as wrongdoers on whom negative sanctions should be inflicted probably serve some important functions. Sociologists have noted that identifying and isolating deviants and law-breakers in a sense helps to establish the boundaries of conformity, and also that uniting to condemn and punish the deviant helps to promote cohesion and bonds of solidarity among the conformists and the law-abiding. However this may be, we should keep in mind that within the limits imposed by the possible "need" to designate *some* acts as deviant and to punish *some* wrongdoers, there remains a considerable amount of leeway. There will never be a serious dearth of potential wrongdoers. What requires our attention is the thorny problem of seeing to it that the objects of our moral indignation and recourse to negative sanctions are selected in as rational a manner as possible.

One reason why such a goal is difficult to attain is that punishment of criminal offenders also seems to serve important emotional or psychological functions for those who do the punishing. Some psychoanalytic theorists suggest that since we all house significant "criminal" urges, punishing the criminal allows the conforming individual to hold out a stern example to his own rebellious impulses. If the criminal were allowed to "get away with it" the conformist's inner criminal might not easily be held in check. While this interpretation may be somewhat open to question, another major theme of the psychology of punishment has more general acceptance: punishing the criminal affords the punishers a socially approved opportunity for the release of aggression and hostility.

This fact may lie at the base of much of our fascination with crime matters—a fascination often exploited by the news media, and which has also served as the basis for several thriving modes of literature and popular art. It may also be an important element contributing to our unthinking tendency to view "criminals" as a breed apart, as well as to the rabid vindictiveness that often seems to color the demand that offenders be brought to justice. These are tendencies that all of us probably need to guard against if we wish to see an atmosphere created in which sane crime policies are possible. And a special danger is that various nonconformists will become an object for the displacement of the deep-seated and free-floating feelings of grievance and hostility—described by the social theorist Max Scheler in the term *ressentiment*—existing in certain not completely powerless yet strongly discontented segments of our population.

It is also well to realize that crime serves definite economic functions. A great many people make their living (in whole or in part) engaging in crime, combatting crime, studying and writing about crime. Respectable industries derive some benefit from crime—the firearms industry is a case in point. We have seen that various kinds of much desired goods and services are provided through crime; such illegal activity represents economic behavior in much the same way as would legitimate efforts to satisfy the same demand. And to the extent that proceeds from such illicit traffic enable organized criminals to invest in legitimate businesses and embark on a wide program of other quasi-legitimate financial transactions, the web of interconnections between crime and the economy becomes extremely complex. While it would certainly be far-fetched to assert that the police, legitimate businessmen, even criminologists really want crime to continue because they have "vested interests" in its persistence, the subtle and diverse interrelationships between crime problems and economic structures cannot entirely be ignored. These ties are part of what we mean when we say that the crimes of a society represent the prices paid for structuring the social order in a particular way. Certainly when individuals steal because of economic need or pressure, crime must be seen as at least partly an economic phenomenon.

These "functional" aspects of crime are, of course, common to most if not all modern societies, and as I have already suggested, they simply imply broad limits within which crime control efforts may be undertaken. One of the key themes of this book has been that while crime cannot be completely eliminated, there is a great deal that we as citizens can do to change the crime picture. For this purpose, we need to focus on the specific crime problems of our own society rather than contemplating the general "nature of crime" in the abstract. In formulating policies aimed at the reduction of crime, we need above all to accept the fact that our present crime situation closely reflects the structure and values of modern American society.

The belief that most criminal offenders are "basically different" has constituted a dangerous form of self-deception. By virtue of it, those fortunate enough to live relatively law-abiding lives have washed their hands of all responsibility for crime problems. And the moral self-righteousness bred through this device frequently strengthens the grounds of resistance to rational and humane crime policies. Certainly it is true that some crime reflects the personal problems of the offending individuals, yet as I have pointed out, the applicability of strictly psychiatric explanations of criminal acts—in terms of the total range of types of crime in our society—is probably quite limited. Likewise, the goals of "treatment" and "rehabilitation"—admittedly commendable ones—must not serve as comfortable evasions of responsibility for the social nature of crime. One consequence of the eager resort to this rhetoric has been the attempt to pass on to psychiatrists and other treatment personnel responsibility for "solving" social problems that reach beyond their professional competence. Another result has been a tendency to ignore the substantive and procedural rights of the individual, as we proceed to take whatever action is deemed necessary to protect "his own interests."

A related and equally well-intended evasion has been the insistence that basically what is needed is more crime research. As a sociologist I would be the last to suggest that research is undesirable. Clearly the more we know about crime, the better we can control it—and indeed my own review of research findings in earlier sections of this book is intended to broaden public understanding of the substantial body of knowledge that has already been developed in this field. However, for policymakers who would prefer to dodge troublesome issues, and who are overly timid (for political, ideological, personal, or whatever other reasons) about making specific policy choices, the call for further research provides an all too convenient out. All the answers will never be in, and we can hardly afford to await their arrival before taking action. As I noted at the outset, we know enough about crime now to take some very large and highly meaningful steps aimed at its reduction.

These steps lie in three major areas: alterations in the social structure, modification of value emphases in American life, and greater selectivity in the use of criminal sanctions. As to the first, no thinking American can any longer ignore the close relation between poverty, unequal opportunity, feelings of deprivation and injustice, and crime. The first order of business in the attempt to alter our crime situation is to mount a meaningful all-out attack on poverty and social inequity. Both the Crime Commission and the Kerner Commission emphasized the crucial need to get at this basic breeding ground of crime. For guidelines we could hardly do better than to follow the recommendations of the Kerner Report—which ably documents the crying need for vastly expanded and improved housing, greatly improved educational opportunities and facilities, adequate health care, consumer protection, and general legal assistance for the poor. A genuine national policy of equal social and economic opportunity could significantly reduce the discrepancies between culturally induced success goals and legitimate means for their attainment, discrepancies which most specialists see as a root of much crime. Likewise, efforts to revitalize urban areas, with special attention to engendering some "sense of community," could make substantial inroads on the prevalent anomie and alienation underlying American criminality. Bringing the Vietnam conflict to a rapid halt will greatly assist in these efforts—since that unpopular war has a distinct bearing on the possibilities for both economic and attitudinal change.

Unfortunately it is probably the case that some segments of our population are already so infused with an overwhelming alienation and hostility that whatever reforms we adopt now may be too late to significantly alter their outlooks. However, the cycle must be broken into at some point; we must prevent similar despair from arising among succeeding generations. With respect to this attempt, I have not meant to suggest that welfare programs can solve all the problems of human life—although they can certainly help to solve many. Nor would I wish to leave the impression that programs patterned along the traditional lines of bureaucratically impersonalized paternalism will suffice. Recent controversies in New York, Boston, and elsewhere concerning decentralization of public schools illustrate that improved facilities are not enough. New modes of providing for basic human needs will have to be developed, ones that take into account the desirability of promoting and maintaining the integrity of the local community as a key social grouping, as well as fostering the dignity of the "assisted" individuals.

The problem of crime-producing values in American society is in many ways a more difficult one to deal with than that of socioeconomic inequity. In a complex, heterogeneous, rapidly changing, urbanized and largely secularized society, traditional agencies of socialization often find themselves hard put to maintain an influence on the young, and frequently the values they would inculcate come under serious challenge. At the same time, as we have seen, there is some confusion as to just what are the "traditional" accepted values of American life —there appear to be subterranean "traditions" that may in themselves be crime-encouraging. I have emphasized that while a return to the example of individual integrity is surely needed, such a change will be dependent upon organized efforts to control and reorient the structural sources of what Mills called the "higher immorality."

In this conection, the mass media may have a special role to play, despite the fact that their impact on individual values and behavior is most often felt subtly and only in the long run. The most useful media reforms may not be ones dealing specifically with the depiction of crime—although some moderation of violent content does seem desirable. Rather it is in the distorted picture of American life the media project, and in their selective dissemination of general life values, that the greater danger seems to lie. The media (perhaps particularly television and movies, because of their ubiquitousness and the relative immediacy of their impact) should be prevailed upon, or forced, to portray the nature of American society more realistically, to reduce their overall reliance (not simply in crime stories) on the "good guys and bad guys" formula, and to greatly decrease the kind of content that actively fosters commodity consciousness and an enveloping concern with materialistic values.

Closely related to, or involved in, such reform is the pressing need for industry or governmental control over advertising excesses. The unnecessarily heavy reliance on inflated claims for products and on downright misrepresentation may well have a pervasive effect in shaping an atmosphere conducive to varying kinds of fraud in our society. Advertising—along with other media content—may also have a direct influence on particular crime patterns, a prime example being that of auto theft. Clearly this offense, which is highly prevalent among our youth (often in the form of "borrowing" a car for a "joy ride") cannot be understood without reference to the activity of advertisers and media in creating an image of the (late model) automobile as both a social necessity and a major symbol of status and adulthood. Along with closer regulation of certain kinds of media and advertising content, there is also a great need for heightened governmental control over sharp sales and business practice, and a general "putting of teeth" into white-collar crime laws. As I have noted, this is an area in which criminal sanctions may have considerable deterrent effect, but in any case there is no reason why the middle-class "operator" should have a preferred status in the halls of justice.

Traditional sources of moral values—such as the family, the school, and the church—most assuredly have some role to play in the effort to promote personal integrity and patterns of fair dealing. While the rapid change these institutions are undergoing is often blamed for the decline of morality, it may be hoped that some of the newly developing bases for their authority will in fact promote rather than curtail their effectiveness. Thus the growing concern of the churches with pressing social and moral problems, the new orientation to this-worldly concerns, may in the long run provide for them a more respectful hearing and therefore actually enhance their role as a socialization agent seeking to encourage high moral standards. Likewise, the new focus on "relevance" and respect for students in the schools, and the increased freedom of individual members within the family situation, hopefully may have the indirect effect of enabling those institutions to act in ways that will encourage law-abidingness.

The third major step we should take is to exercise greater caution in our resort to criminal legislation. I have provided a number of examples of what may be considered unnecessary crimes, instances in which we have unwisely tried to reach out with the criminal law to control situations for which it is not an appropriate mode of control. Since crime is in a sense "created" by the criminal law, we must critically examine its substantive provisions, with an eye to assessing the social gains and costs of particular criminal proscriptions. Sometimes it is argued that such statutory manipulation does not really get at the heart of the problem. Thus, in the cases of drug addiction or homosexuality, opponents of "legalization" have insisted that the legal ban has little to do with the "basic causes" of the deviant behavior. This is an appealing argument (and one that nicely complements the call for further research), but one of the most glaring features of such borderline crime situations is that *regardless* of what the initial cause of the individual's behavior may have been, criminalizing the problem has created many secondary difficulties that would otherwise not be present. Those arguing for statutory reform have never said that research into basic causes should not continue. But in the meantime we should do what we can to control the secondary aspects of these problems through rational policy measures. One needs only to recall the enormous amount of property crime committed by drug addicts (and that the category of property crime comprises the bulk of crime in America) to appreciate the sizeable ramifications of unwise crime legislation. Similarly, the fact that organized crime thrives on the demand for illicit goods and services alerts us to the need to somehow break these pernicious supply-and-demand cycles.

It has not been possible in this brief book to deal with the broad topics of law enforcement and the administration of justice. As the President's Crime Commission extensively documented, there is a great deal that needs to be done to reform the institutions and processes of criminal justice in the United States—in ways that will make them more effective and equitable agencies for controlling and dealing with criminal behavior. A vast need exists for governmental support of police departments, for a general upgrading of the status (financial and otherwise) of the police, for greater professionalization and efficiency in police work, and for enlightened programs of police education, of public education about the police role, and new devices to encourage better police-community relations. Our system of courts and related services (such as probation departments) also badly needs revamping— to reduce congestion and delay, to provide appropriate modes of adjudicating in special problem areas, to ensure adequate and speedy justice for all. Finally our correctional system—at present hampered by gross overcrowding, inadequate financing, obsolete facilities, inadequate and unenlightened rehabilitative programs, and understaffing— also requires thoroughgoing reform.

All of this will cost a great deal of federal money, but something must be done urgently if we are to take any meaningful steps with reference to those individuals who find themselves under the jurisdiction of our apparatus of criminal justice. However, as the President's Crime Commission itself pointed out, the underlying causes of crime problems cannot be solved through more efficient or even more enlightened law enforcement. A key premise of this book has been that insofar as possible we must give priority to policies aimed at the *prevention* of crime—for, to be perfectly candid, our efforts to deal

with it after the fact (and to "rehabilitate" convicted offenders) have
been far from successful. In this connection, increased realization of
the negative implications of "labeling" and of commitment to "treatment" institutions also suggests that we should invoke these processes
only in cases where the social importance of doing so is quite clear.

In addition to the emphasis on prevention (in the broadest sense), I
would emphasize three other major themes that should inform our
efforts to improve crime policy. One is equitable treatment under law
of individuals at all socioeconomic levels in American society. This is
a much professed and supposedly revered ideal of the American way
of life, yet in many ways it is more honored in the breach than in the
observance. In our decisions as to what shall constitute a criminal offense, in the procedures by which we enforce the criminal law, and
in the judicial and correctional processing of defendants and convicted
offenders, this ostensible ideal must be given greater reality. Another
vital prerequisite to adequate crime policies in a democratic society is
that the basic freedoms of the individual be sustained, whatever the
pressures may be for their abridgment. Advocates of a "get tough"
approach to crime often seem to forget that overzealous enforcement
methods could well signal a serious curtailment of the individual liber-
ties we so highly prize. This is not to express a basic "sympathy" for
the offender but simply to restate what should be a governing tenet of
democratic justice—the belief that safeguards against the possibility of
convicting the innocent must be maintained, even if an occasional
guilty man should go free as a consequence of the procedural requirements. Finally, our attempt to evaluate and improve crime policies
must be ever alert to the need for rational allocation of the limited resources available to those who would administer criminal justice in
the United States. This point has bearing on specific police decisions,
and also on broader questions of enforcement and legislative policy—
as I have indicated, for example, in the chapter on overlegislation, and
also in my insistence on giving top priority to broadly preventive programs to combat the basic causes of crime.

During the 1968 presidential election campaign, the issue of "law
and order" became a central one. With a few notable exceptions, public statements about this matter were either misguided in their emphasis on severe enforcement, or else overly timid about highlighting
the need for drastic social reforms to reduce crime. The indiscriminate
bunching together of diverse behaviors that are all viewed as constitut-

ing threats to law and order—mentioned in the introduction to this book—was quite common. In this connection, it must be recognized that politicians are, by definition, seeking votes. The caution with which even liberal spokesmen approach the crime problem undoubtedly reflects their conviction that the taint of "criminal-coddling" must be avoided at all costs.

Whether this view of prevailing public opinion is correct is difficult to say; the political capital candidate George Wallace made of his patently repressive law-and-order stand constitutes ominous evidence that it is not far off the mark. Opponents of basic reform claim that those who are "soft on crime" show little sympathy for the victims of crime, but they produce no evidence that "harder" policies will in any meaningful way really help such victims. They simply assume deterrent and preventive effectiveness, even though the findings of much research show that for many common types of crime these outcomes are extremely unlikely. They tend to oppose strict gun control laws, which could well prevent the fatal escalation of many violence-ridden situations. Such critics argue too that the reformers favor a society in which men are no longer held responsible for the consequences of their acts. Usually this contention is grounded in a serious misunderstanding of the ways in which criminal acts come to be committed. As we have seen, the deliberate plotting of crime (for profit, or for personal gain of other sorts) is present in only a small segment of criminal behavior in our society. Furthermore, those who would rally to the cry of individual responsibility ignore totally the fact that some of us are much freer than others. If we lived in a truly equitable society, this responsibility argument would make somewhat more sense—although it would still slight the situational and psychological pressures that underlie many criminal acts.

All available evidence indicates that crime in America will not be effectively reduced until we make basic changes in the structure and quality of American life. Respect for law and order will not be restored until respect for the nature of our society is restored. Our confrontation with crime cannot be successful if we persist in viewing it as a battle with some alien force. Since America's crime problems are largely of our own creation, we have it well within our power to modify them and to bring them within reasonable control. Improvement of our apparatus of criminal justice can help us do this, but such improvement must at best constitute a kind of secondary holding operation. If, however, we are really prepared to make the necessary commitments—to deal directly with the social and legal sources of American crime—then the goal of a less criminal society might eventually come to be translated into social reality.

INDEX